"Anyone who has been part of corporate America can relate to these stories and inner questions about how to integrate all our human dimensions into doing business. They bring a much deeper dimension to the popular buzzword, 'Re-engineering,' by demonstrating over and over that the true, solid foundation we need to encourage is each individual's wholeness in mind, body, spirit, and emotion."—*Karen D. Lundquist*, *Plant Manager, Dupont Automotive Products*

"Margaret Lulic has created a blend of insight and wisdom enriched with stories about real people living out their values. A wonderful book that touches a deep need in the workplace." —*Daniel S. Hanson*, *Vice President, Planning and Business Development, Land O'Lakes, Inc.; Author*, A Place to Shine: Emerging From the Shadows at Work

"From heads of companies to middle managers to factory workers and union officials, the voices are powerful, and very, very human . . . An excellent idea carried out with originality and thoroughness . . . An exceptional work."—*The Book Reader: America's Most Independent Review of New Books*

"We can create a new world order. All history exemplifies this truth. We must step forward with wisdom and courage." —*Margaret Lulic*

WHO WE COULD BE AT WORK

Revised Edition

WHO WE COULD BE AT WORK

Revised Edition

BY

MARGARET A. LULIC

Butterworth–Heinemann

Boston • Oxford • Melbourne • Singapore • Toronto • Munich • New Delhi • Tokyo

Butterworth–Heinemann

$\mathcal{R}$ A member of the Reed Elsevier group

Copyright © 1996 by Margaret A. Lulic
All rights reserved.

∞ Recognizing the importance of preserving what has been written,
Butterworth–Heinemann prints its books on acid-free paper whenever possible.

Library of Congress Cataloging-in-Publication Data

Lulic, Margaret A.
    Who we could be at work / Margaret A. Lulic. — Rev. ed.
        p. cm.
    Includes bibliographical references and index.
    ISBN 0-7506-9739-3 (pbk.)
    1. Organizational change.   2. Reengineering (Management).
    3. Employee empowerment.   4. Quality of work life.   I. Title.
    HD58.8.L85   1996
    658.4′063—dc20   95-46389
                                                                CIP

British Library Cataloguing-in-Publication Data

A catalogue record for this book is available from the British Library.

The publisher offers discounts on bulk orders of this book.
For information, please write:

Manager of Special Sales
Butterworth–Heinemann
313 Washington Street
Newton, MA 02158–1626

10 9 8 7 6 5 4 3 2 1

Printed in the United States of America

For my daughter, Laura

Each child has something to teach us,
a message that will help
to explain why we are here.
                                        —The Talmud

For my husband, Bob

My rock of support and strength
who has always granted me space and closeness.

For my parents,

Despite their deaths so long ago,
their spirit lives in me and this book.

For all the Children of Earth

May we create a new world community of peace,
justice, and caring for you to inherit.

Table of Contents

Foreword

Having won the Malcolm Baldrige National Quality Award in 1991, many of us at Zytec continually receive calls from other companies that believe we are the best of class in quality and empowerment. They seem to be looking for tangible methods they can practice in order to achieve outcomes similar to ours. There is an assumption that the methods, practices, or measures are the key drivers.

When I ask myself why total quality works at Zytec, methods are not the key part of the answer. The processes we use are available to everyone in the public sector through Dr. Deming's teachings, TQM, and other continuous improvement methodologies. What is different at Zytec is that those tools have fallen on fertile ground. Our people share unconditional trust and respect for one another, and we try to encourage people to operate as whole human beings. These attributes drive out fear, break down barriers, empower people, and allow us to celebrate each other's pride in our work.

In some respects, *Who We Could Be at Work* tells Zytec's inner story. The first part of the book articulates the benefits of being passionate about your mission, of tackling the painful decisions and challenges, and of accepting full responsibility for the outcomes of shared accomplishments. We have been through painful times (salary and workforce reductions) and joyous times (the Malcolm Baldrige Award and moving onto the public stock exchange). We have people who have reached a whole new level of commitment to quality, a new level of involvement, knowledge, and empowerment. We have enjoyed all that goes with that, including financial growth and stability.

I believe the second part of this book describes the key aspects of the next leg of our journey, or anyone else's who is on the same path. As we grow, we find ourselves at the next crossroad that requires still another level of learning. Empowerment doesn't come free. Accountability, both team and individual, goes with it. We are beginning to ask people to look even more fully at the impact of their actions and decisions. Building on our foundation of trust and respect, we need everyone to understand and *choose* empowerment *on behalf of the whole organization*. That takes whole people.

What Margaret Lulic has undertaken in writing this book is to paint a picture of what it takes for the whole person to come to work. This is the missing link that handicaps so many business efforts to change, to innovate, to move into the future. No one has effectively done this before. She and her interviewees speak simply, straightforwardly, and from their own whole persons. I felt like I was almost in a conversation with the many diverse people who share their stories in this book. In the process, they tapped into the heart of what makes all of us tick at work. I have the image that we all wear masks at work. Lulic takes off her own mask and invites not only the people in this book, but those of us who read it, to take off our masks.

This is critical to the success of our companies. Our masks create fear and distrust. We waste energy on unproductive issues. Masks encourage us to see each other as titles, positions, and functions. They reinforce hierarchies and the attitude that "it isn't my job." One of Zytec's methods for helping remove people's masks is to base our decisions on fact and not on the perceptions of people's personalities. We work hard to keep the whole person in the process, but remove the ego that clouds the issues. When the masks disappear and we see each other first as human beings, we begin to form more productive relationships and many of these other things just naturally disappear. We get even more, though. We discover that people have talents we never guessed. The company gains new skills, insights, flexibility, and resources.

Lulic herself is an example of this. She has more breadth of successful work experience than anyone I know. She wasn't necessarily the best technically qualified person available (as far as technological knowledge or educational specialization) for some of the positions she held, but was more successful than most because she contributed her whole self to her work and therefore provided whole perspectives for the organizations to consider. She is living proof that businesses stand to gain tremendous benefit when they recognize and nurture that whole person in the workplace. Now she begins sharing her learnings with us and teaches us how to love living at work.

Annette Cramer
Director of Human Resources
Zytec Corporation
1991 Malcolm Baldrige National Quality Award Winner

Acknowledgments

It has been an exciting opportunity to revise this book and add even more depth and concreteness to it. I appreciate my editor, Karen Speerstra, for seeking me out and giving me the opportunity to take this book to what I hope is an even higher level of value for you, the reader.

Writing this book the first time was a wonderful adventure. I've never felt so purposeful and on track. I have experienced incredible support from beginning to end. That support seemed to come from the Universe itself, and from many diverse people. Every time I needed something, it was there. The same thing happened in this second edition.

My husband's and daughter's daily interest, support, and patience have been sustaining. I'm very blessed to have them in my life.

I'm very grateful to the people who tell their stories in this book. They shared part of their heart and spirit and I am honored that they allowed me to tell their stories. Even after many rounds of editing, I find they continue to inspire me and challenge my thinking. Without them, this book would not exist.

Dorrine Turecamo, my editor for the first edition, was another blessing that appeared in the most unlikely way. Thank heaven for her friendship, patience, and guidance, as well as her ability to help me write with more clarity and spirit. Susan Rosenthal Kraus, my writing partner, and Sally Deke, a dear friend, have been wonderful. In addition to their ideas and questions, their excitement in reading my material in the early stages was very inspiring and sustaining.

There are many other people who have been very important to me throughout different aspects of the creation of this book. Those words of curiosity and support from family, friends, clients, and colleagues sustained my courage. What seemed like random comments inspired new thoughts, resources, and approaches that have been enriching. May you be blessed in return.

This book has drawn upon my whole life and the lives of all the people who share their stories here. We are who we are because of all those lives that have touched us, so I know this book is part of a gigantic web of people I cannot directly name. Thank you.

Never doubt that a small group
of thoughtful, committed citizens can change the world.
Indeed it is the only thing that ever has.

—Margaret Mead

Who We Could Be at Work

> Most people have work that is too small for their spirits.
>
> STUDS TERKEL

We'd like to go home from work knowing we've made a contribution that drew out the best in us. We'd like to go home feeling valued for that contribution. And when we are at home and in our communities, we want much of the same.

Some of the people you will meet in this book not only didn't have these desires met, but felt as though they were dying at work. Many of us feel as if much of what we have to offer is wasted in the workplace. And it's hard to find the time or the spirit to be who we'd like to be in the rest of our lives. We hear the news and we wish there were something we could do about even one of the problems that plague the world. But it just seems so vast and so far removed.

We can begin reforging ourselves so we could be more of who we want to be and who we are capable of being. The workplace could be much more. Our organizations can be major contributors to the well-being of the earth and all her people. We could bring our spirit and heart to work. We can lead more satisfying lives. We are part of a new wave of history that is learning to be whole, more full and complete. Here are people from all sizes of organizations, and from all levels inside those organizations, who believe in more and have helped to create it. You are about to read stories of people whose lives and workplaces demonstrate why a reasonable person can have hope.

We can create something new once we realize that we, our organizations, and the world are all part of one interconnected, interdependent system. We're not isolated islands unto ourselves. In his videotape and book, *The Global Brain*, Peter Russell, the English scientist and researcher, discusses how one characteristic of the new millennium we're entering is larger and larger scale political, social, and technological integration. The whole planet is coming together to function as one community.

In the health field, we're learning that human beings are complex wholes and that we can create better health by treating the whole person rather than just isolated parts. When we act on this same premise in the workplace, we create healthier, stronger organizations. The starting point is for each of us to bring all of who we are to work and to learn to live with each other in that wholeness. When we are boxed and labeled by titles, education, sex, race, and beliefs, great potential from each person is wasted. Everyone loses—the individual person, our families, our companies, and the world. We create such waste when we compartmentalize human beings and define what parts of ourselves we can bring and what parts will stay at home. It's impossible to separate mind, body, heart, and spirit; we are one indivisible whole. When we try separation, we create disease, social problems, and barriers to productive work. We lose vitality and innovation.

Integration is occurring in the workplace on many levels. More of us want to bring our whole selves to work—mind, body, emotions, and spirit. Our organizations need us to do this. We can't separate work from home, business from social responsibility, economic decisions from environmental effects, and personal values from organizational norms without incurring huge repercussions.

We're paying the costs financially, environmentally, socially, and spiritually through addictions, teen pregnancies and suicides, family breakdowns, violence, poverty, and the degradation of the earth.

The stories that follow are gifts for each of us. As these individuals share ideas they are acting out in reality, not just theory, they may help define and encourage our own explorations. It's so much easier to see our own choices—and to deal with the excitement and fears that go hand-in-hand with them—when someone else has gone first and can tell us what it was like for them. These stories can help us explore who we are today at work and who we want to be tomorrow.

To create the changes we desire requires us to use the mindset of the explorer. I'm reminded of my father, who was an immigrant, and of the early pioneers. One of the most important tasks was to write back home to family and friends about what the journey and the new world were really like. Then others could choose their own path: to stay within the old or move to the new. Whichever they decided, they had a clearer picture of the choices and the tasks that had to be done.

There is a poem on a church wall in England:

A vision, without a task, is but a dream.
A task, without a vision, is drudgery.
A vision, with tasks, is the hope of the world.

The letters from the pioneers and the immigrants gave people vision and hope in a new world, as well as a sense of what it would take to make the change to that world. Perhaps the stories in this book can give us a sense of vision that will ignite our own hopes and dreams and give us a sense of the tasks that go with these goals.

The people and organizations sharing their stories in this first section have chosen to try to forge something new. When this first shift occurs, the organization is rewarded with commitment, productivity, quality, and innovation. This section does not try to tell the total story. It asks us to open ourselves to the possibility that things could be different and that difference could be what we yearn for in our deepest selves. The stories don't promise panaceas. They tell the truth of the newfound rewards, as well as of new struggles.

They show that if these people and their organizations can each find their path to a better way of being at work, there is more hope for the rest of us. I have found a much more fulfilling work life, but I found it by leaving corporate life and creating my own business. As a corporate consultant, I have been able to create more of the integrated life I want. I believe the same flexibility, sense of satisfaction, and feeling of wholeness I have can be available for everyone else who wants it. We need to make it available within organizations, for the benefit of the company as well as the individuals in it.

Hope is a maligned word. We've relegated it to Pollyanna and to children who have wishes and dreams. We could learn a lot from our children. Without hope, nothing changes. We have to believe there is some small chance of success before we will take a step forward. Without hope, we stop dreaming. Without dreams, we can create nothing new. The only way hope can be harmful is if we offer hope with no action or hope that is dependent on some external savior. Corrine McLaughlin and Gordon Davidson, in *Spiritual Politics*, tell us, "Hope acts like a spiritual magnet which draws inspiration from Higher Sources. Hope is not an emotional attitude, but a clear intuitive knowing that recognizes good can triumph when charged with courage and unshakable determination."

The stories you are about to read offer an opportunity for self-exploration. Are you willing to explore your current beliefs about the workplace and your role in it? We each have acquired a set of beliefs and values, as well as a way of seeing things that we believe is the truth or reality. If we forget that we ourselves and others created much of this reality, we lose our power to forge something different. If we remember this, however, we will know we can create something else. We acquired our beliefs at such an early age that we frequently aren't conscious of them and their power. They have become fundamental to the way we live.

Once we believe our way is the only way, we give up our ability to see, hear, and feel anything inconsistent with it. One example of this phenomenon would be alternative medical practices. Homeopathy, Eastern philosophies about healing, and Native American knowledge about wellness have validity and usefulness—but most of us won't even consider them. If something like this or any other "different" idea does leak into our consciousness, we plug the leak. We shut out what does not match our own view as wrong, irrelevant, superstitious, or an idiosyncrasy. Then we dismiss all that knowledge, experience, and data, and label the bearer of these beliefs as bad, misguided, or weird. This process stops our learning and growing. A slow, intangible mental, emotional, and spiritual death begins.

To help break out of this mode, companies involved with continuous improvement use *benchmarking*. The idea is to find someone else who is the best of the best at a particular process and examine how they do it. Surprisingly, people in businesses that look totally unlike your own often provide the biggest insights. Manufacturing businesses get insights from Disney Parks and airlines learn from mail-order catalog houses. Many of the people I have spoken with have realized their breakthroughs in attitudes and ideas only after they could see another reality. One of the downsides of experience is that we are taught the "right" way to do things. This creates blocks to openness and creativity because we think we have all the answers. It has often been pointed out that most major breakthroughs in a field are made by people outside that field who haven't been ingrained with the rules.

So, too, we need to form our own benchmarks of what we see as the best of the best ways to live. We can do this through books, articles, discussions, and a revitalization of our own dreams. We need to break out of whatever blinds us to growth and new choices. That is the nature of the journey. The stories in this first section of the book offer us some benchmarking practices that we can apply to ourselves as individuals or to a department, function, or organization.

I've come on my own journey, which still has a long way to go. I've had to let old beliefs and behaviors die and create new realities out of who I really am rather than who I was taught to be. It has been a painful and exhilarating exploration. I wish someone had helped me start even sooner by asking me to imagine there could be another way and to be open to exploring it before I shot it down. Those are the questions I ask you to explore as you read these stories.

Steven Wikstrom, vice president of manufacturing for Reell (pronounced Ray-el) Precision Manufacturing Corporation (RPM), tells the story of a unique pioneering company. Because RPM is so often mentioned in connection with quality improvements, that was what I expected to hear. However, there was much more to their story. This $15 million manufacturer of motion control devices was started in 1970. Their founding name is the first clue as to what is different. *Reell* is a German word meaning honest, dependable, or having integrity.

Here is part of the Reell Precision Manufacturing Direction Statement and in it we find the source of their adventure:

> RPM is a team dedicated to the purpose of operating a business based on the practical application of Judeo-Christian values for the mutual benefit of co-workers and their families, customers, shareholders, suppliers, and community. We are committed to provide an environment where there is harmony between work and our moral/ethical values and family responsibilities and where everyone is treated justly.
>
> The tradition of excellence at RPM was founded on a commitment to excellence rooted in the character of our Creator. Instead of driving each other toward excellence, we strive to free each other to grow and express the excellence that is within all of us.

They have taken quality to a much higher level of understanding than manufacturing and service. They have profoundly answered a basic quality and life question, "Who are we here to serve?" Whether or not people agree with the answer, I like the question.

The benchmarking issue they illustrate so well is clarity of vision, values, and purpose.

Steve Wikstrom's Story: Growing with Integrity

"In 1981, I answered a blind ad placed by an employment agency for the first time in my life. RPM eventually made me an offer. When they did, they said, "Here; take a minute to read through this, and see if you are okay with it." It was their "Welcome to RPM" which is now our Manufacturing Direction Statement. They didn't ask if I subscribed to it. They only wanted to be sure there wasn't a strong negative reaction and that I knew this was the orientation of the company. I read it and found it a refreshing perspective, but it wasn't critical to me at that time. Nor did it cause me any problems.

It made reference to some unique stuff. It wasn't the "Welcome-to-RPM,-we-are-in-the-business-to-satisfy-the-customers-and-make-a-profit-for-our-shareholders" stuff. It talked about coming together in a business relationship and finding a common faith. While the company philosophy is rooted in Judeo-Christian values, they have tried to create a climate where people with wide variations in spiritual perspective (including non-Christian) can work together, respect, support, and learn from each other.

It also said that RPM's primary purpose is not to create a profit. The company primarily existed to allow for the growth of people, to have an environment where one's individual moral and ethical values don't come into conflict with work. They used an analogy to eating. While eating is critical to living, one does not live to eat. They viewed profits the same way. So profits were critical to health, but they weren't the bottom line.

I said "Yes" and took the job. The organization has definitely had an effect on me and I know that I would not be the same person if I hadn't come here. I don't think this would be the same place without me, either. I can look around and say, "This part of the company, this part of the philosophy, this part of the way we do things together, wouldn't look like this had I not been here." I am not saying it wouldn't exist, but it does have my fingerprints on it. That is a great feeling.

I've learned many things. I've learned that many people can be "right" at the same time. I've learned about community, what it means to be working with a group of people who have different aspirations than I do. I came into this company with a strong desire to be the top decision maker, alone in a position of ultimate leadership. Today I don't feel that way at all. I feel that the best way to run this organization is with a shared team of top leaders. It teaches you a lot about consensus, humility, and give-and-take. Independence isn't the ultimate high. Interdependence is the reality and is much more interesting. The world is interdependent, this company is interdependent, and anyone who thinks, "If I just arrive at slot A, I'll have it made," may have a problem.

I've learned that the questions are sometimes more challenging than getting to answers. I've learned doubt is part of growth. What we're aware of in this company, to a very high degree, is that there are ditches on both sides of any road. Can we live with contending opposites, as opposed to trying to solve the tension? Can we live in the question? The challenge is to live with questions, not always to come up with the answers.

We have all the questions that every other company has. In addition, we ask, "Why is the company here in the biggest sense? What are we in this for? What's the big picture? What do we hope to have accomplished when we look back?" What really matters around here is to live with questions about the meaning of life.

There are many concrete things we have done that illustrate how we try to live out our beliefs. We don't have organizational charts. We have a team of three people who provide senior leadership to the company through unanimous decisions. They have found that when they can't reach agreement, it's usually because they find the question is wrong.

We don't have many positional perks that are automatically given to certain people at certain levels. We have no connection between pay and individual performance. We don't even have a performance review. Instead, we call it an annual conference. It's looking at today and tomorrow, without much of a rearview mirror component to it.

A major financial challenge in 1975 provided a test. The payroll could not be supported after a major customer cut back its requirements. The decision was that the right thing to do was not to have any layoffs. Instead, everyone was asked to take a 10 percent pay cut which increased to 20 percent by the end of the year. The founders took a much larger cut.

We've learned that the slow times, the hard times, can be times of great advance and breakthrough. The key is to recognize opportunities and direct surplus personnel in those directions rather than to cut personnel in an effort to maintain short-term profits. One of our best products, the RPM Radial Electric Clutch, is recognized by customers and competitors as the industry performance standard. This product was developed during one of those hard times.

We are an ESOP (Employee Stock Ownership Plan) company, so today, roughly 30 percent of stock is in the hands of the people who work here. We have had years when we have been able to experience really good financial results and have been able to receive bonuses that were allocated equally, regardless of income level. It's like the World Series. There is a pot of money and there are this many players and you divide it equally.

We have a common set of salary change dates, when all of the pay rates change. Executive compensation, by any way you want to measure our ratio, is less than 10 today—that is, less than 10 times the salary of any other worker in the company. There are only 12 salary ranges in the whole company. This includes factory workers. We do not have an all-nonexempt work force because we have people who couldn't, by law, be classified that way. There are no time clocks. We haven't had them for years.

There's a company minimum wage that will be earned by anyone who has had at least two years' experience here and at least three years of other post–high school experience. Today the minimum wage is in the neighborhood of $21,000 a year. That was a philosophical decision on our part, to say we just wanted to have a base that allows a reasonable standard of living for anyone who works here.

We hire by team consensus. The team includes at least the candidate's peers, people who work in other areas affected by the person in the position being hired, and the director of training and development. We have group interviews that are both objective and subjective in content. We're not going to get to the subjective until we have a fair degree of confidence in the objective. Then we ask the person to tell us about what he or she is looking for and to ask us about who we are. What is most important to us is that we are compatible.

As a parent, I have brought my kids here to shadow me for half a day. They'll come and have lunch with me when they're out of school in the summer. Years ago, our sickness and accident policy was changed to read that if your kids are sick, you can take time off. Who I am as a mother or a father is not a separate issue around here.

The ability to be myself at work and at home creates tremendous synergy. I get confused sometimes: Is this stuff I learned at home that I am using at work, or is this stuff I learned at work that I am using at home? That is one of the big pluses to people who are able to work under nontraditional settings. People can start to blur balance into integration so all constituencies, including family, are served. The first time we heard that kind of idea was from Tony Andersen of H. B. Fuller. He made the statement that, as a business, it's fairly easy to be really excellent at meeting the needs of one of your constituencies, but he felt that it is a lot more difficult to be doing well with all of them.

If you have an environment that is the way it should be, it will be attractive to children. We adults have some of the same needs as children, such as making room for feelings. Feelings help create balance, the ability to integrate. Quality relationships equal quality parts, and this requires allowing people to talk about how they feel and what they value, as well as what they think.

Our company has a reputation for high quality parts because we are working on creating high quality relationships between people. How would I like to be treated if I were the customer? If I were the supplier, how would I like to be treated? These are relationship questions. We have made quality decisions based on these questions alone.

I've learned when you try to create an environment that allows people to talk about how they feel, as well as what they do, it creates a better environment. I was able to bring things to the table that were unique to me and others were willing to listen to them. As a result, I became much more challenged and interested in providing the same opportunity for them. We feel free to ask each other broad, deep, probing questions about the business, about our personal lives, about our spirituality. We seek to understand and to listen, as well as to speak.

I find myself shaking hands with forty years and saying to myself, "I'm having a blast." What's really exciting to me is the question, "Do they want just my brains or just my hands or do they want me?" If you want me, you get all of me. People don't leave who they are at the front door. If you try to make them do that, you will have the illusion that they did, but they won't. They will figure out ways to operate as guerrillas behind the scenes. We want to get who people are out in front and deal with it. Let's make it part of the debate and part of the struggle.

The company is committed to maintaining our philosophy. If you asked me how, I'd have no idea. I don't have a map. What I have is a compass bearing. I believe this company knows where north is and knows that they want to go north. But if north is Winnipeg, we have a variety of roads to take to get there. I don't believe we have any idea which one of those roads we are going to be on or how long we are going to be on it. What I do know is that I have never found a company where I sensed there has been a stronger commitment to wanting to maintain and improve upon this environment. What we have created feels different, but good, to a lot of people.

Beliefs make a lasting difference. The president of our company heard a senior officer of a large corporation talk at a seminar about total quality and empowerment. He asked the speaker later, "Do you think that what you are doing is motivated primarily by a sense of enlightened self-interest or by something bigger and higher than that?" The speaker thought about it for a while and said, "Probably enlightened self-interest." At that point our president asked him, "What do you think will happen when the chips are down, when the competition is stiff, when you are losing money? Do you think you will stand by those elements of total quality that had to do with empowerment and building people and those kinds of things?" The man replied, "I don't know if we will." I think the challenge in that is, "What are you in this for?"

If you asked people around here, "What's the worst thing that could happen?", going out of business would not be the number-one response. I believe they would say that the worst thing would be to abandon the "North" we have defined on the compass."

I respect the people of Reell Precision Manufacturing because they ask and answer questions of meaning, purpose, and how to live with integrity. Their answer is to focus on the growth of their people. In Universal Tradewinds, Inc., I found a company that answers those fundamental questions in another inspiring way. Two companies, apparently started very different places, had created some very similar results.

The Universal Tradewinds answer is a product that is meaningful in the world. This company produces and distributes a unique stuffed bear, called SPINOZA™. At first glance, they may look like a specialty stuffed animal manufacturer and an unlikely candidate to meet our interests. How do you create meaning around a toy bear?

SPINOZA™ was originally developed in 1984 by Ruth Grosh and Sherry Goodman. Grosh was a special education teacher and Goodman was a communications specialist. Both are mothers. They had a desire to give their children and the children of the world something special. Their intent was to create much more than another stuffed bear. It was to create a vehicle for emotional healing and love. This intent has affected every aspect of the company and how it is managed.

I met with Terri Lynn, the chairman of the board and creative director. It's one thing to write an inspiring vision and value statement. It can be much harder to live it out. The issue of intention as a guide and measure of integrity in implementation was their benchmarking gift.

Terri Lynn's Story: The Power of Intent

"Intentions color every experience we have. Our customers, employees, suppliers, and community, as well as our families and friends, have a sense of our intentions. This affects how they experience us. The intent behind this company is to help heal the hearts of humankind. That has changed me and how we do business. I have to walk my talk. When we were establishing titles, that came up. The titles in themselves are kind of a joke and an error. Compartmentalizing anything is an error. How can we possibly comprehend all of who we are in a title or a label? It's dangerous, too. We wanted to talk about the questions, "What is my gift? What is it that I have to give to the world?" In my case, we decided to put "Keeper of the Vision" on the business cards. Our CEO's title is Chief Executive Bear. We laugh because we know a company has to have some traditional titles to deal with the outside world.

I am also called chairman of the board, but here we know what that really means. I am the keeper of the vision, the one who brings us back to the focus. It is my gift to help ensure that every decision is aligned with our commitment and that we act out of integrity. As a human being, I am continually learning about that, so it's not that we operate in an ideal capacity at every moment. But our commitment is always to strive toward that to the best of our ability.

I am also director of creative development and that is about being SPINOZA's™ guardian. I must see that he continues to grow and thrive, expand and express in all types of different areas, in ways that are consistent with his intent and the purpose of his life. So, as we partner with groups like the Central Ohio Lung Association to benefit children with chronic illness or as we do ongoing product development, I challenge us to be sure this is the right thing for our vision. In our case, we can embody our philosophy into our product even down to the details of his design.

SPINOZA™ is different from any other bear because of this. When he was created, the idea was for him to be a gift that would contribute toward healing the heart. He communicates basic messages of human kindness in a world where other experiences invalidate that. His whole physical design was developed so that he would deliver openness and love. He is shaped in such a way that when you see him, you want to pick him up and hold him. He is sitting in a totally open body position, upright with his arms and legs outstretched to give you a hug or to receive one. This way he is receptive and giving at the same time.

When you hug him, he's designed to cover your most vulnerable region from your throat down to your tummy. Whenever we feel scared, the first thing we do is cross our arms and legs, hunch over, and try to cover our heart because that is where we feel most vulnerable. He has a tape player tucked in his tummy and a speaker in his throat so he speaks very clearly. His messages come from the heart. They are just SPINOZA™, sharing his experience of being alive. We talk about how each of us has a gift in our heart and the world is waiting for the unique gift that we have to give. SPINOZA™

and his friends help us remember how to live with purpose and vision and to follow our own dreams. Children are so alive with dreams, with just the wonder of life.

We try to run the business in a way that is consistent with this intent and these messages. When we are having trouble making a decision, we ask "What would SPINOZA™ do? How would SPINOZA™ do it?" That is such an easy way to make sure that we are operating in integrity. We measure ourselves by asking how many lives did we touch today, not how many bears did we sell. The motivation and the sense of purpose around what we are doing becomes very different.

In my previous business experience, it was easier to be externally focused and driven towards results. In hindsight, I realize I did sales, marketing, and promotion from a position of manipulation and control, by asking, "How can we provoke the response we want?" When I did sales training and motivational speaking, I would give them the old rah rah. The motivation, of course, was how much money they could make. Here, it feels very different.

Recently, a new sales person was calling hospices. We have objectives like any business and she was having trouble meeting those. I was asked to help. Flashing back to the way I used to operate, I rejected it. I was really challenged. I asked myself, "What matters here? What can I do to support her?" She needed to connect with why this job mattered. She needed meaning.

I asked her to remember a personal loss. She hadn't had anyone close to her die, but she said, "I lost my dog and that was pretty hard." Grief is grief, so I asked her to tell me about that. She started crying and reconnected with the experience of her loss. I would never have done this in any other workplace, but it was right for this company. Then I said, "It is not a matter of, 'Did you get 15 or 20 bears out?' It is, 'What happens as a result of that? Why does it matter that we are calling these places?' "

I told her about a couple of experiences where people had died totally alone because their families were so terrified of dealing with death they refused to be there. Even children are dying alone. People with AIDS are dying alone. On the other hand, we have been told stories of children and adults who died holding on to SPINOZA™, holding on to love. What matters is if just one person doesn't die alone. It makes all the difference in the world for people to have a sense of connection. There is a depth and a richness in that that we cannot tangibly measure, but I believe we cannot live without it.

Many wonderful stories come back to us about SPINOZA™ and this helps us keep our commitment alive. SPINOZA™ is purchased for newborn babies, for young children, for teenagers, for adults, and for the elderly. Drug and alcohol treatment centers for both teenagers and adults use him. For the elderly, he is company and a comfort. He is touching and nurturing during a time of great loneliness. He helps people who are in the healing process from a traumatic experience—whether it is physical or sexual abuse, grieving the loss of someone or something, or separation through divorce. The applications are so broad because the universal experience of love is what the bear is about.

About two weeks ago, a nursing home called and wanted to see how SPINOZA™ would work with their elderly residents. An elderly woman there hadn't spoken in over five years. They felt she had reached an advanced stage of dementia, a disease that leaves people with cognitive impairment. In the most advanced stages, speech is permanently impaired. SPINOZA™ reached this woman; he touched her. She was soon speaking to him with great animation. The nursing home staff was very touched by her improvement.

About a month ago, I heard about a woman whose daughter was murdered. Imagine how intense such a loss must be for a mother. Someone gave the mother SPINOZA™, and she was profoundly touched. On the "Hold on to Me" tape, there is a ceremony for Beatrice, one of SPINOZA's™ friends, who has died. Her friends bring a rainbow of colored balloons to send their love.

This mom called everyone she knew who was coming to the funeral and said, "Bring a balloon of some color that reminds you of your relationship with my daughter and bring a memory of something that you shared with her." At the funeral, they released those colored balloons. She said it was so incredible to release those and to be focused on remembering their love and the special time they had had together. This story is a tangible miracle of healing.

All these issues come up in how we treat employees, suppliers, and others. I was thinking about this, in terms of equality and fairness, as I was walking to work this morning. I was thinking that equality isn't necessarily being treated the same. One of the small ways this shows up is that some people are really good in the morning. It is when they operate the strongest. Others are better later in the day. Others have children to get to school. So to say everyone has to start at a certain time and be expected to perform in a certain way may not honor their gifts or their needs. It isn't a reasonable expectation and it isn't fair.

Honoring both the emotions and the spirit of the person in the workplace are really high on my list of priorities. I don't ask that people come in just with their buffed professional personas, turn in their numbers at the end of the day and go home to deal with the rest of their lives. That isn't a reasonable or a loving expectation.

We respect people's choice to use their time off in whatever way they want. We put sick leave, holidays, and vacation all together so we have a total number of days to use whenever, for whatever. All those ways we compartmentalize people are reflections of our mindset and our approach to disconnecting our mind, body, spirit, and heart. We don't operate that way as human beings and when we attempt to, we shut down. It causes stress, which causes disease and a breakdown in the humanness of our being.

The people who work here have a commitment to the vision, but this isn't just a soft nurturing place. We are whole and that includes left-brain, action-oriented stuff, too. We look at productivity very hard, we care about deadlines and commitments. But we have a different way of doing it. Everybody here has such a fire, a passion for doing what they are doing, that so much gets done. I don't have any need or desire to drive anyone.

If I am living my purpose and vision, I will live from a place of inspiration. If I am inspired, others will be inspired by my presence. They will find their own fire, passion, and reason for doing things well. When we find that, it is bigger than we are; it is beyond us and we will feel a genuine desire to do what is right. I don't want people to work hard because they feel guilty or because if they don't, they'll lose their job. I want them to give what they have because they love what we are doing."

Having heard two stories about doing good and having higher-purpose mission statements leads to an obvious question. Can doing good go hand in hand with making significant profits for more than a few, privately held companies? Benchmarking requires good measurements of success. Many people are coming to the conclusion that methods and financial goals both matter and are turning to socially responsible investing, hoping to prove they can be successful at both.

According to the January/February 1993 issue of *Business Ethics* magazine, assets under socially responsible management grew by 26 percent in 1992 to $2.2 billion. The leveraged buy out (LBO) financial arena is a good place to test this issue on some of the toughest grounds. Even here, new paradigms are already operating successfully. The firm of McCown De Leeuw & Co. came to my attention. George McCown, cofounder and managing partner of the firm, is the president of the World Business Academy (WBA), a network of business leaders committed to transformation for a sustainable world.

There are many stereotypes of LBOs. Few are positive. Yet here is a group using LBOs to transform mature, sometimes poorly performing companies into highly successful, innovative organizations. The way they go about this is what breaks the stereotype. Gauged by all traditional financial measures, they are an incredibly successful firm. Since beginning in 1984, they have raised $170 million in equity capital and invested in 20 diverse companies with total sales exceeding $3 billion. The historical rate of return on these investments has averaged over 40 percent per year to date.

George McCown's Story: Investing in Potential

"McCown De Leeuw and Co. (MDC) is a venture banking firm that's in the business of using organizational transformation to create superior values for our investors. We buy family-owned businesses when the founder wants to harvest his or her investment in the company. Or we acquire divisions of large companies that have more strategic priorities than the division in question. These are existing, mature operations, not start-up ventures, where we see a situation of untapped potential and often underperforming operations.

We are able to use the change of ownership as a "breakpoint" that opens the door to new principles, cultural changes, and new practices. We create space in which an organization can transform itself to reach a much higher level of performance. We don't see this as a one-time-only period of change. When we eventually sell the company—usually four to seven years down the road—that creates another breakpoint, which starts yet another life cycle. We may take them public, we may sell our position to the management and employees of the organization, or we may sell our position to another financial group that can take the company to a level that we cannot.

Our belief in organizational transformation is a distinguishing aspect of the way we conduct business. I believe that developing the right values for employees (integrity, accountability, responsibility) can be a means for creating market value for a business. The best way I know to do that is through individual empowerment, which often requires some form of transformation for each person involved. We believe people want to make a positive impact on their environment and to have a sense of purpose and meaning. They need to know that if they work hard and use their potential, they can enjoy the fruits of their labor.

This is a critical component to the transformations we try to encourage and support in the companies we acquire. We know we have been successful when the management group, acting as owners, leads the change and when employees begin acting like business people responsible for the entire company rather than as specialists with narrowly defined, functional responsibilities. We get results this way. We have one company that has achieved a 19-day order-to-delivery cycle while the dominant international competitors have four- to five-month cycles. This company is now working in stages toward a 24-hour cycle that may decrease total manufacturing costs 25 to 40 percent. In another case, operating results improved by 150 percent within the year following our acquisition and transformation endeavors.

We recognize that to achieve results like this, we and our partners in company management must build new paradigms for the way businesses are run. The historical model of business all too often has been one of exploiting the work force in exchange for job security. I'm not saying people didn't receive a benefit from their employment, but rather that previous behavior toward employees often was based on seeing the work force as a cheap renewable resource.

I believe that in the 1990s we're seeing a dramatic shift toward creating value through the development and empowerment of human capital. This will become critical for the success of any organization. At MDC, we make it happen through changes in management beliefs and behaviors that create a consistent space for new employee beliefs and behaviors. This "management innovation" has applicability often approaching or exceeding any technological innovations in terms of our continuing response to competitiveness.

All this has a life of its own that goes far beyond the workplace. We spend a huge percentage of our lives at work, so work is central to people. What happens there affects everything else we do. If we're satisfied at work, it affects our inner life, our family life, and our community life. Accordingly, business can take the lead in fostering an empowerment that spreads throughout our whole society.

Many experiences and influences have brought me to where I am now. In retrospect, I see all kinds of themes going through my life that seemed unrelated at first, but eventually have culminated here. One of those themes has been empowerment. I started learning lessons at an early age, and although I didn't know it at the time, they were about empowerment and leadership.

As I was growing up, I watched my dad go through a series of bosses. I saw how much energy he had to put into making sure each new boss didn't destroy the values he had built. My dad was an effective salesman and a man who lived by his word. This had a great influence on me. He was good with customers. He really delivered for them, not at the expense of the company, but in a way that maintained an extraordinary market penetration based on always doing what he said he would do. Dad often had to protect that franchise from each new boss.

Since the bosses often would stay at our house overnight to save the cost of hotels, I had more interaction with them than one might expect. What struck me at the time was, "I sure don't want to have to work for a big company and have to deal with this for the rest of my life." I think that is probably the earliest experience that began driving me toward doing what I do today. It remains vivid.

Another profound influence on my life has been my education (and the people I met through that experience). My dad insisted I get a good engineering undergraduate education at Stanford. After leaving Stanford, I spent three years in the Air Force flying for the Strategic Air Command. I had a lot of time to think about what I wanted to do with my life. I had been thinking about law school and politics, but chose to go to business school because I believed business was going to make more of a difference in the world than law. So I left for Harvard Business School in the fall of 1960.

I was given the opportunity to remain for an extra year as a teaching assistant to a famous senior professor of industrial management, General Georges F. Doriot. He taught as a full professor and also had a full-time job as president of American Research and Development Corporation, one of the earliest venture capital firms in America. I would say that Doriot was the best teacher that I have had. He had a reverence for business as a creative process and for the divinity of work. These were chords that struck deep within me, as well.

I also worked part-time for Doriot at American Research. I found I loved the creative aspects of venture capital and the entrepreneurialism of start-up venture capital, but I didn't like one aspect. We knew that eventually we would have to replace the original person we were backing. Most of the people who came through the doors at American Research were inventors or people with ideas. They usually weren't experienced business people.

That bothered me, and I wanted to run something anyway, so I went to work for Bob Hansberger at Boise Cascade, who was an enormous influence in my life. He was a farm boy from Worthington, Minnesota, who went to the University of Minnesota and Harvard Business School. He is a brilliant visionary person who was creating a peak-performing, empowered, and nonbureaucratic company in a very traditional industry by hiring young, energetic people and giving them the opportunity to make a difference.

I was at Boise Cascade for 18 years. The first ten years were phenomenal in terms of my opportunity to grow as a person. The last six or seven, however, were really painful in terms of seeing how a company can be pushed prematurely into bureaucracy through a traumatic event. (We took the largest write-off in the history of American business in 1972.) Ultimately, I left the company out of dissatisfaction with my ability to make a difference and reach for my own potential.

The other important theme for me has been an interest in spirituality and religion, which is something we don't talk about in business. In particular, I remember Harry Rathbun, who taught my undergraduate business law class at Stanford. Rathbun also ran "Sequoia Seminars." This was the forerunner to a program called "Creative Initiative" which later became "Beyond War." Although he was an engineer and lawyer by training, Rathbun and his wife were part of the early human potential movement where people took responsibility for making a difference in the world at the grass roots level. They strove to become conscious of the spiritual side of themselves as they engaged in materialistic pursuits.

Rathbun's final lecture to our Stanford class was "Christian Love." It made a profound impression on me. Interestingly, I was at a recognition ceremony for a fellow trustee at Stanford University recently. He quoted Rathbun's final lecture and mentioned what a profound effect it had had on him. That lecture was thirty years ago. The ability to reach someone spiritually is a powerful thing.

I am also interested in the diversity of personal beliefs. My mother was active in both the Presbyterian and Episcopal churches at various times. When I was in grammar school and high school, I made a friend who was a Baha'i. It's a world-wide religion that believes in a concept called "Progressive Divine Revelation." Baha'is believe that the same truth is there for everyone and that all the major prophets brought something special to the world at the time when it was needed.

When I was at the Harvard Business School, some of my best friends were Mormons and I became very active in that church for five years. Recently, as I have traveled extensively through India, Nepal, China, and Tibet, I have begun studying the history and beliefs of Hinduism, Buddhism, and Taoism, and have found the same underlying perennial truths found in all religions. The idea of teaching, of being a lifelong learner, of valuing education, of being open to the truth wherever I can find it is a big part of me that relates to this. I have been surrounded my entire life by teachers, starting with my mother and continuing with my wife, who today is my most important teacher.

So I have always been actively exploring the spiritual side of things. I believe that society's recent denial of spirituality, particularly in business, is a big mistake. Someday, somehow, somewhere, spirituality or consciousness is going to be a much bigger part of the equation than it is today. I have tried to foster this in myself and, to the extent I can, in those around me.

All these experiences have made me committed to excellence in leadership. A good boss and a good working environment have a more profound effect on people, on organizations, and on society than any one thing I can think of. Good bosses must provide good direction, but at the same time, value people and honor their aspirations in their work and as human beings. They must create an empowering vision people can relate to and constantly communicate that vision. They must provide discipline—rules to live by and work by—while at the same time providing freedom to grow, to make mistakes, and to learn.

Finally, I believe a good boss must be able to relate to people's spiritual needs—if not directly, then by recognizing that our individual desire to touch heaven, to seek that spark of divinity within us is the greatest power on earth. It is the force that motivates all people."

Another benchmarking question has to do with how widespread a practice or need is. In the context of who we could be at work, a question I'm often asked is if this need for meaning and purpose cuts across all lines of work. Do all types of workers ask these questions about themselves and their organizations?

The fact that people ask this question may mean something in itself. To what degree do we personally stereotype people by education and job function, let alone other issues like race, sex, or culture? How much has the workplace, the customer, the community lost because we haven't tapped tremendous potential in all our people?

Robert Killeen, United Auto Worker sub-regional director (retired) seemed like a good person to ask. He has been trying to create a new paradigm for workers throughout his life. He raises issues about the value and uniqueness of every individual in the workplace. Killeen is also one of the founders of the Minnesota Council for Quality and sits on its board of directors. He lives quality out in the deepest way.

Bob Killeen's Story: There Is More to Work . . .

"When I was young, I was a person who would take management on at the drop of a hat. If they wanted to fight, I was right there to fight. Unions are good at it. We react and we have always reacted to what management does. There is a lot to react to, since we are the most antiunion industrialized country in the world. That was a tough way to work every day.

Management has been good at fighting unions and unions have been good at fighting back. When we do that, we get what we have. If this doesn't change, we will just get smaller and smaller. Both management and the unions are going downhill and losing. We have to change that. We have to work together so that when we get to the bargaining table there is something there to bargain about. I am changing and I think many others are changing.

One of the core challenges has been management's basic perspective on workers. Most companies take good workers and make bad ones out of them. I am convinced of that. When we made the products the way we were supposed to, we could see they weren't what they should be. I remember times I came up with ideas for improvements in the manufacturing line and was always told, "We pay engineers good money to figure these things out. You just do your job." Most managers believed that workers really were dumb and treated us that way.

Many still believe that and many business schools are still teaching that form of Taylorism today. That's no way for a person to have to work. I remember being time-studied on the line. A person stood with a stopwatch on the shop floor and measured every motion you made. He would try to catch you making an extra motion and define whether or not you needed to do that.

Right away, it was a threat. It was a challenge between that worker and the man with the stopwatch to see who could outmaneuver the other one. We'd cover up our shortcuts all the time. Nobody knows the job better than the guy working on the line, so when the time-study man left, we went right back to our usual shortcuts again. That's how we achieved productivity. It was insane, but many companies are still using this system. Can you think of a more idiotic way to try to get people to be more productive?

Another example. Companies do a horrible job at performance evaluation. What a waste of time. They can't keep personalities out of it. Most managers start smiling when I talk about reviews. They admit they don't like to do evaluations; it's a horrible job to sit there and judge someone else. Most of them make a horrible mess out of them. There's much change that has to be done around this—peer reviews, for example.

I started looking for solutions back in the late sixties because this just didn't make sense. It was just too hard to work the way it was going. It was self-defeating; we weren't gaining anything for workers. What are you accomplishing if you get a worker out of a mess one day, and two weeks later they are back into it as deep as they ever were because of the system? Much of what I wanted to see I found in the total quality movement.

We have to make a major turnaround in this country, but it's going to take some national leadership to do it. That's the sad part; there is no leadership on a national level to change industrial policy to something that will take us down the quality road. We have to keep improving or this new generation isn't going to have all the advantages we have had. That is a terrible outlook. We need to get union leaders leading the quality movement, involved in the process and on the steering committees because the unions that do this successfully gain far more respect from their membership. They can become facilitators for quality. I subscribe to Dr. Deming's Fourteen Points, plus one. Unions and workers should begin to demand that their companies implement Total Quality Management policies. This could be a future strike issue.

Management and workers must become partners rather than adversaries, or we will all lose. We have to give up our old ways of always trying to write every rule in our contracts. If you look at the Saturn agreement, you'll see it's a thin book. On the other hand, the Ford agreement is three books long and no one knows what half of it is. We have to talk about restructuring and consolidating classifications, which is a problem for unions. They started out as a management tool, but then we built fences around everything so no one can do anything anymore without causing a ripple effect. So we have to look at reducing classifications and restructuring how they are used.

Unions still have a job to do at the bargaining table. I don't know of a single company that has been involved in a total quality movement that has ever decertified a union. Just the opposite is true. When you start involving workers, teaching them in the shop, unions become stronger, not weaker. Workers would much rather see union leaders being creative and solving problems than sitting there fighting with the company all day long. Workers have to be willing to set aside the past and the belief that management is always out to get them, and build up trust by watching new management behavior. If management shows no desire to change, then we can hang on to the past.

What management has to do is start believing that workers have more to contribute than their hands. They also need to learn how to share authority. That is a big hang-up for them. They think by giving up some authority, they are going to lose something, when just the opposite is true. If they start sharing authority with the work force, they are going to gain much more authority than they ever thought possible. They are going to have much more respect and will gain tremendously in productivity and profitability.

Look at training at FMC Naval Systems. Most of the training programs had little effect because they used to be done by management, who didn't really understand the jobs. Over the last few years, two union workers were empowered to set up the training programs. They established programs that are meaningful, tough, and focused on true needs.

People need to be empowered, to have self-esteem, a sense of importance. Who wants to go to work and do a job all day when nobody will listen to you? That's what makes jobs boring. Even with the most repetitive job, you can still figure out how to improve it. Look at Zytech, one of the Baldrige Quality Award–winning companies. Every employee has a $1,000.00 blank check a year to use to improve their job, no questions asked. Ron Schmidt, their CEO, says that program works well. They spend money more wisely than management ever did. They would never discontinue the program.

There are results we can describe and there are results we could realize that we can't imagine. Saturn is one result that many couldn't have imagined. I would love to be able to spend five years working in that operation. There you have a maximum of worker involvement. They work in teams, do their own training, and the union is involved in all decision making. It's an outstanding example of quality. I saw a survey that said there were only two cars that were ahead of Saturn in quality and they cost two-and-a-half times what Saturn does. I think it's the best quality car for the money in the United States or in the world. That would be my example of the ultimate—working under the Saturn arrangement.

Eventually, I think we're going to have unions on the boards of directors of companies. Some unions are going to have to make some concessions, but what they ought to be demanding is that they have someone sitting on the board. I remember Doug Fraser talking about his experience being on the Chrysler board. Most people sitting on the boards of companies have no concept of what happens on the shop floor. Someone from the labor movement, whether a union leader or not, could bring a new perspective of great benefit.

I think there will be more companies like Tennant. I shared the quality counsel chairmanship with Roger Hale, the CEO of Tennant, for the first three years. Tennant was in deep trouble in 1979 because its equipment leaked oil. The Japanese were not willing to accept its sweepers. But through a quality effort with a lot of worker involvement, Tennant turned itself around. Roger Hale has a nonunion shop. The reason it's nonunion is because his workers are happy and he treats them with respect. I really don't care if a company is union or not as long as they treat their people decently and pay a living wage and benefits. We try to unionize places that are treating their people shabbily.

Harley Davidson is another great story of a turnaround. I have taken a couple of unions and companies to visit their plant. When you go in, they give you a two-hour overview of what you will be seeing. We met with the plant manager, the union president, and the full-time union quality man. I asked this union quality guy whether management really listens to the workers and the union. He answered, "You're damn right they do. We're the ones responsible for quality in this shop. We are not going to let this company go back to where they were in 1979 and 1980 when we had all taken concessions, when we had many of our people on layoff and the rest of us were near ready to lose our jobs."

I was watching that manager, and he had a smile from ear to ear because he can now go out and do the things he is best trained for: to manage the company, take care of customers, and find new customers. He will keep his eye on quality, but he won't have to give it all the attention he did in the past. So he's having a great time and so are the workers. That's the way it should be.

The other reason I believe we could have more great but unpredictable results comes from history. There's an interesting story of how incentives grew in this country during the second World War. Managers would set a standard with the aid of the best time-study people. They would set it so that the worker would produce 100 widgets an hour and would get paid an incentive for doing that. He would get more money for going over that number. Well, in no time at all, he was producing 120. Management would go back and tighten the standards up. So the workers' quota would become 120, and the worker would produce 140 or 160. It kept happening.

Workers were so efficient and imaginative they drove themselves out of business on incentive plans. They just became too expensive for companies to handle and it never ceases to amaze me that to this day many companies haven't figured out what that means. Why couldn't they see that these guys are imaginative, they're great engineers, they're great thinkers and they could always beat the best time study? That's why incentive plans are not around much anymore. Workers could take too much advantage of them.

I know companies ought to be making money. They ought to be competitive with anyone in the world, if they are managed right. I know workers' wages can improve. I also know work is important to each individual. Not just money, but to build worker self-esteem, to make a contribution, and to have fun. Self-esteem is developed through worker empowerment. To do all that, we need to understand that work makes you a whole human being. We may be working harder, but we will be enjoying it more. If you're not having fun, there's something wrong with the job. I don't care what kind of a job it is—even a lousy job can be fun.

That's the whole idea of worker participation. Walter Reuther used to say, "There is more to a worker's job than punching in and leaving your brain at the time clock, reporting to your job, then reporting back to the time clock at the end of the shift, and picking up your brain to go home."

A consultant I know, Wayne Alderson, brings love into this whole equation. He has a Theory R, that is focused on doing what is right— real complicated stuff. It's based on three concepts: dignity, respect, and love. We all deserve those basics and will make a contribution of at least equal value in return. I think your work has a tremendous effect on your life. If you have bad working conditions, it affects your marriage, your children, and your community."

———————————

There isn't a category in any of the quality awards that measures the letting-go process, but that is a critical component of a change. If people, teams, and organizations can't let go of their beliefs and practices, one of two things happens. The change effort fails or meets stiff resistance. Or people start trying to hold on to two sets of beliefs and practices, causing double the work, waste, and mixed signals. The next story illustrates the process of letting go from an individual's perspective.

Patricia Hedberg spent 10 years in front-line and middle-management positions at Honeywell and National Computer Systems before changing her career focus. Along the way, she completed her Ph.D. in industrial/organizational psychology. Today she is an assistant professor in business management at the University of St. Thomas.

This story is about an individual who found a significantly different way to be at work and the very personal journey that it took. An understanding that comes through is that we can't just decide to be something else. We are required to explore and journey, whether as an individual or an organization. It's a little easier to see the journey of the individual. Part of what struck me was that to go somewhere else requires us to leave where we are. We need to let go of beliefs, people, places, goals, and dreams.

———————————

Pat Hedberg's Story: Letting Go of the American Dream

———————————

"I had dreams of being the corporate person, of moving up in the pecking order. My dream wasn't to go to the top, but to have power. That was the big thing. I wanted to be in a place where I could influence what the company was doing. I knew I probably wouldn't stay in human resources and that I wanted to get into more line work.

If that didn't work, I felt I would like to be an executive in human resources. When you're in business, you do this nice linear progression up the corporate ladder. I was willing to do a lot to achieve that, but I had little idea what it meant.

I didn't get this belief of "That is what you do in business" from my parents. It was just out there in the atmosphere and I picked it up. I guess this vision of success just came from the American Dream. I don't remember any particular book that inspired me. It's funny how we get "the right way to be" messages. I was at Honeywell at the time, and in regard to women it was as innovative as any company, but there weren't a lot of role models. That was part of my confusion. "How do you do this? How do you live your life?"

My work was burning me out, but I'm not sure I realized it at the time. I was almost obsessed with work, thinking about it constantly, putting in long hours, traveling—which was normal for most of us—and it was taking its toll on me. To get more experience, I transferred to Training, despite rumors of layoffs. I guess we always think we are going to be immune, that we're good enough. My husband could tell that I wasn't being who I could be and that work had much to do with that. I think he almost wanted me to get laid off, even though there would be some financial struggle.

I remember how work almost stopped because we knew layoffs were coming. There were rumors in the business community that Honeywell was being bought by someone else. We were in a constant huddle just standing around talking about, "What is the latest rumor? How many people will be laid off? What percent? What did your stockbroker say?" I almost wanted to be one of the ones laid off.

Then I found out I was on the list. I got through the initial shock. There was shock, even though I had expected it. All the signals were there saying, "You're vulnerable, you're new, you don't have the allies built up." I remember how embarrassing it was to me. This was during the beginning waves of layoffs. Today it seems natural that everybody will be laid off at one time or another. But at that time, I felt it reflected on me personally. I felt singled out, as though everybody was looking at me. That they didn't want to associate with me because I was tainted. It was as if they wanted to protect themselves from what a layoff felt like and were putting up a veneer to protect themselves.

Part of my fear was that I would be tainted for future jobs. Who would want me now? What would I tell people? There was fear that

I didn't belong anymore. If you're chosen to leave, then you don't belong to the group; the group has said that they don't want you. That had never happened to me before. I had always been the person to be chosen, even when I played softball. We carry around that old fear that we won't be chosen and it's hard to shake off.

One of the hardest things to reconcile was, "How do I introduce myself to people? Who am I?" Our identities are so tied up in our professions that when we go to a party and meet somebody, we say, "Hi, I am so and so. This is my job and where I work." So what was I, now? When I went to conferences, I didn't know what to put on my name tag. It was the start of a process for me to learn to feel comfortable with myself as someone different from just being tied up in work.

I realized I had been beaten down by the whole experience. Not just the layoff, but the whole experience of working in that environment, of being the corporate person, of wearing the gray and blue suits and the little bow ties. I knew then that I needed to nurture myself and get back in touch with what I really wanted to do. My termination was really a gift, although I'm sure that's not how Honeywell thought of it.

Several months after the layoff, I was asked to come back as a freelancer to do a specific project. I remember walking in and seeing people looking so oppressed, like they were under siege. I felt I was the one who was lucky to be gone. I realized the experience really was one of freedom. For someone like me who is very loyal, it would have taken a great deal for me to choose to leave. Even though it was the best thing for me, I would not necessarily have chosen that for myself.

That experience gave me the permission I needed to make my own career path. Some of us are so directed toward what other people want, we forget what we want. Then we acquire a lot of fear. It felt selfish to talk about me and what I wanted. You never go to an interview and say, "Well, this is what I want from this job." You are supposed to say, "This is what I can do for you." I learned that when you have that sense of who you are and what makes you happy, people want to connect with you. Then you have something to give back to the people that you are with.

I knew I didn't fit in the human resources game plan, positions, and basic beliefs any more. I was sort of abnormal. In a way, that was kind of fun. By being abnormal, I could figure out, "Well, what does normal mean for me?" No longer did I have to take what other people gave me as the right way to be. I decided that what I wanted was to finish my doctoral dissertation and then search for something different. I wasn't even finished with the dissertation when National Computer Systems approached me about an entrepreneurial position. Having experienced the Honeywell layoff and all the emotional trauma that went with it, it was very affirming to be sought out for this position.

As a result of the layoff experience, the whole hiring process was different for me. Speaking as an academic researcher, one of the things we have discovered about layoffs is that all of a sudden (in the employee's mind), the company has broken a commitment. The implied agreement is that if the employee does a good job, he or she will be secure. I felt as though Honeywell had broken its commitment to me, so I felt freer to negotiate in this new offering.

In the past, I cared more about what the company was getting, what it needed from me, rather than being concerned for myself. I believed I would be rewarded if I focused on their needs. Now, even though I was very excited about the entrepreneurial nature of the division and trying my hand at marketing, I made sure I understood what was expected of me and that they knew what I expected. I took the job with NCS, enjoyed it, and learned a lot. I also continued to watch for what was working and what wasn't working for me.

I did a good job and I was better able to make the decision to leave that organization when I felt the need. When I was eight months pregnant I left. That was another big transition. The last thing I ever wanted to do was to fit into the stereotype of a pregnant woman who left the company. I fight so much for women to have their choice to do what they want. Being pregnant wasn't a factor in my decision to quit, although it probably helped with the timing. There were some good opportunities for me in the company, but I just kept coming to the realization that none of them interested me any more. That was a key for me—the lack of excitement.

There was a particular event that highlighted this for me. I was working 50 to 60 hours a week at my job, teaching an evening class at St. Thomas, and pregnant. One night after a really hard day, I was driving to class and I didn't want to go. I was so tired, I just wanted to go home. But I went.

Driving home after the class, I was so excited. I wanted to tell my husband everything that happened in class. It was great. . . . Then it hit me. If I could go into teaching that tired and come out feeling like this, maybe that was a better life for me. Maybe I needed something different. I didn't decide at that moment to go into teaching, but it made me realize there were other things that could excite me more than what I was doing. I left NCS and focused on motherhood and part-time teaching for about a year.

Motherhood was a gift. We had gone through years of fertility treatment, so the idea that I was having this little one was incredible. I wanted to spend time with my child, but knew I wasn't going to be a full-time mother. This was a transition that gave me time with my son and breathing space to explore some other ideas.

Now I am a full-time, tenure-track assistant professor at St. Thomas. And I love it. I interviewed for the job when my son was a baby and started when he was about one year old. Finding a career that lets me be me, that lets me be a whole person, more than I ever have before, that gives me flexibility, encourages me to be involved in the community and be a mother and a family member has allowed me to thrive. I couldn't even imagine this splendid combination before.

My new goal is to have more and more integration, rather than balance, in my life. In *Seven Habits of Highly Effective People*, Steven Covey talks about identifying your different roles in life and setting goals for those roles. While that model has value, what I am finding is that I want the roles all meshed together. I take my son to my office so he sees where I am. I talk about my son and family in class. And I take home what I learn at work. A constant question for me is, How do I get more integration in the future?

I don't mean to sound overly optimistic or Pollyanna-ish because every day has its struggles. This morning my son was crying, "I don't want to go to day care." We'd had a great weekend. It would have been fun to play a little more. Then there are days that I don't want to leave work because things are happening and clicking.

There is another piece to the integration. When I grew up, I was always told that you wore your grubbies at home and you wore good clothes outside the home. You were always on your best behavior with other people; with your family, you were more real. I am trying to get away from that, to realize that we can be grubby outside the home and not always be on our best behavior. And I am trying to bring more of my best behavior home. I think we need to give our family some of the respect we give people outside the family. I am trying to weave that in, too. I'm letting go of many old beliefs and dreams. I'm much happier with my new ones.

I encourage my students to take risks in their lives and to explore what really matters to them. One of the biggest fears most people have has already happened to me and the world didn't fall in. It was painful and embarrassing, and it caused fear, but I discovered my own inner strength. It's very freeing to learn that we are the constant, that we have our own strength to carry ourselves forward. The organization you work for is a more powerful organization when it harnesses that. Your family and friends are more powerful when you can bring that into your relationships."

2

Dying and Noticing It

Ten years ago . . .
I turned my face for a moment and it became my life.

AS QUOTED IN DAVID WHYTE'S BOOK,
The Heart Aroused

A new way of living for individuals, groups, families, and organizations frequently begins with the death of the old way. There are many ways to die. We can die after a prolonged illness or we can die in an instant from an accident or a heart attack. We're all very aware of this and would prefer not to think about it. We are less aware, however, of nonphysical kinds of dying, especially those related to work. It's critical to begin discussing these emotional and spiritual forms of dying. They're a major source of pain and harm. They are also a source of learning. By addressing them, we can extend, expand, and enhance life.

There is significant dying of one type going on in our organizations today. Downsizing and re-engineering efforts are putting more and more people out of work. Jeremy Rifkin's book, *The End of Work*, documents the huge number of people going through this. In addition, he demonstrates why there are not and will not be nearly enough replacement jobs for those people and why re-training will work for only a small percentage.

I'm happy for those who have jobs and are satisfied in their work and organization. I feel for those who are not. There are people in the workplace who have found a way to accommodate themselves to what they have and don't have. Others are unhappy and without hope. They may have resigned themselves. They assume the only way work can be is the way it is. Then there are those who haven't had the time or opportunity even to think about whether it could be different.

In some cases, the pain is so bad we block it out by burying our needs and dreams. Sometimes we deny they even exist until there's a layoff, no chance of promotion left, or until we wake up and ask, "Is this all there is?" Others discover their work-related pain through personal trauma—a divorce occurs or a child gets in serious trouble. Then we begin to see how work has affected our personal lives. The stories in this section are of people who noticed they were suffering and dying in this nonphysical sense and what they did to regain their health and life.

We can look healthy from a physical perspective, but be dying emotionally or spiritually inside. Emotional death is all about denying feelings, or noticing them and dismissing them as unimportant. That is what we are taught to do at work and we used to believe there were no consequences for doing it. Organizations are trying to move more and more toward teamwork, cooperation, and empowerment, or other types of change. They often fail, and their leaders are left wondering why such good ideas work in other places and not for them. The cause of success or failure can often be traced to how people feel about people. When we deny emotions at work, we create personal and group disabilities by shutting down the part of ourselves that allows us to connect with other people. That is critical to teamwork, empowerment, and cooperation. We are left going through the motions without the substance. Worse yet, research suggests that emotional close-downs catch up to us in the form of illness.

This process happens to organizations, as well as to individuals. An organization has an emotional climate, even if the climate is a cold, fear-filled one. Many years ago, when I was making a career shift, I learned to go to interviews early. I would sit in the lobby and, in many subtle ways, receive clues as to what it would be like to work at each company. Companies can be sick from emotional disorders for a long time, or even die from them.

For instance, we see companies in trouble because they lack new products. We diagnose their problems as having a scarcity of innovation, being out of step with the market, falling behind the technology change curve, or having cumbersome processes for development. For some, these assessments may be true and the truth may stop there. For others, they could be symptoms of something deeper. The real problem may be the emotional climate of the company. People who avoid risk out of fear cannot cooperate because they don't trust each other. In another company, functions may see each other as enemies or at least as competitors. Decisions can be made that cause harm to the whole organization but are good for the individual function.

Spiritual is a word we are just beginning to use in business, but it is very real. I don't know another word that covers vision, values, ethics, purpose, and all the intangibles that are the guts of life. It describes the sum total of our understanding about how life works. When its spiritual aspect isn't working, an organization loses energy, commitment, drive, and cohesion. There is a danger of acquiring legal and ethical problems within the company and between the company and its customers, suppliers, and various governmental agencies.

Spiritual death occurs with the withering of our values. In the more severe cases, this results in the articles we read about fraud, embezzlement, and other acts of desperation. When we feel we are supposed to do something questionable, we are capable of incredible rationalizations, which produce disorders in our intellectual capabilities. We start losing perspective on reality and actually start to believe our rationalizations. The result is poor decision making.

Spiritual deficits appear when employees and management don't share an inspiring vision or from living in situations that cause even mild, but continuous, internal conflict. Ideally, each employee's personal vision will be supported and recognized and tied to the corporate vision. Peter Senge describes this well in his section on personal mastery in *The Fifth Discipline*: "If people don't have their own vision, all they can do is sign up for someone else's. The result is compliance, never commitment." For the majority of us, this is often manifested in a sense that our lives lack meaning, of wondering if there is something more out there, or of just feeling as though some of our potential is being wasted, untapped. Part of our aliveness and energy is gone.

More and more companies have come to realize that trust matters significantly. People measure other people's trustworthiness based on an emotional sense about whether there is honest concern for all involved, and through a sense of the other person's spiritual core. So if we want trust, we have to deal with emotions and spirituality. Without emotional and spiritual energy, individuals and organizations develop many destructive symptoms that can even lead to their death.

I see more and more people wrestling, both consciously and unconsciously, with emotional and spiritual death. Most of them are wrestling with it around issues related to work. This surprised me at first, but after some thought and exploration, it now seems obvious. After all, in our culture, we spend at least 50 percent of our waking lives doing things associated with work. For many people, the percentage is much higher. When you consider that many people derive their main identity from work, and that it's generally believed that emotions and spiritual issues are not acceptable at work, we are looking at a blueprint for trouble.

Steven Covey begins his book, *Seven Habits of Highly Effective People*, with this observation: "In more than 25 years of working with people in business, university, and marriage and family settings, I have come in contact with many individuals who have achieved an incredible degree of outward success, but have found themselves struggling with an inner hunger, a deep need for per-

sonal congruency and effectiveness and for healthy, growing relationships with other people."

When these feelings of spiritual or emotional disease appear,
we don't turn to doctors. One place more people are turning is to
spiritual counseling. Richelle Pearl-Koller, pastoral associate for
Christ the King Catholic Church, has counseled many people
through these difficult experiences. She says,

> The people who are seeking assistance include psychiatrists,
> auto mechanics, business managers, secretaries, and nurses.
> Most are in their forties and fifties, but it seems to be moving
> down into people in their thirties. I'm not sure if this sense of
> dying is becoming more common, or if people simply feel more
> free to talk about it. There is a lot of similarity in how people de-
> scribe the experience.
>
> Some people describe the problem as a sense of not fitting
> anywhere anymore, of feeling as though life is crowding in on
> them, and of having a vast sense of meaninglessness. Others
> focus on how the value system in American business is contrary
> to their personal and ethical values and how it is based on
> competitiveness and getting ahead. They talk about the tension
> between the kind of persons they have to be at work—charging
> ahead, constantly engaged, very directed and task-oriented—as
> opposed to the kind of persons they are as mothers or fathers—
> allowing a realm of chaos so that a child's creativity can develop.
> Others describe the horrendous conflict in the areas of time, so
> that it seems as though work is consuming us more and more,
> like quicksand. . . .
>
> When they describe the experience, the words become similar.
> That inner struggle in people, as I have seen it happen, manifests
> itself physically in a sort of constant gasping for air. It's as though
> we want to take in something more or get rid of something. If we
> look at it from a biblical perspective, the word for *spirit* is *Ruah*,
> meaning breath. When we lose our *Ruah*, we lose our spirit, we
> no longer have inspiration, even though our external world
> doesn't see it.
>
> And then there is the hook: We can still perform our jobs very
> well throughout this experience, but because the inspiration and
> the breath are gone, it's like being brain-dead. We are like ghosts.
> Again, no one on the outside sees it. They keep asking for all the
> things we have always done, and they tell us how good we are at

that. I don't care what we do for a living, there is something about a job that attracts us, something we like to do, and that is what got us into that work. So we feel caught between these feelings.

When we first begin to sense we're dying, we are like the hermit crab, who has to get out of its shell and find a new shell when it grows. If it doesn't, it will suffocate. So it goes along the beach, knowing it should look for another shell. It appears to be easier to stay in the old house, but it will suffocate. To go to the new one is risky: it won't fit in it for a while, the new shell will be too much for it. This is a threshold moment, a doorway, an opening to the new, and this is always a sacred moment. What we need to help people do is dwell in that moment, with all its discomfort and vulnerability, and not push them. We are so product-oriented in our society that there is a tendency to feel we must choose rapidly—to go or to stay—and be done with it. Rather, we must treat it as a sacred time and do the inner work and assessment necessary before we move to the next house.

We should learn all we can about this moment because this is not a nonrepeatable cycle. It is the eternal cycle. It is a myth to think that once we get to the next shell, that's it, because that would be death. This is just the core of living. All of life is just this constant. It's the seasons, it's the earth, it is everything. It is the seed in the ground. All the imagery we talk about deals with the eternal cycle of death and birth. And that's what business is about. That's what work is about. Sometimes it is a major shift where you move totally out of that system into a new one, and sometimes it's a minor shift where you stay and retool within the same system. Dying and birth are closely connected and go on and on.

The stories that follow help us explore what it's like to be in this space and on the other side of it. We can examine whether we are experiencing our own form of dying, understand it better, and so choose if we want to plunge more willingly and deeply into the process of change. If this process seems totally alien, we need to wonder how we are avoiding such a natural growth cycle.

These stories also help us investigate the experience of non-physical forms of dying, both individually and organizationally. We may recognize ourselves, someone else, or our team in the dynamics of the stories. We could learn to identify this kind of death before another ten years of our lives have passed.

Sometimes we have to be willing to walk away from a lot of safety in order to keep living. Would you walk away from a vice presidency of a major corporation, from a position with money, perks, and status? Most of us find it hard to imagine that someone at the top of an organization would do this. We find it hard to believe they can be as miserable as we are some days. In fact, we don't give them much space for having feelings at all.

Intellectually, we know that happiness is not acquired through status and material gain. Behaviorally, however, we seem to believe it is. James Bowe, former vice president at Control Data Corporation, had it made by all social standards of success. Yet he knew he wasn't satisfied. His is the experience of dying at work because the work itself didn't seem to matter enough and the work process was not inclusive enough.

Jim Bowe's Story: Walking Away from It All

"About ten years ago, I was in the executive ranks at Control Data. I was in the power structure and I was dying, hating it. I was absolutely unsatisfied, not getting anything that I needed, and not being able to admit it. To admit it would have probably made me feel weird and ashamed because who wouldn't be happy with money, title, position, status, perks, and a warm place to park my car?

I know that dying is a strong word, but I realized how accurate it was when I got a wake-up call one morning. I was driving to work and suddenly this big dump truck, filled with a load of concrete slabs, looked like it was going to dump over on me going around a curve. My first thought was, "My God, I could go into the hospital for a while and I wouldn't have to go to work." That was really startling. So I began to realize that I wanted to get out.

I learned something from the book *Ordinary People*. There is a boy who is depressed and suicidal. He went to see a wonderful psychiatrist who explained that depression is an escape from feelings. When we have intense, painful feelings, we go into a depression that will kill all feelings. It's a way to escape the pain. Then there is no joy, there is no anything, there is just "blaa." That was the first time I really understood anything about depression.

I think half the people in the workplace are in a state of semidepression because of the need to keep all our feelings under wraps—we can't do it selectively. We just get flat. So we have a flat workplace and we don't have terrible grief or wonderful joy. Therefore, we don't have the spirit of creativity, excitement, energy, and all those things that are necessary to make any individual or organization thrive.

I began to realize I wasn't alone. I was talking to a senior person in my organization about this and he said, "Jim, please do me a favor. Figure out a way for somebody at my level to cut back without losing face and without being thought of as a total failure to the company." He said he had all the power he wanted at the company and he didn't want to have the level of responsibility and the pressure anymore, but he still had plenty to contribute. He was afraid that if he asked to back off and was allowed to do that, everybody would think, "He's through. He really must have done something terrible. He fell on his face. Look what they have taken away."

More and more people are waking up. I'm in a men's group that meets once a week and this is happening to several people in it. They are finding they are totally dissatisfied with their workplace. They are learning how to be full-life persons outside their work. They are seeing they have to be someone else in their work and they are just getting more and more unwilling to make that sacrifice. It's not worth it.

In my case, I need to be consulted about what I do, and I didn't feel there was enough of that. I work very poorly simply taking orders. I am a creative person, so I have things to add to projects that can make them better. In the beginning, it was the greatest thing in the world because they said, "Bowe, you know how to do this stuff. Come in and do it." But things changed. Finally, I wasn't able to put my stamp on things and say, "This is mine. This is my best work," and stand or fall on it. I need to feel respected and valued enough to be asked. I think that is one of the main things wrong in organizations today; that people are not being consulted. They are not being asked to participate in the choices, the decisions, the plans. I was not. That was one thing.

The other thing was, I didn't believe in the value of the end product. My responsibility at that time was communications. I was in charge of internal communications, public relations, corporate advertising, stockholder communications, and also executive communications—booklets, expressions of who we were and what we were aiming to do. There was a lot of that to be done and that's what I was most personally involved in. I came into this corporate executive communications spot and realized just too much of it did not ring true. And, indeed, it hasn't stood the test of time.

Lastly, I think there were attitudes developing that were very counterproductive and not unusual. It seemed as though a sickness had begun to pervade the company. We did not bring bad news to the boss. Like in a Greek drama, the messenger got eliminated. When we can't bring bad news, we're going to have some terrible surprises. We were beginning to act as though we believed in certain things because important people's names were involved and at stake. Suggestions that something might not be the wisest thing for us to do were unwelcome.

I need meaning in my life. There is no way to get any meaning out of living a flat life, not being a part of something worthwhile or contributing to the creation of things valuable to humankind. I just think that people do have a value system that requires something meaningful. One of the most impressive books I ever read was Frankl's *Man's Search for Meaning*. I just reread it last year. It was ten times as powerful as it was when I first read it about 30 years ago.

I realized I wanted to undertake something on my own. I decided to take a "wake up and get well" process and build a business around it. I wanted to create workshops and services to help people examine their work life in the context of their whole life and purpose. I wanted to help them explore what they really wanted in their lives, not what they had been told to want. It's a very hard sell because what we are asking management to do is pull back and let people have a say in what they do instead of just telling them. There aren't that many top people who are able to do that, although they talk about it.

I am one of the most optimistic and hopeful people around, but I still get very discouraged about that. My generation, those of us over 50 or 55, is still in charge of most of the big outfits. We learned how to gain power and exercise it. We didn't learn anything about wholeness and empowerment. We haven't had any practice at that stuff. So how are organizations going to change? Must we have an epidemic of heart attacks of everybody over 40, so that there will be a generational change over to people who are younger and more open? Then the problem is that those very people are still being groomed by the older people and being shown the old model of what we have to be like and sound like and look like. I am helping change this in my own way, as best I can. That is meaningful to me. It takes time and real dedication and hard work.

CDC decided to invest money in my enterprise to help me get it launched, because they were going to use the service. They were going to buy the workshops for people, for career development within the company, at least within the management ranks. So I had a wonderful send-off and an optimistic departure and was well funded. By the time the product was ready, though, CDC had begun to lose money and they weren't the customer for it that they had expected to be. It was rough for a while.

If I had known that earlier, I wonder if I would have had the guts to pull out. I grew up in the depression. For a kid who was really poor at one time, I was making it by every definition. We don't just walk away from that unless we think some bigger and better changes are possible. But I am not at all regretful that I did it. What I have done has tremendous value to the people in the organizations that use it. And it has been extremely satisfying for me. I'm living and growing now."

One side of death is waste. Susan Anderson's story illustrates that experience of dying at work that comes from feeling wasted. This is one of the hardest things about the process of dying—the wasting away that can precede death. If you have watched a loved one go through the fight against cancer, for example, the pain of watching them deteriorate can be more devastating than death itself. We have a tremendous amount of wasted human beings and talent in our organizations. We label people as fit or unfit for different kinds of work as they come in the door and we may begin their march of decay, rather than growth.

Today, Anderson is the executive director of the Bloomington Arts Center. If you look at her budget, accountabilities, and management responsibilities, she operates as a small division manager. Her energy and creativity, and the growth rate of the art center at a time when most art enterprises are shrinking, are good news for her community. Her former corporate employers think they lost an executive secretary. Actually, they lost skills, energy, and knowledge that far exceed their assumptions. And they don't even know it. This is a serious blind spot for organizations.

This story speaks of the deplorable waste in our current organizational paradigms. It is an example of what happens to an overwhelming percentage of people who are not executives or middle managers. It happens in higher ranks, too, but significantly more to people who carry titles like worker, administrator, secretary, or operator. As an executive secretary, Anderson felt trapped in a box, prevented from using all her skills and denied recognition when they were used.

Even more lamentable are the times we don't listen to someone because of his or her position in the organization. These people try to warn us of problems, try to offer insights about an issue or an innovative idea to solve a problem. We are blinded even to demonstrated skills by title, education, sex, race, and other differences. We end up killing a person's spirit or, if they have the resources to leave, we lose their contributions.

Susan Anderson's Story: So Much Talent, So Much Waste

"After 20 years in executive secretarial and administrative positions, working for good companies, I left corporate life because I couldn't live that way anymore. I took about a 25 percent pay cut when I left and I lost all the benefits: my 401K, employee stock options, health insurance, and life insurance. Losing all of that was really a shock. But I would do it again in a minute.

In my last position, I loved the people, I loved the work, but I continued running into issues about how people are treated as expendable in corporate America. That may sound odd, but it was true. There is constant rhetoric about people being a company's greatest asset. From my perspective, even in the best companies, it seemed as though there wasn't enough consideration for how corporate decisions would affect the employees. I am very people-oriented and I felt my values were pitted against what I perceived as corporate values. It caused frequent internal struggles. I finally said, "OK, it's always going to be like this, and I can't live this way."

I was treated well and not so well in my jobs at ADC Telecommunications, Inc., National Car Rental, and Chun King Corporation. I'll always be grateful for the training ADC provided and for many good learning experiences at my other jobs. At the same time, I kept feeling stuck.

I left college after two years because of personal reasons that, in retrospect, probably were foolish. At that time, the way to break into the business world was to begin as a secretary. I was lucky to become the secretary to a senior vice president at Chun King Corporation. I had the capacity to learn and I learned quickly. When anybody asked me if I wanted to take on a project, I always did. I liked the tremendous variety and learning that provided. As long as I worked with people who allowed me to take on higher-level projects than my job description called for, I thought I could be satisfied.

Over time, though, I found myself working at that higher capacity, doing the same kind of work other people were doing, but never getting the same kind of money, recognition, or appreciation because they had different titles and education. When I started as a secretary at National Car Rental, the whole marketing, advertising, and sales department consisted of two people—my supervisor and me. As the company grew, I trained new college graduates on the marketing programs my supervisor and I had initiated and that I administered. These included a national co-op and yellow page advertising, and the internal company newsletter, which I completely wrote and produced.

Then new marketing people were added; they took over the programs, and I went back to sit behind the typewriter. While I didn't resent the people and actually became good friends with them, I felt others in the company placed higher value on the programs I had nurtured and implemented as a secretary just because they were now being administered by people with higher titles.

Companies make too many decisions about people based on hierarchy. If my boss was a director, I couldn't make as much money as a vice president's secretary, who might do half the work. At another point, I was turned down for a sales administrator position because I only had an AA degree and not a BA degree. My twenty years of experience in the business world didn't count against 22-year-old BA grads. I felt like I was never, ever going to have an opportunity to grow out of my box and be recognized for it.

It wasn't just me and it wasn't just people without degrees who got hurt. I would say that careless layoffs and shifting of people can destroy a group or department. I am an intensely loyal person, so I'm very affected by what happens around me. I have seen many reorganizations and many changes in leadership. So it really disturbed me to see new people brought in who usually rehashed the same ideas as their predecessors and then got all sorts of glory until they, also, were replaced. I experienced about eight changes in senior marketing officers, with all the starts and stops that go with that. We had two women in the department who could have done the job better than any of them but were never given the chance. It's hard to live with that amount of waste and lack of productivity when you care about your customers, your colleagues, and your company. I wanted to tear my hair out.

I have been in groups where we really worked hard to come together as a team to create new business opportunities, and where we were succeeding according to all the ground rules, and then we had the rug pulled out from under us. A reorganization would happen, plans would change, and we would be reassigned for reasons we didn't buy. Leaders who were not close to the business and didn't understand it had the power to destroy what we had built together. What happened to me, as it has to many others, is that I lost confidence in upper management. I started pursuing avenues to get out of the corporate world.

I think companies take away part of a person's spirit, their lust for the job. We get stifled, we shut down, and then we don't work as well. I started shutting down my creativity as well as my output. I became dissatisfied with myself and with what I was accomplishing.

In contrast, I've been at my current job for four years and I haven't had time to sit down yet, much less get bored or feel like I'm being squashed by any hierarchy. As the director of a community arts center, I manage a $200,000 operation with five staff people and 18 faculty members. Each year we serve about 1,100 students of all ages and interests. We manage three gallery spaces, with 150 to 180 professional artists exhibiting annually. I am the producer of two children's plays a year and we do eight performances of each play.

I report to a board of directors and am responsible for fundraising and revenues, grant writing, budget administration, operations, and planning. We have grown about 25 percent since I took the position, and I am having a wonderful time. I receive a tremendous amount of gratifying feedback from the community and that makes me work even harder. Some days I get so many ideas I think my head is going to burst. I finally feel as though I'm working to my potential and getting recognition for it. While money is very tight in a nonprofit and I can't offer the benefits I would like, I feel I can treat people in a way that matches my values.

All my staff is encouraged to create and innovate. No ideas are treated as unworthy. Everyone has input to all programs, regardless of position. For example, our custodian also does data entry and assists in hanging exhibits. We all pitch in and do whatever needs to be done to accomplish tasks and complete projects. We are more of a team than a hierarchy. I don't want to put anyone in a box, ever."

It's hard to know when to let go when we are dealing with death. When we find that someone we care for is seriously ill, we want them to fight, fight to survive, so we don't have to let go of them. Watching people I love suffer and fight, especially when there were relapses, has finally moved me to say, "I'm willing to let go. They can't take any more. They're just shadows of themselves. God, please take them." A hospice nurse once told me that it is sometimes a relief and a necessity for the dying person to be given permission to die by their survivors.

Perhaps our culture is too afraid of death. There are companies and organizations that probably should die. Some industries are more of a problem for society than a benefit. Others suffer from changing markets and technologies. They fight against regulation or changing social trends or competitors when it might be wiser to put those energies and resources into starting something new.

At the personal level we face big questions. Many times our health care institutions make enormous efforts against all odds to extend a person's life for days, weeks, or months. Yet the technology itself contributes to diminishing the quality of the life that is left. And the cost of all this is astronomical. About 40% of our financial dollars are absorbed in situations like this that support only 3% of the insured population.

Is there a good time to die and a good way to die—both for organizations and for us as individuals? I don't have these answers. I do have questions about the millions of dollars that are spent to keep organizations alive that should die. Millions more are spent convincing consumers that dying products are the only road to happiness. This next story looks at a similar issue that comes up for the survivors of corporate downsizings. It is the other side of the coin, of needing permission to leave or to admit something is dying in us or our organization.

The Observer is an anonymous storyteller who is still inside her organization. As vice president of finance and human resources for a subsidiary of a *Fortune* 500 company, she's trying to determine her course of action to deal with the disillusionment and loss of motivation caused by a sense of destroyed purpose and lost progress in her organization. The duration of emotional and spiritual death can be very long and wearing. When talking to her, I felt as though she was in a suffocating environment.

This story demonstrates how hard it is to know when to walk away from something, to let go. The Observer has stayed through many changes, positive and negative. She believes a large percentage of employees do this. Many have done it out of loyalty, some perhaps out of fear. She has tried to re-energize herself and her employees and help them shift from a focus on the negative to the positive. But she wondered aloud, "Would it have been better for us to let go sooner? Would we have paid a lesser price? Would the company culture have changed faster? Would it have become more troubled and then have had to see its problems and respond?" At the time I interviewed her, the jury was still out.

Sometimes companies are like people. They are in a state of denial. In that case, we need to allow the pain to worsen, so they will see that change is necessary. To the extent we improve things or fix things, we reduce the pain of the symptoms and allow the company to stay in denial longer. Our efforts to help may actually hinder.

The Observer's Story: One Step Forward, Two Steps Back

"I've experienced many types of organizational change in my company over the last 15 years: the entrepreneurial growth phase, the changing of the guard from a more technical/business entrepreneur to a business/marketing-oriented person, an acquisition by a much larger organization that now has been acquired by an even larger industrial organization. My experience with these changes has taken a heavy toll on me and on the other employees of this company. I don't think it was the number of changes but the sense that we were going one step forward and two steps back, especially with the last few changes. It's hard to keep up your commitment when you suspect all your efforts will be reversed.

The most important pattern I've noticed through these experiences is how much difference it makes when the employees feel they still have control. When we felt we still were in the driver's seat, we remained focused and personally committed. Every decision that took away control ate away at people, and what we really lost was each person's sense of personal responsibility and enthusiasm.

The first major change we went through was a new CEO and a change in investors. It was a case of a new person with a different set of skills for a different stage of the business. The previous CEO had created a very caring environment and had brought good discipline and planning skills to the company. He managed the company by developing and introducing new products for new markets, which set it on a path of high growth and superior quality. People felt they were in control with him. They understood and were part of the whole decision-making process to its conclusion. As a result, the spark was there in each of us.

The new person brought a strategic vision of what we could be and critical thinking skills. That was invigorating and helped each of us grow even more, although his style was less personal. We gained a sense of greatness, of potential. While many people in management positions appreciated the need for change on top, we still had camps. There were those who were so loyal to the former CEO and his way of doing things that it was difficult for them to make the transition. In the short run, we had a lot of conflict. Over time, some managers left, but most stayed. Half of them continued to be successful under different leadership, but they didn't necessarily feel the same way about it.

Our new CEO's leadership helped us successfully bring a new critical product to the market. With this product, growth was on our side. We added people we thought would fit into the new culture. They were more aggressive and added new talent and capabilities to the organization. This helped us change our environment quickly. We built the organization we wanted. When the longer-term people saw all these new people come in and be successful by approaching things differently, they became a little more comfortable with the changing culture. Growth kept us going, kept the motivation up, and provided a reward. It was a positive time for most people. So we weathered this first change well and we grew from it.

After several years in this cycle, we were acquired by another company. The parent company retained our CEO for several years. He tried to keep local control but, little by little, changes were made and they started to affect how we did things. Politics began to play a bigger role because we had to anticipate how the parent company would respond to what we wanted to do. The whole nature of how we operated began to change.

Our business started to decline. A product we were supposed to introduce was late. Then, when it was introduced, it was a flop. It was the result of our CEO not staying involved enough and making some wrong technical decisions. We were less focused, too, because we had to deal with all these other issues. Consequently, he left and they brought in someone else as CEO from the parent company environment.

We had been moving toward an empowering management style, operating systems, and philosophies. Now we are back to what we had five years ago. We had implemented a results-based performance management system, moving us away from the traditional performance reviews. We had to change that. We used to have a profit-sharing plan. We lost that because the parent company doesn't have one. Just that one decision totally refocused people. Everybody was concentrating on the results of the company and what they could do to improve them, because there was a clear reward. Much of that has gone away just from that one decision. All the headway that was made is just down the tubes. Now with the acquisition of our parent company, I expect more of this will happen.

The significance of all these changes on employees shows up in physical stress and in their intellectual and emotional responses. We have experienced more lost time over the last few years. People complain more often about stress, even individuals who were rarely gone or, when they were, would make it up. We see less and less of that positive behavior. Even when they are here, it shows up in lost incremental productivity. People spend more time complaining and that's very disruptive. It's hard to feel positive about what's going on when people are complaining.

I see more frustration and anger coming out. Emotionally, I see people grappling with the issue that if they embark on something else, three years from now there's a high likelihood it will go down the tubes as well. Intellectually, this sense of start, stop, one step forward, two steps back takes a heavy toll on the employees and the business. I needed to help my people deal with the change as positively as possible. Even though I don't like some things and can't change them, I still have a responsibility to help my organization know what is happening. It's my responsibility to do what I can so we can get on with it. I'm not saying that I try to change how they feel about the turmoil, but they have to let go of it and move on.

I have tried to help people concentrate on identifying a problem and solving it, rather than just complaining about it. We can't fix everything at once, so what's the most important thing right now? I can see that that has really made a difference because my group is functioning better than others. It comes out in different ways. For one, other departments see us as more cooperative.

As I have gone through these experiences, I have learned more about myself, particularly about what really motivates me. I have always set most of my goals and they were far more aggressive than any of my bosses would have expected. But I did them because I thought they were the right thing to do. The first two CEOs had a vision of what they wanted for the company, for employees and customers. I knew they would go to the wall in helping me overcome obstacles. I was very motivated in that environment and worked long hours. Most people were telling me I worked too hard and I should have more balance in my life.

It's totally different now. Dealing with the change in my motivation, my values, and work is difficult. I've gone from a person who was driven—almost too driven—to a point where I am struggling just to keep my mind on my work and to be here 40 hours a week. This new CEO is a very corporate controlling type. No longer are we working for something greater in a vision, but for profits and career promotion. Personal relationships are superficial. He takes little risk and is more focused on how things are going to influence his career. So his motivation and mode of operation is quite different. I can't get motivated to do something when the goal is to make some executive look good.

His point of view on people is that they are dispensable. While I know that any company can deal with people leaving, you still need to have a philosophy of retaining your most talented people. If you want to grow and develop, you must care about what they are doing. Because we have been up and down in sales volume, this puts additional stress on the organization.

As if this weren't enough, he treats me differently because I am a female. I see it and so do my peers. The company was unique, from a female perspective, under both the first two CEOs. I always knew that. Some of my female colleagues are just now realizing it. When we talk about career goals and aspirations, the current manager sends me a message that the parent company doesn't really promote women. Many of my responsibilities have been taken away to a headquarters functional group. I have chosen to take on different areas of responsibility to provide new challenges.

I'm not sure staying here is going to be helpful. In fact, it may be damaging because I am going backwards or at least stagnating. I have paid a high price to stay here so far. Emotional commitment to my work is what motivated me before. I have to let go and be less committed emotionally. This doesn't mean that I won't get good results, but over time, the lost passion will hurt me and the organization. I don't necessarily feel good about that, but I do see it as survival. I doubt I'm alone in feeling this way. A decision will have to be made. I sometimes wonder if it would have been better if more of us were less loyal and had left faster."

The last story of this section is different. I don't know of a company that would want to state publicly that they are dying from emotional or spiritual disorders. I don't blame them. It's easier to talk about the pain and disease after the cure is at least starting to take effect. Plant 126 is very real because it's based on the words and experiences of real people and companies. It is mythical because it's in a composite form. The first two stories you have seen were the stories of individuals. The third story was of a whole company as seen through one executive's eyes. This one combines what I have heard and seen in many diverse settings.

When an organization is ill, it tends to be a system of illness, with different groups unknowingly playing out a role in the disease. It's similar to what happens in the body. One part's deterioration affects another, which affects another, until you have a total collapse. To see the problem, we need to be able to get inside many parts. This story is written as if we could drop in and hear many people's perspectives. Plays and fiction are peculiar that way. You can be anywhere the author wants you to be. That would be a wonderful ability to have. If people really could hear how everyone else in their home or workplace is feeling, we might be able to make some breakthroughs. So often, what prevents change and healing is our beliefs about other people and their intentions.

So this is the story of how it might feel to be in a company that is near death, as told by the voices of people throughout the organization who can't always see and hear the other voices. Look for the dominant feelings and beliefs. Some of the predominant feelings I see in dying organizations are fear, anger, suspicion, apathy, helplessness, or a sense of victimization.

Major characteristics of a troubled spiritual state in an organization can take the form of unethical behavior or subtle sabotage. Unethical behavior includes lies, overcontrolled information, trying to maneuver around the law, and any kind of harassment. These are usually conscious acts. Subtle sabotage appears in various forms of undermining others, in suggesting the worst possible interpretation of events and of people's intentions, and in trust-destroying behaviors and words. It's subtle because these usually aren't conscious actions.

The effect of these feelings and behaviors is to suffocate change and improvement. It's the organizational version of what Richelle Pearl-Koller described as losing our breath, our *Ruah*. A glimmer of hope, of energy, of change appears, and it's snuffed out before it can take hold. It's why a leader can make a difference only if there's some critical mass of supportive people large enough to offset the negative energy of the prevailing disease.

Plant 126's Story: On the Edge of Death

"Hello, I'm Plant 126. I've been a manufacturing plant for 30 long years. I haven't been doing too well for quite some time now. I might die. They have talked about pulling the plug, but are giving me one last chance. Between you and me, I'm scared. No one wants to die. What will happen to all my people? Once they're gone, I'm nothing. I'm also scared of this major life change they want and I'm confused as to whether I'm doing it or not. I have so many different voices, I don't know what I really believe or what I want to believe. In the movie *The King and I*, the King sings, "The world has changed a lot. I am not sure of what I absolutely know. I find confusion in conclusions I concluded long ago." That's how I have been feeling.

Some of our years were good years, some were OK, but lately things have been pretty bad. Then about a year ago, I was given my last chance to change. Some of my old voices went away and I got some new ones. A voice is a voice, I thought at first, so it doesn't really matter. It'll be more of the same. Now, I'm not so sure. One of these voices was Sarah, the new plant manager. She talks differently. Maybe it's just because she's a woman. But you know, I'd like to believe her, even when I don't totally get what she's saying. Listen to some of my voices. Maybe you can sort this out.

The Voices of Employees:

Voice #1: I don't see much changing. All this stuff is just another program of the month. There are some cosmetic changes, but not deep down. When I came here, I couldn't believe how much people were head to head against each other. Now I feel the same way. I don't think it can change.

Voice #2: I don't see any changes. Same old thing. We've had it rough at this plant and I don't see it getting better. Maybe they'll close it down soon.

Voice #3: I'm more optimistic than that. I wonder if we are turning things around, but we can't see it.

Voice #4: It's hard to know what to believe. Some days I think some managers or supervisors are changing and the next day they are back to their old selves again.

Voice #5: I'm not sure either. Sarah is different and trying lots of things.

Voice #1: Maybe, but she won't be here that long. This is just a stopping place for her. Then we'll be back to the same old thing.

Voice #2: That's right. You can't trust anybody here. The Plant 75 people were told they wouldn't close down and look what happened. We can't trust the unions or management.

Voice #6: I'm here to make money, not to feel good. The bottom line is the executives are just looking to make money, quarter to quarter. If we complain, they just threaten to close us down. It's not worth doing anything.

Voice #3: I'm almost afraid to say this because you guys always shut everyone down who says anything positive. But I don't share all these negative feelings. I can see change and I like coming to work. I used to work at a place that was negative like this one and it doesn't exist anymore. I don't want to see that happen here.

The Voices of Supervisors

Voice #1: I think we're improving, but it's hard to put my finger on what has changed. There's more involvement and more efforts to work together.

Voice #2: Our vision is changing. People matter a lot more now. We still haven't altered our management style the way we need to on a daily basis, but it's beginning. When things get critical or when we sense suspicion or hostility, I think we drop back to the old way of doing things.

Voice #3: There's more untapped potential in people. They're ready to go faster than management thinks. We're ready to go faster, too.

Voice #5: I think Sarah is trying to change the management group. They act like they're trying to change sometimes, but I'm suspicious that they're just getting their cards punched and aren't sincere.

Voice #3: Maybe we all need more faith.

Voice #4: I just want them to manage me the way they're asking me to manage my people.

Voice #2: They're nervous over the plant goals and demands from headquarters. I wouldn't want their jobs.

Voice #4: Isn't that a double standard, though? If we are all on the same team, shouldn't they share their concerns with us and get us involved in planning to reach those goals?

Voice #6: I'm busy enough with my own changes. I haven't been trying to analyze other people that much.

Voice #7: I'm still holding back some. I'm not sure where I stand. If I tell the whole truth of what I think, it could come back to hurt me on performance reviews. I'm watching out for myself.

Voice #6: The problem is this change in people stuff is like a ping pong ball bouncing in a small room. When it goes back and forth without any new whacks, it starts to lose energy and it stalls out.

Voice #7: I'm concerned about time. Our buckets are already too full and more keeps getting added. And the list of what needs to be done keeps changing. Management wants changes, employees want changes, we want changes, and headquarters sets aggressive goals. We're getting new tools to help, but who has time to use them?

Voice #5: The bottom line is that we aren't using all the minds in this plant yet. The good news is we're beginning to want to use them and we're using them more than we did before.

The Voices of the Plant Leaders

Plant Leader 1: I came to this plant from a very progressive plant, in terms of working together and empowering people. The baggage I found here was unbelievable. Everything that has ever happened just kept getting thrown in my face. There was no desire in the former leadership group to think about moving forward, either. It was a very frustrating experience for the last two years. I started thinking I should stop banging my head against the wall so it won't hurt so bad.

Plant Leader 2: I want a place where we roll up our sleeves together and make this plant what it needs to be in the face of outside reality. Nothing will ever change if we just keep walking away from each other, stay mad, and watch the ship sink. I want a place where people talk to each other with respect and where we recognize each other's contributions and abilities. I don't think people understand that if they want change, it requires an individual decision by each of them to let go of the way things used to be, let go of stereotypes of each other, and get on with creating the future.

Plant Leader 3: I'm amazed at how difficult it is for one person to recognize when someone else is trying to change. I have made changes that I felt were major accomplishments. Then I've had someone look me straight in the eye, describe exactly what I did, and tell me there's no change. Or, if they do admit there is a change, they look for the worst possible motive.

Plant Leader 4: I know we have changed, but I don't know how to measure it. I've had customers and people from headquarters visit us and tell me they *felt* the change. I guess there's something, some electricity that is different. Somehow, it relates to the way people treat each other. That's been hard for me to accept. I'm beginning to understand that feelings do matter at work. If we really want and expect people to come in and use their minds, there has to be more respect and trust.

Plant Leader 5: When I came to this plant, I was appalled by the apathy and distrust. I thought I was going to be part of the solution. Like everyone else, I got bogged down in the way things are. I came into an environment I didn't create and got blamed for it. I guess in a way I said, "The hell with it." I don't know that I consciously did that, but on reflection I can see that happened.

Plant Leader 6: I don't know about all this stuff. This isn't how I was raised or trained. All my adult life, I've been rewarded for controlling, deciding, getting results. I feel like the rug has been pulled out from under my feet. I was so close to the rewards I had been promised for playing by the rules and now they've changed the rules. I don't know. I just don't know.

The Voice of Sarah, Plant Manager

Sarah: I've been here a year and I think things are starting to change. I see glimmers of light here and there. Our productivity is up, quality is improving, people smile occasionally. I even got a group to laugh last week. But the minute I start to think we've turned the corner, something happens to cast gloom over it all. I'm paying a very high price to try to turn this place around. I'm tired. I feel like I spend every day hitting my head against the wall. My credibility is on the line with headquarters. . . . Stop this. I can't afford to fall into this kind of thinking.

I'm doing all the things I should be doing. We have clear, well-communicated goals; we're sharing more company information; training is going on; we've started improvement teams; we're working on customer service; and we've cleaned up the performance and salary review system. I still feel as though something is missing. We need a sense of pulling together for something that really matters. I thought saving the plant from closing would be enough, but we still don't have that spark that could propel us forward. We need something that's bigger than the plant. *I* could use something bigger than the plant or a promotion. It just isn't enough. I need to understand what people really care about. . . . I'd better go back to listening again.*"*

3

We Could Have Purpose

A calling is when a deep gladness in your heart meets a deep need in the world.

FREDERICK BUECHNER

Purpose is critical to coming out of the dying process and beginning to create something new for our organizations and ourselves. This is the core ingredient. It has to do with an inner sense of potential and truth, which often challenges the prevailing cultural norms and beliefs. Individuals don't have to create it. We are born with it. It's our most natural, positive way of being in the world. When purpose is tapped and nurtured, things begin to happen. Without it, we stay dead in the waters of the current way of doing things. One of the most significant things purpose can do for us is to keep us learning and growing. It inhibits complacency.

The strangest thing about purpose is that we can act on it with or without being able to articulate it. Some of us need to engage in the effort to put words to it and some of us just need to learn to trust and act on these positive internal impulses. We know it in the doing. We know we are on course. Sometimes we follow a particular passion or interest and invest in much learning. It doesn't seem like work, though, because it is fun. Then we get that delightful surprise one day when a new opportunity falls in our lap that requires some knowledge of that area. We get that synergistic feeling of "I couldn't have planned this better if I had tried."

Purpose is hard to define precisely because the same purpose can manifest itself in different ways in our lives. It's the common threads that seem to weave throughout our whole lives when we're operating at our best and truest for a good beyond ourselves. One of the people featured in this section describes her purpose as being a truth teller and how that has been her core throughout her personal and professional life, and in and out of various career changes. This means seeing and speaking of the deeper truth in each instance, not superficial factual truths. It's what is most essential to who she is.

Organizations need to expend more time discussing purpose, especially if they truly believe in becoming learning organizations. It provides the motivation, the fuel. Our united purpose rises out of the needs around us and our individual purposes. It isn't so much the creation of the next statement to hang on the wall. It's the learning and coalescing that happens in the discussion and the continuous effort to keep the question in front of us. We need to be sure we never think it's fully answered, because then we think we're done and put it aside.

Business is undergoing a transformation of historic proportions related to this. At the macro level, business has a unique, global capacity for creating major change. Government, churches, and other social entities are vitally necessary as well, but they have different gifts. Business can offer resources, expertise, speed, a global reach, and a freedom that no other social organization can match in such a direct manner. It can improve or harm the planet and its inhabitants daily. It can help create a decent standard of living for the many or the few. At the micro level, it allows individuals and groups to create meaning or meaninglessness in their lives, to live out individual purposes. In the next few years, I believe we will begin to ask even more profound questions about the purpose of business organizations. Why should we ever think we are done?

At one time, we believed all organizations had the same purpose, which was to make money for shareholders. Companies didn't go on management retreats to discuss their purpose. In fact, such a proposal would have been viewed as unnecessary and wasteful, because the answer was obvious. Today such meetings are common and organizations are expected to have unique purpose statements, missions, visions, or all of the above.

Organizations have started differentiating their purpose in terms of how to make money, defining their focus in regard to products, markets, or unique capabilities. This did require discussion because there were many options from which to choose. Once they've passed through that stage, many companies have started to rethink purpose in more fundamental ways and to decide they have an even bigger vision. They are talking about serving people, the community, and even, perhaps, the world. This discussion takes more than one or two strategy sessions. Throughout all this, the understanding of purpose has been broadened, deepened, and legitimized. Not all organizations were this linear, but many were.

Many companies are struggling with this. They believe it's easy to have inspiring purposes when you're in health-related areas, for example. But they say, "We just make widgets. You can't add inspiration to that." You can for some widgets, and for others you can if you go beyond the widget.

Ben and Jerry's is an example of a company that provides ice cream, operates with a higher purpose, and has excellent financial results. If the founders of this company had confined themselves to the product they make, they would have been stuck, too. They go beyond that. They try to provide an enriching place to work, contribute to an improving environment, and contribute to their community. They encourage employees to find meaning and inspiration by being participants in these activities.

This respect for the power of tapping individual purpose isn't accorded much attention or respect in the general business environment. Nor has the same evolution of understanding occurred within our culture about personal purpose as has begun to happen with businesses' purpose. Sometimes our jokes tell the truth of our beliefs. We say things like, "We live, we die, and in between we make enough money to pay taxes and outdo our neighbors." Our various religious faiths suggest other purposes, but our mainstream lives frequently ignore those suggestions or cause us much internal conflict. We don't discuss these things at work.

Within ourselves, though, we know much about purpose. We come into the world filled with purpose. We demand to be cared for, to be loved unconditionally, and to be the center of the universe. This is like a business focused unconditionally on its shareholders' wealth. Shareholders are the center of the business universe.

As we grow, we become aware that we need to be here for a purpose beyond ourselves. And we know this purpose is to be accomplished within a community—so much so that for quite a while we cannot distinguish ourselves from our families. We learn, though, that we should meet the needs of our family and friends and not just take from them. So, too, business has learned to care for customers and the community. No one gets their needs met if they aren't giving as well as receiving. When we are uncomfortable with the spiritual tones here, we call these behaviors "enlightened self-interest." For many, growth stops here.

Could there be more? I think so. Some people keep growing and come to know that we also have a distinct purpose, just as Cardinal John Newman has written: "God has created you to do Him some definite service. He has committed some work for you which He has not committed to another. You have your mission. You shall do good." We sense this in our thrust to be unique, to be recognized. Our sense of purpose matures with us. It's like reading. We learned the basics of reading. The minute those were mastered, we found out there were different levels of reading and we worked through those one by one. It almost seems like Life is challenging each of us, throughout the world, to move to a new higher level of purpose and service. If we don't, the problems that face us may bury us.

Many individuals and companies are awakening to their journey through a form of mid-life crisis or economic strait. Something within us causes us to start questioning if there isn't more to life, to growth. This questioning process is critical and takes us into the death/birth cycle. Though the questions and events take different forms for different people, at their core they are the basic philosophical questions of life: What is the meaning of my life? Why am I here? What unique gift do I have to offer? Why does this organization exist? What makes us unique?

This perspective assumes that we each do have a unique gift to bring to life and to the workplace. It also assumes that love is part of work. Not romantic love, but love in the sense of caring, or *caritas*, which means compassion. Caring about what we work at, as in doing what we love. Caring as in concern for the effects and results of my actions on others. And compassion as in how I treat everyone I work with and for: co-workers, bosses, customers, and suppliers. Out of that caring and compassion comes commitment, energy, and innovation.

For many, this is more tough than exciting. Our culture and educational system reward people who have answers, not people who ask questions—especially thorny, hard questions. Our value is in knowing the answers, not exploring the questions. One right answer only, please. Produce it now or it doesn't count. Produce all of it now, not part today and part tomorrow. Learn the answer from the teacher (expert). Now here is terror. How do I learn the answer when the teacher, parent, boss, expert isn't there or, worse yet, doesn't know the answer? There is no outside expert for these questions. The answers need to come from inside. We generally conclude it's better to steer clear of the questions.

Life doesn't see fit to allow us to do this indefinitely. When we don't voluntarily take up the questions, life hits us with an emotional punch. It may be an addiction, divorce, illness, or a death. It may be a failed product, a frustrated career, a lost job, a failed business with mass layoffs. Today's organizational downsizing is creating the external stimulus for many people to ask new and old questions and to begin a new phase of life. The maturing of the mass of baby-boomers is another stimulus.

When a business stops evolving its understanding of purpose, it loses its competitive edge and may stagnate. As individuals, we can also stagnate without purpose. We may invest too much of ourselves in pursuing money and acquiring status. We lose much of our spirit and spend our time wandering in a wasteland of meaningless activities. We stop learning. We feel empty. In severe cases, we become victims of cynicism.

The following stories speak to various aspects of understanding and exploring our purpose and identifying our core. They suggest how to act on this, consciously and unconsciously, in our individual and organizational life. For those interested in Peter Senge's book on organizational learning, *The Fifth Discipline*, I'll point out how these stories also illustrate the human side of some of the learning disciplines.

Charles (Chuck) Denny recently retired as CEO and president of ADC Telecommunications, Inc. His early career and development was at Honeywell, Inc. He joined ADC as president when it was close to bankruptcy in 1971, due to an unsuccessful merger and other difficulties. He left it a thriving $250 million telecommunications provider. This first story explores how much we can live out our purpose if we stay in touch with our deepest sense of our core. It also illustrates Senge's principle of personal mastery: "individuals must have their own visions before a shared vision can exist."

Denny seems to be continuing his process. For a recently retired person, he is very busy. He is an active part of a project at the Minnesota Center for Corporate Responsibility, wrestling with the creation and utilization of a unique document (discussed in a later chapter). He was pondering whether they, in collaboration with others, could lead the business world toward a new international standard of values and ethical behavior. It looks to me like more of his core is operating on a global level.

Chuck Denny's Story: Knowing the Core

"I learned a great deal in my early years at Honeywell about managing change through relationships at a variety of levels. Beginning in 1968, I spent a number of years managing a French subsidiary. The first year I was in France, I was vice president of sales. Then I became president. The company had not performed well for years and morale was terrible. Employee relations were hostile. Somehow, I needed to turn this around.

The organization I inherited was patriarchal, paternalistic, and dictatorial. It relied on the capacity of the organization's very top officers, to the point that everyone below those levels was considered in the servant class. I was not comfortable with this, so I asked, "Do I continue in the same fashion or do I seek to implement an environment in which I will be more comfortable in my work relationships with others?" I don't think I had a management philosophy, theory, model, or book in mind. I simply had a need to breathe freely and know that those around me shared that same privilege.

I began the difficult task of discharging many of these senior managers, despite continual warnings that I would find myself in the French civil courts for the rest of my life. Somehow or other, I was able to work my way through those terminations without any trouble and few, if any, hard feelings. I spent a year recruiting and replacing them with 28- to 32-year-olds who were bright, extremely well-schooled, and enthusiastic.

I was ignorant of all the products and markets. I certainly didn't know the customers. Because I had come out of the military operations, they were all strange to me. Even though I spent every morning and evening learning the language, reading the literature, and trying to understand the politics and culture, I was obviously at a third-grade level. I had to rely on the people I worked with; it was the only way I could survive. I learned that when you carefully select people and then empower them, your chances of success are greatly magnified. They took the company by its ears, they charged everyone else up and started climbing the peaks on all sides.

Another of my favorite memories is learning how you can unlock some people's potential without even knowing you are doing it. The day I became president of the company, the entire French nation went on strike, led by worker walkouts in the industrial park where we had our plant. What a way to start.

We had a vice president of administration who was brilliant and intuitive. He had a sixth sense that something was going to happen and came to me about four hours before the strike started. He said we needed to do something. I asked what he'd recommend. It's always good to have money and gasoline, he pointed out. So we took $4 million from the bank and locked it in our vault. We made arrangements with a sister company in Belgium to run gasoline across the border at night. Then I got in my car and drove to the factory, north of Paris.

During my first year in France, before becoming president, I used to go to the factory weekly because the design group was also there. I always got up early and drove to the plant, drank a cup of coffee and smoked a cigarette on the front steps. I loved being out of doors. The first people to arrive were always the stewards of the three separate unions. We would drink coffee and smoke. I would speak in my fractured French, and they would help me along. We would talk about this and that. This served me wonderfully at this crisis time.

I got to the plant and called them all together. Because of our relationship, we were able to speak honestly about the problems, and inside of three hours, we were able to resolve every issue. They asked to return to work. Since the entire zone was out and the whole country had gone on strike, I asked them not to come back to work that day for fear something bad would happen.

I drove back to Paris and was having dinner when I received a call from one of the stewards. He said that the industrial workers were going to march through the zone that evening and trash all the factories. They intended to turn over the inventory bins, empty the file cabinets, and do petty damage—the kinds of things that tie up a factory in knots. They were asking permission to occupy our factory and defend it. I had to say that was a wonderful offer, but I couldn't accept it for fear someone would be hurt. I'd rather have the factory destroyed than our workers injured. We had a friendly argument, but they agreed to stay home. I did ask, though, that they spread the word to the unions led by the Communists that they would appreciate it if our factory wasn't trashed.

They did so. The march occurred that evening and every factory in our zone was trashed except ours. We returned to work the next day, six weeks before any other factory. Six months later, the largest factory was still out. I hadn't set out to curry favor with the union stewards during that first year. That wasn't my job or my intent. It's just weird. This was a wonderful object lesson that employee relations is a contact sport. It isn't by theory. It has to have flesh, warmth, and perspiration joining perspiration or it's meaningless.

My learning continued. We were growing so well that we had to acquire another factory. We found the perfect facility with a totally open space surrounded by four walls. The engineering department was to move in here, too, so they promptly began planning to put their offices all along the wall so they'd be sealed off from the factory. I knew the French were class conscious and I felt it was destructive to what we needed to do. So I decided to build the engineering offices in the center of the factory with glass walls all around it.

Everyone could look in and out. The engineers had to walk through the factory to enter and leave, go to the canteen and to the bathrooms. Well, you can't walk past someone day after day without looking at them. Then, having looked at them, it's hard not to say "Hello" and eventually, "How are you?" After six months, they felt guilty for not knowing each others' names. Within a year, they were all talking and were pleased with themselves for knowing everyone on a first-name basis. This was very rare in France. The whole dynamic changed. They did an incredible job together.

This was a simple, dumb thing, but it was what was lacking. It reinforces the idea that if you allow people the freedom to behave nobly, most of them will. People changed deep cultural behaviors, at least at work, once artificial structures were removed. When individuals changed, the organization changed and we had increased results.

My greatest psychological need is to feel in relationship with other human beings. I think that desire unconsciously shaped most of my behavior over those years. I have intellectual interests, but they are secondary to being a member of a group. My idea of nirvana is to be intellectually challenged, working on meaningful problems with wonderful people, as a team member. Sometimes the more difficult it is, the more rewarding. That is a real joy.

Unfortunately, I wasn't able to replicate the experiences I had in France. I was never really successful at doing what now, in retrospect, I wish I had done. Ross Wagner and Don Moersch were senior vice presidents I brought into ADC Telecommunications soon after I became president. We had a lot of ideas about what we wanted to do. Twenty years ago, we wanted to increase empowerment, enrich jobs, flatten the organization, and share more of the rewards of business.

Through my own fault, it never prevailed. In talking to larger groups of people about our ideas, we would experience severe resistance. I'm not attributing blame to anyone, because I had the power to remove those people. With all the turmoil caused by growth and change in products, markets, and technologies, I ultimately backed away. In the early years at ADC we were in survival mode. As time moved on, the excuse was that the company was doing so well—growing 20 percent or better per annum over 21 years. Also, we were so busy changing markets, products, technology, organizational structure, adding people, adding facilities, equipment, systems, that it was just consuming.

One of my worst defects, which is at the same time one of my immense psychological comforts, is that I would not and could not take action against people who did a B- job but were outstanding people and brought ever so many other good things to the company. And I consider it inhumane treatment to let people go who are unlikely prospects for finding a new job, if there's any way to avoid it. Sometimes their less-than-able performance was costing the company mightily in our ability to bring about change. To this day I don't know the answer to those Solomon-like judgments. But I chose not to and it took almost five years before we made real changes.

I believe all of us in the work force need to learn to understand ourselves better each year as we continue throughout our lives. Many years ago, I took a test related to profiles of CEOs. I discovered I was in the acceptable boundaries on only two out of twenty issues and these were right on the margin. The psychologist suggested that, although I was succeeding as a CEO and probably would continue to do so, it was at a terrible cost to myself. I was forcing myself to do things that were destructive inside and I didn't understand myself well enough to know that. The things that really energized me probably were not to be found in the business world.

We're all conditioned by society to prefer certain paths and goals. We notice that success in this world is defined by following some career track, so that's where we want to go. We figure we're smart enough to succeed in that environment, no matter what our psychological profile may be. We think we will be able to manage our needs. And we often do externally, but internally we're short-circuiting our entire electrical system without really knowing the damage until decades later. We're not very healthy and that affects everyone around us, the organization and beyond.

I've learned about the unused power of people. I backed some managers way too long in hopes they would use their total capabilities. I watched how many of us, including myself, are incapable of the personal discipline required to use all the capabilities that our parents gave us. They are there. We know they're there, but we can't seem to take that last final step to make them employable. I wish I knew how we could allow and/or help individuals to make the most of themselves. How do you do that? How much management, company time, and money would it be worth to do that? That's one of my great regrets. I never found a sufficient way to help others achieve all they could be. I wasn't sure what my role was.

I have also learned that corporations can and will become involved in changing behaviors that I never would have predicted. The changes in the past forty years in such areas as environmental compliance, employee safety, equal employment, sexual harassment, respect for the individual, drinking, and smoking behaviors are examples of these.

Going forward, I think managers will be called on to ask these questions more and more. The ideal work force that we need would be composed of totally healthy people—intellectually, physically, emotionally, spiritually—who are ready to meet the challenge of our world. When I look at the future work force, now enrolled in our school systems, I am concerned. I know many are emotionally deprived, an increasing number physically deprived, and most spiritually vacant. No matter how good the intellectual system, it cannot work in these conditions. These students then become employees who are crippled human beings. Is the employer to become the recuperative means for all these people? Given that no one else is doing it, it is in the corporate interest to undertake that work. But what skills do we have to do that? None.

We also need to be more prepared to deal with human relationships. They are the very base level of the social contract. How much of ourselves do we surrender in return for the perceived good that can be given to us by the bodies called government and corporations? The tide has swung too much to the organizations, I suspect. They have more rights and privileges than they deserve. When I look to the future, I think there will be more flexibility in the working schedule and more independence in the employee–employer relationship. I think we will see more collegiality and, therefore, flatter organizations. We need to be ready to respond."

In his book, *Man's Search for Meaning*, Viktor Frankl describes the power of purpose that keeps people going in the worst of situations, even in death camps. He goes on to explain that a sense of purpose or unfinished business sustained life rather than whether one was healthy, strong, or wise. Purpose can also help us handle suffering better, because it gives meaning to the suffering and pain. Otherwise we feel punished, victimized, or hopeless. A sense of purpose makes a profound difference. I was struck by the number of people who referenced this book in my research.

Life frequently surprises us with suffering in different forms and often it is through the working of our organizations. These surprises can seem like totally negative experiences, or they can also take us into the deeper recesses of ourselves that need exploration and expression. In that sense we can gain much from our pain, if we choose to see it this way.

Susan James is director of marketing at Personnel Decisions, Inc., a firm of organizational psychologists who assist clients in building successful organizations through consulting and the selection and development of managers. At the time I met her, though, she was living through a crisis in her career and a major disruption in her mental models. This is when our sense of reality gets challenged, especially through our own inner work and ability to ask ourselves new questions.

Things had been rolling along well, when life surprised James with a layoff from her position as marketing director at a medium-size manufacturing company. Unfortunately, that's a trauma many people, of all levels and types of jobs and education, are sharing. James' story is also about taking that experience and choosing to use it to empower herself in her search for meaning and purpose. She asks probing questions about all aspects of a meaningful life. She is engaged in exploring her core.

Often we hesitate to share these types of questions, because we think we are alone in asking them. That makes us wonder if we are crazy or if there's something wrong with us. Peter Russell, author of *The Global Brain* and *The White Hole in Time*, said that as he travels the world, he notices that we really share many questions, fears, and concerns. Until someone takes the risk to share his or her thoughts, everyone else sits there thinking they're alone.

If we started sharing our personal questions and thoughts at work and at home, what would happen? Would we find out we aren't alone? If we started asking and sharing our personal purposes in life and connecting those with our organization's, wouldn't that make a deep difference?

Susan James' Story: The Search for Meaning

"I'll never forget getting laid off. I was walking down the hall when two senior managers said, "Oh, Susan, we want to talk to you." They proceeded to tell me that the CEO, my boss, several other vice presidents, and many other people were being let go and so was I. I was stunned. We had just introduced nine new products and we didn't even know what the results were, yet. I hadn't been there long enough to know if I had had an impact. Having an impact is very important to me. In addition, I had just come back from having lunch with my husband. I had told him that I wanted to leave the company. They weren't going to grow as expected and things just weren't the way I had been led to believe. I didn't plan on leaving that quickly, though. It was strange.

I remember going in and talking to my boss. I couldn't believe what the company was doing. At the same time I was incredibly calm. I was dazed, but I wasn't upset. I said, "This is really strange, but I have the feeling that this is the way things are supposed to be. If you think about it, this is our path. This is something that is happening to us so something else can come from it. We will grow from this." He thought I had lost my mind. He was looking at me as though, "I have just lost my job and this woman is talking to me like it is the great journey." Interestingly, we have talked since and he shares more of my feelings now.

It was some time before I actually believed I had lost my job. It felt like I was on an extended vacation. Rather than start thinking about putting my resume together, I cleaned my house. Because I had been working my brains out, I had all this energy that I didn't know what to do with. So I started cleaning like a mad woman. It was really bizarre. It was almost a month before I calmed down and thought about what I wanted to do. The reality of not having any money had not yet come to mind.

Fear has struck terribly. It comes in waves. It doesn't manifest itself in a particular feeling of fear: it's more in my actions. I notice that when I am feeling fear, it affects my thinking. I start thinking broadly and then it gets narrower and narrower. It's hard for me to keep the walls from closing in. That's when I see my fear. I also see my fear in my relationships. I can feel the fear because things start bothering me that haven't bothered me for a long time. I start worrying about my husband's work. I start worrying about the kids and what we're going to do about school. I think it's a way of taking the focus off myself.

I have no doubt that I will find a job. I will be employed again. I know this isn't going to be a lifetime experience. I start to bring back that spiritual side, "What is it that I am supposed to be doing and am I really watching for that or am I missing the boat?" I start floundering. I am used to having a very set, structured business life and, all of a sudden, there's no structure. It's hard for me. I am good at structuring myself within a work situation, but when I got out of one, there were so many questions it was hard to keep the noise out and the focus in.

I guess one of my fears is, "Where is a meaningful job and will I see it?" Things could go in so many different directions. What are the right choices? What could I pick out of each of these that I would really like to do? There are also questions from a family standpoint. I have had five and a half months of spending much more time with my children. I never had that when I was in a corporate situation. I worked long hours and traveled. There's the feeling that my kids are starting school next year. They're growing up and I wish I had more time with them. How do you balance all of that? How do you get those things fulfilled in your life? How much is the corporation responsible for and how much are we responsible for, as individuals? I have all these questions going around in my mind. How do you make those choices? In what way should I have an impact?

My father-in-law died recently. They had a very unusual funeral where they played all these wonderful jazz and big band tunes and they talked about the impact of his life. He had been an educator and had started schools and had done all sorts of wonderful things for the community. He really had created change in many different ways. That's when my husband and I hit the wall. We both thought, "We have to do something different so that when we die, we will have done these sorts of things." The question is, "What are those things, and how do I want to accomplish them?"

I wonder if there really is a magic answer or if it is just a process that we are always supposed to have to work through. I am realizing that I have to find the answers myself. No one else is responsible for them except me. I think that we all have to go through periods in our lives that are full of turmoil. There's no way things can stay the same. That's not the way life is. We age, we die, we get sick, we get bored. All sorts of things happen, so we just can't stay in the same place forever. When we were first married, I remember thinking that it would be nice when things finally calmed down and we could get on with life. Then I realized—change and turmoil are life.

It helps me to remember some ideas from *Man's Search for Meaning*. I can choose how I respond to this situation. I can act like a raving lunatic filled with fear and anxiety and get really crazy with my family or I can choose not to do that and to take it in stride and think that things are going to be OK. I am not going to starve. Nothing terrible is going to happen. It's a personal decision if I'll handle a situation with grace or without it. We can blow the crisis up and make it really chaotic or we can sail through it a little more smoothly.

I have discovered that I am not alone in wondering about living a more meaningful life. I have had many informational interviews with people who are doing things in which I am interested. Many of them have been in new product development, business development, and marketing. I have been looking at the industrial and the consumer side and different types of product ideas. I have talked to people about what they do, and what they like and don't like about their jobs. Most of these people have been between the ages of 35 and 45. Ninety percent have been going through some kind of crisis within their jobs. People were happy with certain parts of their jobs, but almost all of them wanted to do something else. Most of them wanted to start a business of their own.

I have the feeling that a great number of people are re-examining their lives and asking what they really want. My husband is doing the same thing and so are many of my friends. It's a questioning time. It's like we have hit a period called mid-life crisis. All of a sudden, you realize, "I have now lived half of my work life doing this. Is this it?" The majority of the questions that I have been hearing people ask boil down to, "What am I giving to society from a personal stand-point?" They feel there is an emptiness. It's "OK, I have been making sweeping machines. So what?" Or, "I have just come up with disposable paint brushes: What does that mean?" The other part is, "Am I meaningful in this job and what do I really bring to it?"

I would never have predicted that I would think, let alone talk this way. As I was growing up, I felt that it was much more important to be intellectual than it was to be spiritual. Over time, I found out that didn't work. Many years ago, I had a boss I'd go to when I was really upset with people for not responding to logic, facts, and research data. He'd looked at me and say, "Susan, have faith." It made me angry that this man was telling me I had to have faith. Then I went though a difficult period of trying to figure out how things really work, what was working and what wasn't working. I was trying to manage every outcome it was possible to manage and even trying to control uncontrollable ones.

Finally, it hit me that having faith meant that I didn't have to control every outcome. I can't control every outcome of every project or every life situation. I just don't have that control. The only thing I have control over is the Zen of my own work. I can do as good a job as I possibly can, but other people are involved and can't be controlled. I am responsible for being ethical, respectful, honest in my communicating, and then doing the work that I feel is necessary to be done. That's what I can contribute. Everything else is faith. Everything will not turn out as I expect. But whatever does turn out, I will learn from and I will continue in the direction that will teach me more of what I have to learn in my life.

I wish I had known that sooner. But we only hear new messages when we are ready. It's as though we are blocked somehow or just can't hear. For a long time, I couldn't hear what my boss was saying. Things would be easier if, when we hear something we resist, we could just say, "Maybe, but not now," rather than "No, never." It would give all of us more breathing space."

What can happen when a company is sure of its core? H. B. Fuller was a small company when it was acquired in 1941 by Elmer

L. Andersen. Today, it is a $932 million manufacturer of adhesives and coatings and, in attaining that growth, it has been one of the most philosophically consistent companies I have ever seen. They started practicing customer service long before it was in vogue and have valued their employees for an equal length of time.

Anthony (Tony) Andersen, president and CEO, gives his father full credit for creating the company's philosophy and culture and says he absorbed it over the dinner table. More than once, he said I should really interview his dad, not him. The best way a boss, teacher, or parent knows what lessons have really been learned is to hear and see them in the behavior of the employee, student, or child. Based on this interview, Elmer Andersen is an excellent founder, teacher, and father.

When a company is sure of its core, it seems to be able to do good and do well financially. This core seems to help the company move through the pain of change. The issue of doing well and doing good is still hard for many people to digest. There are companies that do well financially for a long time, but whose practices turn out to be unethical. We wish they would have failed sooner. There are other successful companies that, while not focused on doing good, certainly aren't trying to do harmful things. There are others that have done good and been successful and then fail due to market issues.

The truth is that the coupling or uncoupling of profits and goodness isn't a guarantee of market vitality. That's too simplistic. There are many factors that influence a business's success. The important point is to know that there are viable choices. Then we each have to decide how we want to live—individually and as organizations.

It was reinforcing to have another example of a company that has done well while doing good, and whose track record spans so many years. There are people who still deny it's possible to sustain both, even when the proof is in front of them. However, for those of us who are open to believing, it's invigorating. Why others don't want to believe baffles me. Perhaps they're afraid it would take away their excuses and they would have to engage in a change effort that frightens them.

H. B. Fuller is a company that keeps learning about systems thinking, another learning discipline that is critical for more people to learn. Systems thinking demonstrates the search to understand how to meet the diverse needs of different stakeholder groups, to see all of these as part of an interrelated whole.

Tony Andersen's Story: Standing Firm When the Wind Blows

"Our value system and our rank priorities put us in a firm competitive position. Whatever wind may blow around us, it isn't as threatening because we know where we're standing and why we are standing there. We're working very successfully in the marketplace against competition that doesn't always share those same basic beliefs and we win that battle far more often than we lose. I believe our strength is in having an organization of committed people with a common bond of beliefs that operate in 33 countries of the world, and many languages and currencies. That's tremendously satisfying.

We have ranked priorities of served constituencies that reflect our beliefs. Customers are our first priority. It's really simple. If you don't have happy customers, then you don't have a business; at least, not a long-term one. That's not hard to understand. Secondly, we serve our employees. If we have good people in the company who have a commitment to the company values and objectives, then there's a symbiotic relationship and each feeds the other. It's a strong and powerful force.

If that is in place and customers really are first, then with some management over the long term, we're going to be profitable. Then we can serve the third constituency, which is the shareholder. When we have success with the company, we ought to share it with the community, which is our fourth priority. After all, it's society that created companies in the first place. It isn't rocket science stuff. Yet a lot of people don't get it.

I didn't create this. My father, Elmer Andersen, had created a culture that was strongly in place when I came. Of course, I knew about the company and its culture. You don't have your feet under Elmer's table very long before you learn a whole lot of things and I had been exposed to that my whole life. Those four rank-ordered constituencies seemed to make a whole lot of sense to me. Over time, the culture meant more and more to me. I'm so sold on this today and so absolutely convinced that we're right, that it's easy to fall into the trap of wanting everybody to do the same thing. So sometimes I try selling the concept to everybody. I suppose I'm even trying to do it right now. All I can say is that it has worked for us in spades. We're all about doing well while doing good.

When we have those four priorities tucked away in the back of our heads, it makes life so much easier from a decision-making standpoint. We don't have to search for a place to stand. When people don't have anything to believe in or any confidence that the beliefs are going to be right over the long term, they'll be subjected to the kinds of uncertainty that make decision making scary. They're not sure they're going to succeed. When there's a fear of failure, you're not going to make the same kind of bold decisions you really ought to be making.

One of those times for bold decisions happened in 1982. We went from a geographically driven to an industry organized and driven sales force overnight. About half the people in the company experienced a significant job change all at once. They were in a different territory, industry, town, with different customers, or working for a different boss.

To be successful in that situation, we had to work with a lot of worried employees. That's an enormous change for a company to undertake. I don't know if I would want to do it again. Many people thought we were doing the worst possible thing as a company, since we had been so successful the other way. Many were worried about their jobs and their performance under this new scenario. What we did then was to guarantee these sales- and incentive-based managers that they would not make less than the year before, guaranteed, no matter what happened. They would not make less and they might make more based on their new profit and loss statement. We gave people stability in all the chaos. Now that was an underpinning of confidence for people that really helped.

Some of us believed the customers' needs were changing. We wanted to have specialists who knew more about specific applications of glue than even the industry experts. Today we have people who do know more about how to laminate this and how to put this edge banding on here and all that sort of stuff, more than the industry itself knows. Well, who is the industry going to call, then, when they get a problem? H. B. Fuller. But we had to be willing to let the company take the negative side of that. We paid out a lot of money to folks whose profit and loss statement didn't look very good at the end of that year. It didn't make the shareholders very happy, but over time the decision has paid off.

We've also been clear on our commitment to our responsibility for the planet. The word "planet" usually refers to the environment. We've gone after environmental health and safety issues very, very aggressively, since 1985. I was convinced that we had to take a strong stand as a company, internally and externally, to deal with the whole subject of the environment, not just on a country or community basis, but on a world basis.

Some of the biggest problems for an international company like ours are the multiple country, state, county, and city requirements. It's a challenging world of rules and regulations. So in all of our capital spending, our plant design, and in process work, we want to know who has the most severe requirements anywhere in the world. We let that be our standard and then exceed it. You're going to have to do that ultimately, so why not now, when your costs are less than they will be later?

Our commitment to our employees is to make H. B. Fuller a great place to work. We recognize that Maslow's Hierarchy of Needs is real. That description of needs goes from basic safety, food, and clothing to the need to belong and for self-actualization. We really have to meet those needs, if we're going to have a place for young people to come and build a career working in a free association of people. That's terribly important and it isn't just about money. Surveys tell us that money is not the driving force that keeps people attracted, retained, and motivated in a company; it's things like respect, appreciation, and challenging work.

We keep the question in front of us, "Is Fuller the kind of place you are proud to work?" We're not perfect, but we try to make it an interesting and exciting place to come to when you're young and then spend your whole life. The first time we were ever in the *Wall Street Journal* was in 1948. We were on the front page but not because of sales or profits or dividends. It was because we started giving a person's birthday as a personal holiday.

To be thirty years ahead of a trend is kind of fun. More importantly, it shows people in the company that we care about them. We want to pay as much as we possibly can in salaries, for example. That salary may or may not be what the employees think they're worth, but at least they know we're trying to do as much as we can.

Fifteen years ago, we started a bonus vacation. In the tenth year of employment and every five years thereafter, a person is given two additional weeks of paid vacation and a check for $800 after all the deductions. There's only one hook—you've got to take a vacation. You can't buy a new television, or paint the house, or pay down on a car. A trip to Hawaii, a trip to Europe, a fishing trip to Canada can be done under that program. Some folks have had opportunities they never in their wildest imagination thought they could have.

Retirement is another major area that needs attention. It strikes me that to have a happy and satisfying retirement, people need a couple of things. They need health, income, and shelter. If you have those three legs of a stool, your chance of having a happy retirement is significantly enhanced. Therefore, the company has in place a retirement health care program that is significant. More recently, we have begun to fund the future liabilities of that, as well as of a retirement pension plan and a 401K. The third thing is the most important part that nobody is really addressing—the issue of shelter.

We see more and more people reaching retirement without a house that is paid for. It's much harder to buy a home today than it was twenty to thirty years ago. Many people never seem to be able to save enough money to make the down payment.

We're looking at a program right now that would ensure employees the opportunity to buy their own home, if they wish. It's a company-sponsored, one-time down payment. A home not only applies to retirement, but provides the personal net worth of individual capitalism—capital owned by an individual for all kinds of uses throughout a lifetime. It can provide a college education for kids, it can provide strong retirement positioning for a person, it can be the capital for somebody in the family to start a small business. It can have very significant positive ramifications for all members of that family for decades.

One thing disturbs me in all this. We have a lot of "soft subjects" that are very important to us and we take a lot of flack on them from some Wall Street groups. It's as if some of them can't or, even worse, refuse to believe that we're going to do a job for our shareholders in profit, dividends, and capital gains. The fact is, we have. We've compounded our sales growth at over 17 percent per year for over 51 years. Our profit has compounded at just about the same rate. What we do works. We've been in the top 100 of the *Fortune* 500 for total return to shareholders, six or seven out of the 10 years we've been in the *Fortune* 500.

We've performed with excellence for our owners and for our shareholders. Those are two words that are a world apart. If you're an owner, you care about what happens tomorrow because you're going to be an owner tomorrow. Owners don't come and go by the hour. A person who feels that he or she owns a company has a long-term interest, concern, and commitment. On the other hand, many shareholders think of themselves as owning a certificate in a company that they may sell this afternoon or tomorrow, depending on how things go.

We are blessed in all kinds of ways at Fuller. For one, we have many shareholders who really are owners of the company. I have been blessed to have had tremendous support in my position as president of this company for over 20 years by a board of directors who want this company to perform over the long term. They're willing to endure the slings and arrows that may take place over short time periods. That personal support gives a president an enormous amount of confidence to do the things that are the right things to do in the first place."

It takes courage to explore and to live out one's sense of purpose. William C. Norris was the founder of Control Data Corporation and today is chairman of the William C. Norris Institute. He took Control Data Corporation from an idea to $6 billion. After dramatic restructuring, CDC has been split into two companies—Ceridian and Control Data Systems—with combined revenues of about $1.5 billion.

CDC has had impacts far beyond its own size, employment, and technology. Over 15 years ago, a chart was developed that showed approximately 100 spin-off companies from CDC. The company was also among the great social experimenters of the seventies and eighties, trying to solve social problems through profit-oriented organizations. Norris was roundly and frequently criticized for these efforts.

At a time when we need creativity and innovation, we hold off out of fear. Fear of making a mistake, of people thinking less of us and, as a consequence, of losing our jobs. The more visible we are, the higher up we are, the more we're watched and the more likely it is someone will try to tear us apart. So I wanted to know how this head of a huge organization sitting in the public eye deals with that. I was especially interested because he could have stuck to his computers and been much safer. If we had the secret to his courage, it might free the rest of us. Without this we will never apply what we do learn.

I liked Bill Norris and found him to be many things the press accounts had never described. He has a spirit, or core, that I respect. He seems to have the ability to let go and trust that good will come from good, whether it's in the form we planned or not. We are always part of a bigger process that's going on. Other results will flow from our efforts in ways we least expect and may never personally see. I noted that three other people in this book mentioned that they or another officer in their company had learned much through some kind of affiliation with CDC's efforts. Norris had never heard of any of them, but they confirmed in my mind that his trust in the larger process was validated.

Bill Norris' Story: Let Them Laugh

"When people get out in front, they'll be criticized. You just have to make up your mind that you're not going to let it bother you. I have gone through that many times. I was born and raised on a farm in south central Nebraska. My father died in 1932, a month before I graduated from the University of Nebraska. We were right in the middle of the depression and the worst drought that ever swept through the Great Plains. Many people were losing their farms, partly because they couldn't feed their cattle and other livestock. We had a fine herd of Hereford cattle. The neighbors were all selling theirs, because there wasn't anything to feed them through the winter.

I remember feeding the cattle, as a kid, and noticing that every once in a while, a cow would pick out a Russian thistle and eat it. Well it was dry and hot and there were Russian thistles growing high and beautifully green. In fact, they were about the only things growing. I decided there must be some food value, because animals don't do things for the hell of it. So I stacked the thistles. I had a terrible time, but it was really a godsend. I remember saying to my mother, "People may get a big ha ha, if this doesn't work, but so be it. At least we tried." She said, "That's right," and supported me. I couldn't get the other farmers to help because they were afraid of being laughed at.

It worked out very well and, 15 years later, I read a report by someone at the University of Arizona. They had done a research program on the nutritional value of Russian thistles and it turns out that they have a very high protein content. So I decided very early in life that I was going to do what I thought was right and if somebody wanted to laugh at me, then OK—laugh.

I ran into the same thing when I was in the Navy. I was in an intelligence division and we had an idea for a new technology. This same issue came up and someone said, "What if it doesn't work?" I said, "So what if it doesn't work? At least we did what we thought was right." I have always followed that. It's easy once you make up your mind.

When I was leading Control Data, we began to get involved with some projects to address societal needs. They evolved as the environment changed and we grew. Its genesis was in the racial strife that started in the middle sixties and then the fires and riots, including the one we had in North Minneapolis. I had been at conferences where the gravity of the situation had been discussed. That caused me to start thinking about what our society and company should do.

As I saw it, the root cause was lack of jobs and job creation was the purview of business. That led me to thinking that maybe business could do more with respect to job creation at the same time it was carrying out its other major functions. I never had the perception that business, by itself, could solve that problem. I wanted to get business and government working together.

All of the efforts were worthwhile. Some made or exceeded objectives, both social and financial. Many did not. People have been too focused on the financial results. There were no failures because a great deal was accomplished, even in those instances where performance fell short of expectation.

For example, we put seven plants in poverty-stricken areas. The first one was in North Minneapolis. The program was tremendously successful and lasted for about 10 years. At its height, over 2,000 people were employed in good manufacturing jobs. Changes in the world economy and in the computer industry meant those plants were no longer needed. But during the period they were there, they provided jobs for a lot of people.

Plato was a program that trained hundreds of thousands of people, especially the handicapped. We taught a large number of talented, dedicated people in the utilization of technology in education. While they have left Control Data, they are out there and today, technology in education is moving forward. It's almost a given that you must have computers in your schools. The issues now are how many and how are they going to be used. I planted seeds and, in some instances, they have grown into oak trees and they're still growing. Many people who learned from those experiences are using that learning today in schools, new businesses, and government.

For instance, I have been a great proponent of wind energy. When I was at CDC, we helped set up wind farms in California and Hawaii. But the government eliminated the tax credits and that pulled the rug out from under the whole thing. I was criticized for using bad judgment and chasing and jousting with windmills. I remember when people laughed at that. I have a wind generator and solar system at my home that provides part of our heat. I recently heard that Northern States Power is going to put a wind farm in Southwestern Minnesota.

Many things got in the way of our goals. Some were uncontrollable and unpredictable like the economy, the advances of other countries, changes in technology, and changes in government regulations. I have been criticized from hell to breakfast because I went off on all these social junkets. Well, the so-called "social junkets" were never more than 5 or 6 percent of the effort of the company and they were really aimed at long-term business development. That wasn't understood, and in retrospect, I didn't do a good job of communicating it.

The main reason we fell short in expected performance was simply that the idea of a partnership or collaboration between business and government to address job creation wasn't there. It's still not there. The perceptions were that business ought to help through contributions and volunteering, but that it shouldn't be involved with schools, if it related to making a profit.

Collaborative efforts still drive me. Growing up on a farm affected my views on a lot of things. I think you come by a better appreciation of nature and the interdependence of people. Our society still doesn't understand the potential for government/business collaboration. I started to think in terms of collaboration early in the history of Control Data. We were manufacturing large computers and our competitors were much larger companies, like IBM and Sperry. I felt like David and Goliath and the old sling isn't very effective in today's world. So how do you get help? Very simple. You get others to work with you.

I began to think seriously about that and I had great difficulties within the company. Engineers would say, "But I would give away all my secrets." I would say, "Well, yes, but what if you get some secrets in return?" and they would say, "I don't know if I could do that." We got started down the path, but there was quite a bit of grumbling. After two years we met to discuss our results. There wasn't a single engineer who felt that we didn't get more than we gave. From then on, the concept of collaboration outside the company really took off and became part of the culture.

Today, I am working largely on innovation and collaboration in education. It's the very fabric of our society. We're not going to be able to compete unless our people are better trained and have the skills that are required in the world economy. Beyond that, life itself is so much more enjoyable if your mind is trained to evaluate new things that occur. Knowledge is certainly a part of wisdom and a part of character. Second to food, it may be the essential of life.

I have 17 grandchildren who I worry about. I'm also concerned about my children. They are struggling to maintain the standard in which they grew up. That's very hard to do. Their children are going to be at an even greater disadvantage because we have a population that is largely technically illiterate. They don't understand the role that technology has in society. That's part of the reason it took so long for technology to be recognized as essential to a better education system. Our most serious shortcoming is our individualism; second is our lack of understanding of technology and innovation.

Our society is highly individualistic and more inclined to compete, rather than collaborate. I'm not against sports, I love sports, but we introduce that spirit of competition and it carries into the classroom, the workplace, and the relationships between government and business. Education should be based on teamwork and collaboration.

Even the brighter students discover that they learn more by helping other students. There's nothing like trying to teach someone what you think you know. You usually find out that you don't quite know as much as you thought you did, so that's a challenge. This was one of the advantages I had when I went to school. I went to a one-room country schoolhouse and the teacher was busier than a cat on a hot tin roof. She had eight grades, so she relied on some of the older students to help the younger ones. That's a great experience. I have always regretted that my grandchildren don't have that.

These things have to start at an early age. I have talked to my grandchildren about the process of innovation and after a couple of sessions of light conversation, they get it. I sometimes think children are born with wisdom and then we educate it out of them. Once they connect with the process of innovation, careers and school are more meaningful, especially math and science.

We also need a highly accessible education system that will provide people with these needed skills at a much lower cost. The Norris Institute fosters collaboration to utilize technology better in education and in the process of innovation. This will help lower costs and increase access. We have three consortia, one in K–12, one in engineering schools, and another we call the academic quality consortium for colleges.

The K–12 consortium includes 60 schools in 13 states. It's focused on a particular set of tools for transforming education. It includes a personalized education plan for each child, outcome-based education and instruction, appropriate use of computer-based interactive multimedia technology, distance learning, and total quality. These tools and processes were selected by people on the policy board who represented all members.

We started with a concept involving personalized education. Nebraska had tried to develop a system by hand and failed. They and others felt there was no suitable software available and this was the necessary foundation for a personalized plan. The Institute paid for the development and the teachers worked hard in laying out the design of the plan, what it should include and the parameters of the software. They donated parts of two summers to do this. So now we have set up a separate company to develop and market the software.

Each child has a plan they can print out and take home to show parents. We want to keep embellishing it so that parents can get more involved. Progress is updated by the student and teacher. Cost-saving comes in because the role of the teacher changes from lecturer to facilitator and the child takes more responsibility for his or her own learning. The teacher will have more time to monitor and work with individual students. As a consequence, the student–teacher ratio becomes less relevant. This personalized plan starts with kindergarten and goes through twelfth grade into higher education and the workplace, where appropriate. We hope eventually to include preschool as well.

This is what collaboration allows. It's people and organizations working together to accomplish more than they could in isolation. That old business of a committee not designing anything that works doesn't really apply to modern society. It may have been true before, but today's problems are so complex that the benefits of diversity are needed. The process involves the pooling of both intellectual and physical resources. Pooling provides economies of scale, but more than that, things can be accomplished that otherwise wouldn't be possible, particularly for small organizations.

I have some regrets looking back, but not a lot. It was too bad that Control Data had to go through restructuring, but what company hasn't? I recall with great unhappiness that we had the leading position in data services and we couldn't get into Japan, the world's second largest market. Had we been able to, the course of CDC would have been quite different. But that wasn't possible, so on balance I feel good. We had some deep roots that made it possible to come through and still be a very strong company. Ceridian is a strong company; it has a solid product line in the service area. Control Data Systems is not quite as strong, but I think it will do fine."

The final connection we need to explore is the power of individual purpose when aligned with organizational purpose. This radical idea is just beginning to sink in, so I needed a rare person to help me explore it. I found her at ColorAge, Inc. in the Boston area. This company is a leading developer of products for color imaging and computer connectivity in graphic arts and desktop publishing. It was ranked number 174 on *Inc.* magazine's 1992 list of "500 Fastest Growing Privately Held Companies in America." Part of what has fueled that growth has been the integration of several diverse technologies to provide state-of-the-art color imaging solutions. Wynne Miller, their director of human development, seems to mirror the company through her interesting integration of a multifaceted background.

Miller has done career counseling, organizational consulting for business, and cofounded and managed a nonprofit organization. She integrates her management background with holistic health training and experience. She feels it's natural to combine these because of the connection between well-being and work. (She points out that she has read that most heart attacks happen around 9:00 AM Monday mornings.) This diversity of experience and background allows her a unique perspective.

She used a powerful metaphor that comes out of physics to talk about purpose. Metaphors give us new insights, help shake up our way of looking at the world, and clarify the more subtle aspects of behavior. As Gareth Morgan explains in *Images of Organization,*

> Metaphor is often just regarded as a device for embellishing discourse, but its significance is much greater than this. For the use of metaphor implies a way of thinking and a way of seeing that pervade how we understand our world generally. For example, research in a wide variety of fields has demonstrated that metaphor exerts a formative influence on science, on language and on how we think, as well as on how we express ourselves on a day-to-day basis.

I encouraged Miller to explore her metaphor some more, almost in a thinking-out-loud mode. As she did, the disciplines of shared vision and team learning came out as well.

Wynne Miller's Story: Magnifying the Humm . . .

"I was excited to join this company as director of human development. Even the title said to me that this was the right place for me to be because I have always needed to help people appreciate themselves, see more fully who they truly are, and support them in being more of that. When I was asked to come here, I was told that when things were going well there was a hum in the company and my job would be "to keep the humm . . . going, the energy flow flowing." The fact that it was the company lawyer who said that impressed me even more.

A start-up organization frequently has a special feeling to it. It has lots of energy, the vibes seem right, and it's as if everyone is on the same wavelength. Sometimes, people almost seem to read each other's minds. We're near becoming big enough and diverse enough so that may not continue to happen automatically without some assistance, some nudging. The challenge we face is to keep that original spirit as we grow. That takes some conscious effort. People have to stop and think about who needs to be involved in a decision or action and know that the team decision needs to be supported. It may not happen by itself anymore.

Seen in this way, human development goes way beyond intellectual development. It is the development of and full expression of the self, which means the mind, body, emotions, and spirit all integrated, all having permission to be part of the whole. Someone said "putting the soul into action." I'm not sure we know how to do this. What I am sure of is that an opportunity has come my way to help build a young, fast-growing company based on truth, permission to be as we are, and the ability to feel safe so we can take risks. Being who we are and taking risks means revealing our gifts and making mistakes sometimes.

In a broader sense, it means supporting each person to fulfill his or her personal purpose and mission through the mechanism of the organizational mission and purpose. I think of mission as more concrete and specific. It's what we make or do. That can change, depending on technology, markets, and economics. Purpose is different. It doesn't change and, in a sense, is on a higher playing field or a deeper one. Purpose is broader, more intangible, more lasting.

It's a quality that is present when we show up as a whole person. It's the impact you have on those around you. In action, as someone said, "It's what you can't not do." In essence, "It's what you can't not be."

A simple example of what this means on a daily basis is a conversation I had with our shipping assistant the other day. He's one of the newest hires. In a more traditional company, the position could be considered "lowest man on the totem pole." I had asked him for a small box to place near the copier where we generate a lot of paper; this could then be dumped into the larger recycle bins elsewhere in the company.

He went beyond my simple request for a box and talked about recycling and its importance. He checked out who we use for recycling now, what the best arrangement is, and he offered to learn a graphics program to create signs. He suggested we invite company members to have a small recycle box at their desks as well, since we all use printers and produce a lot of scrap. Then we talked about how to communicate this throughout the company with a memo over e-mail. I suggested he sign the memo himself. This is an example of evolving leadership, a seeming follower in the shipping department becoming a leader on an issue that sparks him, that somehow touches his purpose.

When we touch people's sense of purpose, it can be electrifying. A charge goes through the person and the organization. Part of my charge in my current position comes from being so closely aligned with my purpose. I discovered, years ago, that my purpose is to tell the truth and to help other people to tell theirs. Now, that isn't much of a job description, but the more I've lived in that space, and the more I've lived in this company, the more I'm humbled by how much of my job is to do just that, to describe things the way they really are to everyone, including the two founders of the company. To be their mirror is another way to think of it. When I do that, I open the safety net because people know exactly where they are and they know they can say what needs to be said. If that causes conflict, then we deal with the conflict.

I notice how often we talk about electricity, charges, hums, vibes, and so on. That's very interesting to me. I read an article in *Advances, The Journal of Mind, Body, Health*. It was titled "Life Energy and Western Medicine: A Reappraisal" by Eric Leskowitz. This article says that health can be seen as a state of electromagnetic expansion, and illness a state of electromagnetic contraction. It also suggests that the phenomenon of electromagnetic field resonance underlies the skill we call clinical intuition. I'm neither a medical person nor a physicist, but I think there's an important idea here that correlates with purpose and organizational energy. I've learned enough about this to be convinced that it's true, but I'm not yet at a level to be able to explain it well.

As I understand it, scientists are saying that the whole physical universe is energy, including us, since we are made up of atoms just like everything else. So everything, our bodies, the rocks, the trees, animals, products, even our thoughts all share the same basic components of energy. We're all connected in an energy field. One of the laws of energy is that similar energies or vibrations attract each other like magnets.

I'm thinking about how many human dynamics this helps account for. I'll have a conversation in one corner of the company and then the same ideas appear magically with a whole different group of people in a different corner almost simultaneously, as though there's a readiness for things to be transferred. This isn't a grapevine phenomenon. It's people getting the same idea at the same time. When there is readiness, the idea travels and things happen synchronistically.

Organizations also tend to attract certain kinds of people. I think a healthy organization is successful as a culmination of the right spirits coming together. If we live true to our purpose we attract the right people in a very physical, electromagnetic way. We develop very strong bonds that give us a unique capacity and competitive position. I hear people talk about the glow that you sense going through the Baldrige award–winning companies, and I have this image of chemical elements bonding to each other. Unhealthy organizations pull in more unhealthy people much of the time.

To play that idea out, I think it implies that life has meaning, that we do have purpose, even if it's just to learn and grow. Another way of saying that is we're all here to make a contribution. There's some piece of a jigsaw puzzle that is uniquely ours and if we let the pieces fall into place, they actually fit with each other. Organizations are beginning to recognize that when we express ourselves fully and encourage personal and organizational purposes to become aligned, we have a powerful dynamic. Then each of us can take our rightful place.

If there is this universal energy field that we're all plugged into, then we would each see ourselves as a sort of transmitter and receiver in this field. The more clear we are about our purpose, the better we transmit. The more we become an open receiver, the more we have all those important experiences that appear coincidental, like getting that phone call we didn't expect, or making that happenstance comment to a customer that made all the difference, or catching those two lines in a newspaper we otherwise would not have read. When we have trouble it may be that there is too much resistance in the air, too many people unaligned.

For example, we've all had the experience of an employee who just didn't seem to fit. We had an employee who was not well suited to the work he had been doing, so we transferred him to a different group. It turned out the new group was upset. No one liked him or got along with him. I talked with him privately and learned how hard he is on himself. He identified his own fears and defensiveness. I reminded him about some tools for staying centered like breathing, yoga, watching his physical responses, being truthful and vulnerable. He was willing to try. Within a few days he realized some things that were getting in the way of his being able to see his part in the company and to give and receive effective communication.

Then I needed to look at the signals that were going between him and the group so I met with his new group. We got everything out on the table: why they've had problems with this person and what behavior it produces in them. We agreed that we need honesty in the company, that each of us has our problems and if no one tells us, we'll go on doing the same offensive things. We talked about ways of communicating this.

He was subsequently given the feedback, narrowed down to a few troublesome areas, and asked to come up with ways he and others will know things are working. Meanwhile, the group saw that instead of scapegoating or ostracizing the person, we could take a forgiving position, realizing it could be any one of us. I suspect the group members also saw that if they have a problem, they'll get the help of the group. The rest is up to them. We had made it clear how we needed to be connected. To use the analogy, that set of discussions and insights helped this person and team become better receivers and transmitters.

These are conditions that need to be nurtured. They're new models, where human development is considered every bit as important as product development. It seems ironic that we could ever have missed the significance of this. We need the hum in human beings to be vibrating to achieve breakthrough products. Then we will move toward purposeful organizations and beyond the norm described by Studs Terkel, who said "Most people have work that is too small for their spirits."

4

Empowering Mirrors for Change

We must be the change we wish to see in the world.

GANDHI

There is a desperate need for leadership and empowerment at this time. I see many who do want changes in who and how we are at work. We desire change because we want more purposeful lives and organizations, but not enough of us are actively seeking it. One of the most frequent comments I hear is, "I wish it could be like that, but it will never happen where I work. It (he, she, they) won't change."

I feel their pain and wistfulness; it's a mile high and wide. They'd like to believe it's possible, but can't imagine their organization will ever be different. For some, the idea is such a stretch I almost sense they're patting me on the head and telling me to grow up and forget the fairy tales. Occasionally, I must unknowingly strike a nerve because there is anger that I even broach the ideas. In both cases, the message is, "Leave those dreams buried. It's better to not think that way."

Most people don't feel very empowered to do anything about change without quitting their jobs and taking risks they really don't dare to take. Others tell of change programs that never quite made it. These two issues bog us down because they erode hope. For every success story, there's a failure. Therefore, many people are frustrated. Some cynically watch for the next program of the month to appear.

I don't think these have been wasted efforts and that we should quit. If anything, it is becoming more necessary to move forward. My concern is about the issue of responsibility or leadership for forward movement. Too many people feel that they have to sit on the sidelines and wait for someone else to lead or to change. This is dangerous. It's too easy to let ourselves off the hook. If we're the executives and decide to change the employees or the organization, we don't tend to look at ourselves. If we're employees and decide we have to change the organization or the bosses, then it's likely we won't do anything.

We need to let the best of our natural selves arise, to let our heroic selves emerge. Robert Greenleaf, in *The Servant as Leader*, describes this: "It begins with the natural feeling that one wants to serve, to serve first. Then conscious choice brings one to aspire to lead. The difference manifests itself in the care taken by the servant—first to make sure that other people's highest priorities are being served." I believe this urge is buried in many of us.

Part of our problem here is that we are engaged is some disempowering thinking patterns. Anne Wilson Schaef, in *Women's Reality*, names this type of thinking "dualistic" and argues that current Western patterns of thinking are heavily dualistic. She states, "We are trained to simplify the world into either/ors. . . ."

One must always choose between the options. One choice will be the 'right' choice. The other choices are 'wrong.' If we really want to realize potential and creativity, she believes we need to be thinking in "ands." When we think in "ands" we see a greater truth, a larger picture of reality, and can combine these into a new insight.

When it comes to leadership, we are filled with lots of either/or thinking. It's either the executives who have to lead or it's the change agents or department heads or a team leader or an outside guru. But usually it's someone other than me. And in terms of who has to change, it's seldom me or us. It's always you or them. Some "and" thinking might suggest anyone who's willing to grow and improve themselves is leading, so therefore we all could be leading.

To understand this personal emphasis, we must grasp that we and the organization are part of one system, and that the organization changes—in some way, shape, or form—when individuals change. The metaphor of mirrors helps explain why this is so. Mirrors are a multifaceted metaphor or lens that can help us understand some underlying dynamics. In the negative sense, many change efforts make employees feel we're only doing tricks with mirrors; the changes aren't real or lasting.

However, mirror images can be used positively and powerfully. When we're trying to intervene in an organization, a department, or with an individual who is in denial, we speak of holding up a mirror so they can see reality. We supply them with facts, events, data, and feelings. Many breakthroughs are achieved. Other times we speak of mirror images, looking in the mirror, two-way mirrors, and reflections on the water. In all these cases, we see, gain insight and may decide to act in new ways. And that's how change efforts are: they can be frauds or powerfully enlightening.

What people do is constantly look in the organizational mirrors to see what's a fraud and what's a reality. Examples of organizational mirrors are vision and value statements, the behaviors of people from the highest to the lowest rank, the attitudes of different departments, or the reward system. Different mirrors have different degrees of influence. We take our cues from them. They act as feedback loops to us.

"And" thinking about mirrors opens the possibility that we can be changing the organization while changing ourselves. It's similar to the phrase, "Think globally; act locally." Acting locally is something we can do and, at the same time, we are changing the global scene. The counterpart in the organizational sense is, "Think organizationally; act on me." Changing me is changing the organization.

If that seems like a stretch to you, remember that in *Seven Habits of Highly Effective People*, Steven Covey introduces the concept of our areas of influence and how they expand or contract. We extend our influence outward by focusing on what we can influence today. So to change the organization, our boss, or our group, the focus must begin with ourselves.

One of the reasons change efforts haven't been working is because we haven't had this personal link. We've become too entangled in the mechanical aspects of our change efforts when the problem is that we need to go deeper, to find the heart and spirit. Many change agents know this and are already engaged in trying to learn about a new dimension of change. The business world hasn't, until recently, been at all open to this concept and its personal nature. The door is beginning to crack open as we realize we don't have a choice. We must empower ourselves and our organizations to go through the door.

The stories that follow illustrate different mirrors at work and their interplay. They demonstrate the ability of leadership at all levels in the organization, using all kinds of approaches, to be productive and successful. The intent is to encourage each of us to find a way to be a leader, regardless of where we are in the power structure.

Medtronic, Inc., is a billion dollar, worldwide supplier of medical devices. Many years ago, I saw a Medtronic document. It had the graphic form of a person rising from a prone position giving a sense of rising from the dead. I read the mission statement associated with that image and never forgot either the graphic or the statement. Medtronic exists "to alleviate pain, restore health, and extend life."

There's been much discussion of *vision* in the business arena—unfortunately, so much discussion and so little action that we're in danger of wearing out another wonderful word and turning it into a program of the month. We write vision statements to put on the wall or hand out. Often, we stop there and say, "That's done." As William George, president and CEO talks about Medtronic, it's obvious their purposeful vision could touch and excite people. It has continued to guide the company since its founding in 1949. He describes where Medtronic's vision comes from and how it affects an organization. In this story we see the dynamics of a vision and values mirror being used as a large-scale feedback loop.

Bill George's Story: The Soul of an Organization

"All organizations have a soul. The soul of our organization came from Earl Bakken, our founder. He has given us a mission statement that focuses our efforts on products that "alleviate pain, restore health, and extend life." With that mission have come strong values about understanding the real work that we're doing, and the importance of customers and employees. Even though he has been retired from the business for about three years, Earl continues to be very present in the company in conveying those values.

It's my job to increase and extend the vitality of our organization's soul. In order to do this, we are trying to reinvent the company. Another way of saying this is that organizations have life and we need to pay attention to renewing their blood. An aging organization, like the human body, sometimes loses its vitality.

It happens to many organizations. Once you lose your soul or sell it, it's very hard to get it back. There are very few companies that have succeeded at the kind of goals for continuing growth that we are seeking. That's why 40 percent of the companies that Tom Peters describes as excellent are out of business or losing money five years later. He isn't looking at what things really are needed to sustain the success of the enterprise.

One of the ways you lose your vitality is by having the wrong purpose or losing sight of the right one. Companies in the eighties that said their purpose was to enhance shareholder value are in trouble. There has to be more to purpose than just that. It's not just about getting rich. If we asked our employees for 100 percent quality so that we could make more money, we would have a very different response than when we ask them to do that because our purpose has to do with furthering human life.

Employees feel a certain hollowness when the company purpose is something that lacks value. What they do becomes just a job. The older employees hang on, hoping they can get their retirement. If they have the opportunity, younger employees probably move on. In the meantime, you don't get any truly valuable work done because people are just going through the motions. Companies lose a great deal when that happens.

Medtronic has tried to keep itself clear, centered and vibrant in many ways. That's a big challenge when you have over 9,000 employees and numerous diverse customers worldwide. Earl Bakken still goes to every major medical meeting in the world. He stands in our exhibit from 8:30 AM until 5:30 PM every day, so any customer from anywhere in the world can see him and talk to him. His behavior reflects the value he places on customers.

He meets, individually, with every new employee in the company everywhere in the world, stressing leading by values—as opposed to management by objectives. As he talks with our people, they want to talk about values. Many leaders aren't comfortable with that, nor are many business schools. It makes them feel vulnerable, and many leaders see that as a sign of weakness. We think it's a sign of strength.

Another thing Earl initiated was our annual Christmas event. It really is a spiritual occasion. Spirituality and values are hard to separate. Patients come and tell their stories, and they're so powerful and touching. We invite six patients and their doctors, one for each of our six major businesses. They tell their story, what their disease state was, what happened, what Medtronic product they received and what the impact has been on their lives. It's a very powerful occasion. We have about 1,100 people in our atrium, we put it on video to our skyway conference room and then we send out videotapes around the world. The Christmas program is probably the most effective team-building thing we do and a vivid reminder of what we are all about.

Since coming to Medtronic, I've had to learn to be open and share my emotions. I've been opening up in expressing beliefs, being more of my true self, and have been supported in evolving and growing. I've also had to learn a new business, so opening up about that feels vulnerable. This is something I needed to do. I was picked on some, as a kid, so I learned not to be vulnerable. I've spent the last twenty years trying to be more vulnerable again. In a position like mine, if I don't learn to do that, it's too easy to set myself apart from people and to appear less human. But vulnerability doesn't come naturally to me.

At the first Christmas event I attended, an 18-year-old who had spastic cerebral palsy spoke of his pain and how it had debilitated his life. He told how the implant of one of our devices has transformed his life. As he talked, I had tears in my eyes. I was embarrassed for a moment, until I looked at the guy next to me and saw he did, too. We really can be more open at work. I think most of our worst problems are like malignant tumors inside us. They start small and they grow large when we don't let them out.

Encouraging feelings and emotions is not always pretty. Anger, vengeance, sadness are part of our emotions and part of being a whole person. When they aren't dealt with, though, they get more severe. I don't want to departmentalize my life and be one way in the community, another at home, and yet another at work. It's like taking down the walls of my personal house and being the same person on my bike and in the board room. Other places make you feel as though you should be on your best behavior at work. I wonder why. It's a lot easier to be internally consistent and real than to be on stage.

Medtronic is a young organization. It could be compared to a person coming out of college with much idealism, with enormous potential. We're doing good work, but we still aren't a fully mature organization. As we get larger, there's a danger that we can stagnate and become bureaucratic. We're an organization built on creativity and innovation and being vital and responsive to the customer. If we lose that, we lose the essence of what we are. There is a huge risk if we ever lose our creative juices, our creative spirit, or become less risk oriented.

Part of keeping the organization alive, healthy, and on the cutting edge has to do with being honest. We have to be willing to look inside ourselves, avoid denial, and see what our shortcomings are. We need to admit them and then address them. Sometimes those are painful things to do, but unless you're willing to face them you cannot have a healthy, vital organization. Unless the whole company continues to do that, we'll stagnate.

When I came to Medtronic three years ago, I began instilling an even greater customer-focused quality effort. Our emphasis on quality has expanded significantly. This gives us a methodology and tools for learning, challenging ourselves, and using external and internal measures to see our weaknesses. Internal measures may say we're doing a fine job of serving customers; we may or may not be doing so in the customer's mind. We need to keep the whole organization learning through this process, just like we do as individuals. If we stop our education in our twenties and don't continue to renew ourselves, eventually we'll stagnate.

Earl continues to model this value. He's involved with a major new hospital in Hawaii. He continues to learn about health and healing. The hospital is focusing on the merger of Western and Eastern medicines, using all the Eastern therapies, massage and acupuncture and various other forms of healing techniques. Part of that modeling is taking risks to try something new.

Meditating twice a day has helped me through changes. My wife persuaded me to take a course on meditation at the University many years ago. I was at a different company then and I think it would have been viewed as weird within that culture, particularly at the corporate level. I was quoted several times in newspapers about it and was a little self-conscious about that. But we're more open here. In fact, Medtronic has a meditation room. It's a quiet place for meditation and reflection and study. It includes a small library, art works, and artifacts of all the great religions of the world.

I've been doing this since 1975 and it has been a godsend. I'm an intense person, so meditating lets me break that pattern and reflect on events of the day and my life. I am enjoying life so much I almost don't want to move on to another phase, but I must. My father died recently and my son graduated from high school the week after that. Clearly, I have new transitions to work through. All of this has to do with who I am at work.

People often ask me how to keep a balance in their business, personal, and community life. This is important. People who work sixteen-hour days won't be effective for very long. We have to nurture each aspect of ourselves. I continually try to take stock and take time to tighten control over how I spend my time and review my priorities.

For example, I love coaching soccer. For 10 years, I've coached and watched my son and a group of his friends grow up to be men. That's a real joy. I really think it makes me more effective at work. At one point, we were involved in an important issue with the Food and Drug Administration and there was a major inter-soccer tournament that I wanted to attend. I managed to find a way to do both, so I was walking around with my beeper. I wouldn't have it another way.

I like to think I've spent my whole life changing, overcoming weakness and growing, and I've done it from a solid core of values and spiritual beliefs. These have developed, evolved, and matured as I have grown. What happens with the individual is analogous to what happens with the organization. We have to work at change or we fall back. Whether we are changing jobs, communicating an idea, being a parent or spouse, each experience is different from the last experience and that keeps us evolving, alive, and dynamic. Every time we learn from one change, we take that on to the next one.

Medtronic's continued growth has much to do with keeping our soul vital. We must be responsive to environmental changes inside and outside the organization; that will mean more and more change. We can't resist change, because it's our lifeblood. At the same time, people need stability. If they have that, change is easier. Stability of identity is created when you have solid roots. We have that in our mission and values.

This is not a one-person kind of thing. Management literature places far too much focus on the top person in the organization. You have to have a broad group of people really committed to those kind of objectives. There's not enough sensitivity to the larger team at the top and the role of middle management. In many organizations, they're fighting with each other and aren't really on the same wavelength. When that happens at the top, people all the way down will choose sides.

I want a vital, healthy organization that is a dynamic and fulfilling place to work for all our employees. Then we can use all our potential to have a major effect on eradicating disease and restoring the people of the world to a full life through our technology, rather than drugs."

Our organizations want more empowered employees who take actions and make decisions in a more heartfelt and personalized way. An article in the April 1993 issue of *Inc.* magazine, "A Company of Businesspeople," describes an emerging shake-up of the mindset and practices of the us/them, employees/managers view of life. The article includes this hypothetical mission statement: "This is a company of partners, of businesspeople. We are in business together. Our economic future . . . depends . . . on our collective success in the marketplace. We will share in the rewards just as . . . we share in the risks. No one in this company is just an employee."

When I reflect on a number of trends, I am convinced we will either all become owners in our organization in ways that may not have been created yet or we will become self-employed. Companies need people to have this businessperson/owner mindset. They also need the flexibility of buying services that to date have been centralized inside the organization, so there's a trend evolving to a form of outsourcing. So more people may become suppliers to their previous employers.

I look at the change in the needs, education, and aspirations of the work force members who are beginning to realize that the dream of lifetime security or of rising to the top will happen to very few. Coupled with increased awareness of the needs of family and children, we have a greater need to be our own bosses with more flexibility to make decisions about our time and our financial tradeoffs. The pendulum may be swinging to a new balance.

Wynn Binger is president of Construction Materials, Inc., a $20 million supplier of heavy construction materials. In addition to work, Binger loves to sail and travels around the world every year. He's been to Tibet five or six times and is assisting with a Tibetan resettlement program. He volunteers at a grade school, teaching children about world cultures.

This story sheds light on how much of one's leadership is a mirror of one's total being and consciousness. It also begins to explore the nature of change when it is led by the top officer in a smaller, privately held organization. We see one of the optional mirrors in action in this company.

This interview also set me to thinking about some of the other CEOs I had talked to, like Chuck Denny, and how much ADC is a mirror of him. ADC is 21 times the size of CMI. Yet it clearly reflects Denny. Binger describes a profile of employee characteristics that guides him in hiring. It was one of the documents I felt mirrored his spirit. Denny had also clearly hired with some kind of profile in mind. Some of his key hires were mirrors of his values. Perhaps in a larger organization, the CEO can't have the same immediate impact that the leader has in a smaller organization. Still, there seems to be a mirroring of mirrors that spreads and sustains a set of values and beliefs throughout larger organizations.

Perhaps each of us is more like a prism. A mirror feels too identical. We certainly have our individual contributions to make. We need that diversity. Are we all prisms of and to other people? If we are, then we are each capable of creating change. As we change or grow ourselves, we affect others. This is a different view of change than what many of us have been taught. Change was doing something to someone else or having it done to you. It was more like combat. This thought feels very different.

Wynn Binger's Story: Mirroring the Leader

"I'm often asked if it's easier to change a small, privately owned company than a large one. I don't know. The dynamics are different, to some extent. The implementation to make change happen is probably easier, but that's often offset by the more direct and personal innate fear that goes with a decision to change. When the change depends on resources and staff, a small company is more limited.

From the perspective of culture, attitudes, leadership, quick decisions, and selling your story, change is probably easier. I'm dealing with fewer people and layers so change can be more immediate. If I as the owner provide leadership, there's little bureaucracy. There aren't a lot of committees, meetings, or written communications, and there isn't the necessity for feedback through various layers.

The hard part is that the results are so close to you. In each instance, we quickly—consciously or unconsciously—weigh the economics and the consequences of errors. It's hard to be 100 percent certain any change is totally positive with no downsides. So you see risks and you start to weigh those—finances, reputation, relationships with employees and co-workers. What will their reaction be? Will it upset the cart? I think a lot about those things. Risk is less personal and direct, perhaps, to the head of a large company.

What is similar in any size organization is that there are people—good people, good employees—who are more comfortable with the status quo than the idea of change. It's as if people have a personal standard such as "I'm getting my paycheck, my raise," or "Things look fine," and as long as that standard looks OK today, they want to hold on to it. It's almost like a nostalgic longing for the past. We forget the harshness or problems that were also part of how it has been.

Sometimes people voice those concerns. Other times, they don't say it but I see questions in their behavior. "Why would we change here? We're well accepted in the industry and doing well. We have good customers who keep coming back. Everything is fine. Why would you want to change anything? Let's leave it alone." I wrap that up in my definition of status quo, which is not rocking the boat. I've felt it's one of my responsibilities over the years to overcome that attitude consistently, but gently. I see less of it today.

At CMI, we have had constant change but I try to make it uniform and transitional without problems. If someone wants to see change they have to look at more than a year because it's been gradual. My industry allows that. Construction doesn't change that rapidly. Our industry has its dynamics, but not as rapid as that of the computer, communications, or entertainment industries. Maybe I'm taking the easy way out emotionally. We are progressive, we take risks, but my style and attitude has maybe kept us from other opportunities. It's a balancing act.

Our changes have been pretty concrete. Every new employee, every new product or product line is an important change in a small company. The integration of new employees always gives me a feeling of great satisfaction, especially when I see a new employee become what I call a "five-year veteran" in two years. One of the ways I've dealt with this is in hiring decisions and coaching when people come on.

I have what I call a "CMI Personal Profile." It's a list of ten characteristics of a CMI person. The characteristic that most relates to change I have described as curiosity: "The curiosity of CMI employees has led it into new areas, new products, and new relationships." I use this with new employees, but I also use it with existing employees for performance feedback. I've used it to assist people to leave who fit the profile in every way but for whom we couldn't offer enough challenge. I hate to lose a good person but they deserve to be allowed to use all their potential.

I think any new product we take on gives me a sense of that, as well. We see a new product, have a sense about it, and make some commitment to explore whether it could fit. This subtlety is important. We don't ask whether it *does* fit, but whether it *can* fit. If we just took the ones that do fit, that would be limiting. When we take these product ideas from a whimsical dream to reality, I always have a good feeling. Success encourages us to try another one.

I would be interested in knowing how my employees feel about my initiating, allowing, resisting, and encouraging change. I suspect their perception of me would be quite different from mine. I got a hint of that one evening after work. A few of us were talking about style. I saw myself as easy going. Jokingly they said, well, sure I was—as long as I got my own way. The message I got was that when I had strong feelings, I wasn't as flexible as I thought I was. That surprised me because I thought I had changed a great deal in my time with the company.

Len Shope had founded the company and I soon joined him. As we grew, I became heavily involved in managing the operations. I wasn't a very good delegator. We kept doing more, adding more people, increasing our involvement in the industry, and adding more activity. I was emotionally and physically overloaded. It came to a point of building anxiety and frustration—with myself, not with other people. It was crazy. I decided I'd better do something about this.

At that point, I made a choice to change. I remember some key growth issues. I realized I measured the company's and my success by the number of tasks I took on and completed. I also realized how limiting that was for me because I got so caught up in tasks, I couldn't do other important things. It was also limiting for other people who wanted those tasks and responsibilities. That was a big occasion for me, to step over that line and be comfortable with delegation. The second part was to learn to leave it delegated. That came much later. I had to accept that things wouldn't be done the way I'd do them. I still work on this second part today.

That personal change for me was a significant step in the growth of CMI and it was also a big growth step for me. I know it's carrying over into my personal and professional life in learning how to say no. I grew up on a farm, where you do the job when someone asks you to do it. In my personal life and business life, I never said no. It was letting someone down and that was selfish and inappropriate. It would get me in trouble in a lot of ways, and it robbed me of pure energy. We all take on things that we shouldn't, don't want to do, and don't fit for us because someone has taught us we have no choice.

Personal changes can also reflect back into our business careers. Ten years ago, I was going through some counseling. Eventually, we got into spirituality. Up until that point, I was uncomfortable thinking about spirituality, even about what it meant. I thought everyone else had it figured out so that was why no one talked about it. Because I didn't want to look weak and inadequate, I didn't talk about it, either. A friend has since given me a good definition: having a spiritual sense is understanding how life works. I thought about it and gave myself permission to go on a spiritual quest for the rest of my life.

It's taken different forms. I changed my reading choices, some of the ways I look at things and how I listen. It's an interesting feeling. I still have that innate feeling inside that—whether it's my relationship with other people or family or even business—spirituality is a big issue. I haven't figured out how much of it to bring to the office. I know I'm asking myself new questions about the meaning of life, the next horizon of my life in business, and, in general, what I bring to life and what I take from it. For people who have children, those questions may get answered daily. I don't know.

I think it's especially important for those of us with technical backgrounds to explore these issues. Technical companies are loaded with brain power in technical areas, but we generally lack a broader understanding of the life we are in. My engineering degree was a five-year technical degree. I grew up on a farm in the forties and fifties, got out of high school at 17, went right to the University of Minnesota, knew I was going to study engineering, and lived in a dorm. We had very few nontechnical requirements and electives. At that time, we took whatever was there that was easy and took the least time. Our attitude toward liberal arts was to take it and get it out of the way.

I have made an effort to change what I feel are real gaps. I've had to work on my own liberal arts in the classical sense of reading, music, opera, philosophy, and religion. I think I really missed something. Most 18-year-olds don't ask for advice, but I have told the few who have to get the best liberal arts degree at the best school they can afford and then get their technical degree. At least we'd know there was a world other than the technical one. Perhaps it comes back to the greater context of spirituality—understanding how life works."

American Paging, Inc. is a subsidiary of Telephone and Data Systems. They sell and service pagers and paging services throughout the United States. The company has grown considerably in market share over the last 10 years, but at the expense of profits. They're changing that situation now in a big way and at a fast pace. To understand their story, I met with a few members of the leadership team—John Schaaf, president; George Orr, vice president of human resources; Donald Sporer, vice president of sales; and Terry Busse, vice president of finance. While their story includes strategic planning elements and quality, service, and productivity efforts, it also was interesting to hear the story of changes in their leaders' behavior described as the critical ingredient.

This is a clear example of a change effort that started with leaders focusing on their own change, as well as on changing their people and systems. This leader looked in his own mirror and the mirror of the organization. In a sense he did what Wynne Miller suggested in her story about becoming clearer transmitters and receivers. This seems to have made all the difference. American Paging's turnaround—and the speed with which it is being accomplished—is impressive.

Leaders who don't do this find it backfires on them. It's insulting to the people throughout the organization when the message comes that the top group is just fine, but the rest of you had better get your act together. And that is often the message, regardless of how it's disguised. Since the rest of the people are very aware of the weaknesses and blind spots of those at the top, it doesn't hold much water. Mirrors reflect all these messages.

This message isn't just for leaders at the top. It holds true for all of us in our daily work lives, regardless of title, and in our personal lives. Whenever we have a problem or a need for a change, consider starting the way John Schaaf did. Ask, "How is this situation a reflection of me and my group?" Even when we know there are other elements that are causing the problem, we'll get more cooperation when people see we're setting ourselves in order first. This is empowering; the former is not.

American Paging's Story: Inside Out Changes

Orr: American Paging is turning around in a time of recession after 10 years of lack of profitability. The most visible change that set it in motion was our new leader, John Schaaf. His change has created a whole new set of changes.

Busse: You could say a wake-up call was really delivered by TDS, our parent company, through the change-out of the president of American Paging. It suggested that maybe we weren't on the right track. That alert was felt by all the cities, the field people, and the corporate people. There had to be some changes if we were going to continue our corporate existence.

Orr: The least visible change was in John, himself, as he took the reins. Without that change, though, I'm not sure we'd have the same results. He was a 10-year insider, and was perceived by some of the people in the company as a real pain in the neck. They saw him as far too self-righteous. He knew the right answers and was too dogmatic about telling people what those answers were. This would irritate people. The company was going in the wrong direction and he said so. People didn't want to hear, "You're in trouble and you're going the wrong way, but if you do things this way, everything will turn out all right." He had made a lot of enemies.

Sporer: When John took over and worked on his own changes, as well as ours, we started taking the shackles off our people who did want to change. We have also removed the people who were holding our company back.

Schaaf: Motivation to make a change was easy. If I could turn the company around, we could all become heroes. If I didn't, that would be the end of my career with AP. After ten years with AP, I had a lot of sweat equity involved. Leaders sometimes find they have to change themselves as part of changing their organizations. If I expected the company to change, then I had to be ready and capable of change. I took responsibility by acknowledging that part of the reason the company was in the shape it was must be because of me. There must be a piece there that I needed to examine.

I accepted the position on a Friday and spent the weekend doing some journaling. I tried to mentally put myself into another company that was going through the change and examine what I should do. The obvious answer was to take a look around and do a lot of listening. I made up my mind to do that. That was a big change for me. Secondly, I felt it would be better to communicate in a sense of "we" rather than "I." Another big change for me. I also had to change my mental print pattern to accept that I couldn't know everything that's going on and that that's OK. I had to get over being afraid to say that I'd made a mistake or didn't know something.

I talked to a number of people. Jack Militello, a professor from the University of St. Thomas, was very helpful. From a business standpoint, the best thing that ever happened to me was going back to school at St. Thomas at the age of 46. Had I not done that, I probably wouldn't have been appointed president, wouldn't be as agreeable to and capable of change. You're forced to listen and to do things you may not want to do—reading, discipline, time commitments. It was a tremendous experience.

One of my moments of greatest satisfaction in this whole process happened when I was going on a series of traveling sprints. I was visiting developers of new technologies and talking with employees to find out what was going on. Then I was bringing that back into the strategic planning process. I'd come back from these sprints and I'd find the corporate staff was still behind me and I had widened the gap. After doing this two or three times, I was discouraged. I tried to talk with them about it and I could see by expressions on people's faces that they didn't understand at all.

When I came back from a sprint in early January and looked back, there wasn't anybody there. I said to myself, "It's worse. They're even further behind." I lamented about that to an associate who said, "Did you ever think of looking out in front of you?" I turned around and there they were—out in front of me. They had accelerated past me and didn't even beep when going by. They went by in the middle of the night at an incredible speed. I think they were taking the time to reorganize themselves and to reshape or retool themselves in those depressing months and I hadn't understood.

It's been a thrill. We sit at staff meetings today and I will find that 75 to 80 percent of the information discussed is news to me. That's the way it should be. The teamwork is remarkable.

Busse: From an earnings standpoint, the company's previous financial trend downward is reversing itself up to a more profitable level. A lot of that is due to a different approach to our sales efforts and the realization that the company *must* be profitable and produce earnings. In the past, many people in the organization felt we were successful if we just grew and never made any money.

We've set some extremely aggressive goals to move this organization from the bottom quartile in our industry to the top in terms of profit and growth. We're also bringing the organization into the top 10 percent in terms of quality and service.

Orr: We've gone from people feeling they're on a losing team to being part of a winning team. That makes all the difference. But it didn't start that way. When the previous president left our company, there was a feeling of mourning, a feeling of passage. We were not getting rid of somebody who was causing great harm to the company. He was a wonderful guy. What we had clearly lost touch with was that he didn't have the capability to fly the plane through the turbulent weather we were in.

So the first change we had to go through was a kind of period of mourning and a realization that it was absolutely essential for the first officer to take over because he did have higher skills. We had to believe there was a mountain out there that we just couldn't see on the radar. Now people are really getting excited.

Schaaf: Some people resisted because of honest doubts about the change. The way you remove the doubt is by consistent performance and involving them in change. I took a very positive position with the doubters, saying, "It's OK for you to feel this way. If you want to express your doubt, then you also have to participate. Apply your experience to say how to improve it. Then back it up." At a certain point, though, I will terminate people.

Sporer: To make changes in an organization, you have to face that reality. Some people may have to be moved or retrained. And some people, even in high places, are going to be obstructionists and they have to be replaced.

Orr: People who couldn't accept the change have left the company. Most left voluntarily, but some had to be helped because they were stuck and weren't making progress. They struggled with it, they tried to deal with it, and they couldn't. There are always people who are so rooted in the past that they simply cannot accept a change. They so firmly believe that what was done before was the right thing that they can't let go of it and accept something new.

Out of five departments, two vice presidents left. In the general manager ranks, there were probably five or six out of 25. Some sales managers couldn't adjust, as well as key productive sales people. They thought that the right way to sell our product was to sell a zillion of them and sell them at low prices. When we said, "No. You don't understand. This is a quality service. We want a fair price and a fair margin on it and if that means we sell fewer, then that's OK." Those people said, "I don't know how to do that. I have to go away."

Busse: This was particularly hard for us because we've always sought general managers and field managers who were very aggressive, not particularly team players. They were told to run the operation as if it were theirs. Now we're changing the playing field. We're saying we still want you to treat this as though it's yours, but we want you to use our values. Bringing in consistent values or methods of operation is very different from what the company did in the past. Once these values are internalized, those particular individuals may make the operation more successful because of their high level of motivation and their get-the-job-done approach.

Schaaf: In addition to personal role modeling, there are two particular mechanisms we used to send new, clearer messages. We had a preliminary tune-up to the strategic planning process with TDS. Then we involved many people in a full-blown, strategic planning process. We had done this before, but I don't think we were serious about it.

The second method relates to communicating. If we had had a slogan before it would have been, "Damn the torpedoes, full steam ahead. Get units, units, units." All our incentives and recognition systems were geared toward that. Rick Millington, one of our marketing people, synthesized the whole plan down into today's slogan: "QP2—Quality, Productivity, Profitability." All of our decisions, the way we act, the directions, the employees we hire and train, the systems we build are being challenged by those points.

Busse: We went through years of an annual strategic planning process. We would show up, go through our agenda, and when we got done, we'd take our nice three-ring binder filled with 50 pages of ideas and shelve it. In the latest process, we tried to make it a living document, a focal point, and tried to involve more than the senior management of the company.

It was supposed to help communicate where we were going, what we wanted to do, and the direction of the change. Soliciting input from all levels of the company helped make everyone aware that we were going through a change. We discovered, in the process, that communicating this throughout the company is extremely difficult. No matter how many times you say it or send it out in a letter, people really don't grasp it. Everybody talks at different levels, and we probably don't break it down to the centers of interest or activity that particularly affect various groups of employees. The question is "What the heck does it mean?" or "How do we achieve it?" We haven't totally figured that out yet. We keep trying different approaches.

Orr: As a result of all these things, we have brought values and dealing with emotional issues to a higher level in the company. For one thing, we terminated a manager this year for sexual harassment. This company has never done that before, but we're different now. We're a company that couldn't condone it or ignore it. The company believed that sexual harassment and other destructive behaviors were bad things, but we didn't seem to be able to act on that belief. We've talked about being a people company out of one side of our mouth, and out of the other side, we've condoned behavior that is absolutely contradictory to that.

Quality is as much a people thing as it is anything. This means finding the right people, developing them, keeping them through benefits and compensation, creating a healthy workplace, and helping them be successful. We all want to be fulfilled and successful; so it's really just helping people get there.

This quality is connected to the second quarter results that show all indicators are going in the right direction. We're enlightening managers who are realizing that when you have to keep firing, hiring, and training people over and over and over again, you spend a lot of productive time going through that process, but you don't really get anything done. Customers don't like high turnover, either. Now we hear, "I like the fact that I've been with you for three years and I've always been dealing with the same person. That's important to me because they understand my business."

Schaaf: I needed to learn and so did our managers and employees. Overall, I believe in a lot of the things in the children's book, *The Little Engine That Could*. We're capable of learning almost anything when we want to do it. My hope is that if you asked any employee about where we are they would say, "We have a focused direction, no more mixed signals; we know where we want to go and, at least to some degree, how to do it. It's just a matter of time."

One of the most accepted ideas about change is that it has to start from the top. So far, I've probably sounded the same way. It seems easier that way. Change is more extensive and faster if the leaders are practicing changing themselves as well as the organization. But it isn't the only way. If enough people in the middle empower themselves and mirror something new, that can cause changes throughout the organization.

I spent over 15 years inside three very different organizations before going on my own. I helped create a lot of change from the middle. My earliest training was from a liberal arts and social science perspective, not a business program. I had learned that the individual does makes a difference. I hadn't learned that everything had to come from the top. That was an excellent hole to have in my training. I retained that despite my subsequent business education and experiences.

Peter Block's book, *The Empowered Manager*, is instructive about mirrors and empowerment at the managerial level in companies. It speaks to my spirit when he says,

> As managers, our fundamental purpose is to build a department and organization that we are proud of. Our unit in many ways becomes a living monument to our deepest beliefs in what is possible at work. We strive to create both a high-performing unit and one that treats its own members and its customers well.

Each time we act as a living example of how we want the organization to operate, it is a positive political act.

Malt-O-Meal Company (MOM) turned out to be a good place to explore that model. I talked with a middle management team composed of Donald Price, director of quality assurance; Jeffrey Zibley, director of human resources; and Carol Lynn Courtney, organizational development specialist. They are in the middle trying to lead Malt-O-Meal's change efforts. Their story helps us explore another set of mirrors—those internal to ourselves—and to investigate the role of mirrors in the middle, and to some extent from the bottom of the organization.

Don Price's Story: Mirroring from the Middle

*"*When I joined Malt-O-Meal in 1970, we were much smaller. I thought it would be a short-term thing. But as time went on I realized that I wanted to stay with this company. Around the mid-1970s, we began to see we were going to have to change, particularly in the production area. Many of those efforts were driven from the middle of the organization, but with concurrence from senior management on the general direction. We decided we wanted to be a quality company, from products to service to relationships with customers and employees.

Perhaps one of the reasons so much has been driven from the middle is that we have always believed that the person doing the job is the expert. I think management may recognize that they can't lead the change because they aren't the experts in change. They are marketing, manufacturing, and finance experts, but change isn't one of the things they know very much about. And they aren't experts at some of the new things we're trying to do.

We did a number of things inside the company to start changing. We tried a management by objectives program. We tried a zero-defects program in the early eighties with Crosby, which didn't really go anywhere. Then we started our reading campaign with things like *In Search of Excellence*. We went to seminars, including

Schoenberger's "World Class Manufacturing." Twenty of us went to that seminar together, a major shift for us. To be cost effective, we usually sent one person who reported back. For the first time, we had a shared experience of the whole thing. We learned we can't change a company using one person's viewpoint and training. After that seminar, we tried some cross-functional teams. Then things started to happen.

One of the things that has always slowed us down, and continues to do so, is our rate of growth. We've been growing at a fast rate for some time. When we're growing fast, so much is going on. There are new products, markets, and equipment to deal with, new employees to be hired and trained. It's hard to get people's attention to do anything except run fast to keep up. We're all faced with having many competing needs. Change seems to be over and above the normal job.

Despite that, several things have helped us keep the change going. A company needs at least one challenger or risk taker. For us, that is Myrl, our director of research and development, who has done many things in the company. He's one of the driving forces here. He's the kind of person who keeps things loose. He constantly challenges ideas and asks questions, and sometimes we don't even know what he's talking about. He's also the kind of person who makes most upper managers very nervous.

A second thing has helped us. About 10 or 15 years ago, we started getting more women in the company and, recently, more women in middle management. As a group, they have different ideas from the men and we are beginning to take note of them. One of the things that I sense, more than anything else, is that women do cross-functional teaming naturally. They like to include people in the group, so they seem to be good at so many of the things that we say we need to be. They have wonderful ideas, especially about human issues. Our challenge is to bring in enough of those ideas to change our workplace so that it's better for women and men.

One of the things I have learned about driving change from the middle is that we still need to educate top management as to what kind of change we want to bring about. Every change we make is going to disrupt the company somewhat and they have to be able to understand that and support it. That's very difficult to achieve. It takes time because they have their own particular viewpoint, which is frequently a functional one, given their backgrounds. Many did not grow up in the computer age. Most of senior management and many of us in middle management who have been here for a number of years are in the 45 to 55 age group, so many of the new ways of operating were not around when we went to school or for most of our work experience. Part of the problem is that we speak different languages.

The other big lesson I have learned is that if I have an idea, I need to try it. And keep on trying. Our atmosphere supports that. There aren't any dire consequences for me if I make a mistake. I need to involve other people, do my homework, and get other people to buy into the idea. The problem comes in trying to figure out what I want to do and getting the resources to do it, because there are so many competing ideas: self-managing teams, high-performance teams, employee involvement efforts, and zero-defect programs. We also have talked about statistical process control and how we're going to use all these technical tools to help improve our company.

Related to that is another lesson. Many people-skills go into making a change. We're to the point now where we're saying, "Technical tools will help us, but we have to have employee involvement and empowerment." I've come to believe the human side is probably as important as the technical side, if not more so. The technical changes come fairly easy. Maybe that's why we generally focus on them."

Jeff Zibley's Story: Mirroring from the Middle, Continued

"When I came to Malt-O-Meal about ten years ago, I felt I was going to have an opportunity to lay the groundwork for a new, more vibrant human resource structure. I also liked the philosophy here. Malt-O-Meal has always been an organization that has valued, respected, and rewarded people fairly well. So we had the philosophy and values in place that provided a foundation or framework upon which we could build employee involvement and participation. What we didn't have was the structure by which people were able to get more involved in the business.

We were viewed as a good employer, but we were still tradition bound with narrowly defined supervisory structures and jobs. Ten years ago, we were talking a better game than we were playing. Some organizations will say the right things and not care if it works out or not, but we did care. We just didn't know how to put some of our philosophy into operation. We have changed a great deal, but we have much more left to do.

All the textbooks and most of the articles say that change has to start from the top. That's what I believed eight to ten years ago because that was all I knew. MOM illustrates that change can start somewhere else in the organization. This kind of change has its own problems because there isn't that executive mandate. People sit on the fence and say, "We'll wait and see what happens, whether the executives buy in." Many of the case studies, though, say that the same thing happens when the CEO gets up on the podium. So I don't know how different it turns out in the end. Our advantage was that nobody got in the way. No one was opposing what we were doing. By the same token, nobody was jumping on the bandwagon and leading.

Starting from the middle can be very slow. We had to go out and touch people and develop a small group with a single vision. We now have a critical mass, 25 percent or more, who are going in a single direction. And we have had staying power. We keep talking about change, we keep planting seeds. We have built our base that way. In the beginning, we thought we had to have this grandiose, perfect plan to announce to everyone. We got stuck in the mud with that. One of the things we learned was just to go do something, take some chances, try some things, and use it as a learning experience. Then go back and revise, revamp, modify.

There is a major advantage to changing from the middle. When the people in the middle lead the change, you're living out empowerment. We're modeling exactly what we are trying to talk about, so that's a plus. It illustrates the whole concept because nobody is directing us to do it.

Sometimes it feels lonely to do this; other times, it feels incredibly challenging. I've learned about myself and about getting other people to work together. We talk about being experts and not having boundaries, but that can still be confusing to people. We hesitate to test that. It's a two-edged sword. We have a unique opportunity if we can get beyond the emotional hang-ups of taking risks and wondering where our support is coming from.

I have learned that I probably create my own boundaries more than I ought to. I think, "Well maybe I shouldn't try that," then I come back the next day and say, "Well maybe I should try that." There's always a matter of "How far should I push?" and "What are the limitations?" I have expanded my boundaries farther than I ever imagined. So I'm thinking that maybe, in general, our boundaries aren't really there. They may be self-imposed limitations.

The last 10 years have been exciting. I wouldn't have traded them for anything. They weren't without dilemmas and problems, but there's a high level of ethical thinking, values, and principles that the company tries to emulate, both within and outside Malt-O-Meal. There are many people who are very involved in the community, so we are talking about a holistic kind of issue. People are extending their skills and services beyond the walls of the company and that's encouraging."

Carol Lynn Courtney's Story: Mirroring from the Middle, Conclusion

---

"I joined Malt-O-Meal $2\frac{1}{2}$ years ago. Trying to drive change from the middle has been the most frustrating and, at the same time, the most rewarding experience for me. I was hired to help the organization to define and implement team processes further and to implement skill certification programs using my background in industrial/organizational psychology and my experience with Motorola, Quaker Oats, and consulting.

I thought Malt-O-Meal would be unique and challenging. We have all been taught some basic rules of change: that change has to be driven from the top, that it's harder to change when things are going well, and that change requires a systems perspective. MOM wasn't following any of them, yet change is happening, so we're proof that change efforts can at least start from the middle.

The main advantage has been that we can try many different approaches with minimal risk, because there aren't any clear boundaries. For many people, that has created a sense of adventure and creativity. We have an underlying value that each person is an expert in their job and that supports this risk taking. Others are uncomfortable with this looseness, especially when one of us crosses an un-known boundary and gets zapped. When the senior management group is less involved, there are unwritten rules, taboos, or "invisible electric fences" that can zap people and that takes away momentum.

We have made progress, though. It has been extremely satisfying to see people do things they didn't think they could, like make pub-lic presentations. Recently, one of our board members came to a pre-sentation given by one of our teams. They were delighted by his interest and support. He observed that what he thinks is happening is that there has been this ground swelling—or grass roots—change and that triggers interest and change in top management. So we aren't just changing the middle and lower levels in the company.

I tend to focus on what is the next leg of this journey we're on. What do we keep doing more of and what do we need to change? Part of me still questions if we can keep going without more senior management involvement. An important comment came from some team members who said we need to change together, not have change done to anyone. I wonder whether the rug would be pulled out from under us if there were a crisis. We have had the luxury of being in a very successful organization.

Secondly, I am concerned about the mixed signals that can be sent if top management makes decisions that don't support what we have been promoting in the middle of the organization; then we would have a clash. I sometimes feel managers think they have changed and are empowering, just because they have agreed that it's something good for the organization. We all need to practice new behaviors, not just agree with them conceptually. To do that requires everyone's in-volvement.

For example, we have advocated data collection, empowerment, and teams' responsibility for their own learning. We have told peo-ple they need to know the information channels and how to get what they need to do their jobs better. Employee groups have taken us at our word. Some managers have been comfortable with employee re-quests for information, decision making, or equipment and others have not. That sends different messages.

It's hard to ask these kinds of questions, especially when the or-ganization is successful. They can be seen as signs of disloyalty or criticism. My experience, though, is that it's dangerous not to have people asking them at all times. Myrl, who's a unique resource in the company, does this continually. I also think new people are a critical resource for helping an organization challenge itself. They can see so much more clearly. People often feel that because the new person hasn't been there since the beginning, they don't really understand the organization—what has happened, the history—so they can't have any answers. An organization needs both perspectives: the inside, long-term one and the newer, outside one. It's hard to stay honest or objective when we're inside too long.

I would like a community of trust where we could openly disagree without consequences. We need to be all of who we really are at work and at home and to welcome other people's diversity, regardless of the nature of that diversity. I'd like everyone to feel supported in growing and changing in all aspects of their lives. We have leaders throughout this organization who really want to create this kind of place. We're an organization with good intentions that's still going through the transition from a good company that takes care of people to a more empowering one that helps people learn to take better care of themselves, each other, and the company. The intention of being good to people hasn't changed, but what that means is evolving."

When the organization changes, people have the chance to respond personally to the broader changes. We've seen how a change inside a leader can create changes inside the organization. These next two stories are related and allow us to look at what can happen to a front-line employee when the leaders and organization change. We also have a chance to look at someone who had much to lose in that same circumstance. We see that empowerment and changes at work get mirrored into homes and community.

Sandy Miller has worked as a front-line manufacturing employee for Schott Corporation for ten years. Robert Suelflow was the plant manager for 22 years and helped attract the plant and start it up in a rural town. The company story is told in detail in Chapter 6, "Going Through the Pain." In short, the company decided to undertake a rapid change effort to go from dictatorial management behaviors to an empowering, team-leadership approach. These stories tell how that change affected these long-time employees.

I heard Miller make a presentation to First Bank about her change and how it had allowed her to blossom. I wanted to know more. The company allowed me to interview employees privately and to do a survey of all the employees who had been through the change. That's when I met Bob Suelflow, the former plant manager, who now is part of the quotation team. Employees told me about the remarkable change in him and how much they now valued him. I wanted to hear this story of transformation from his perspective.

Change was embraced in these stories by most people largely because the change effort honored people and the whole tone was that of helping people be more, to use more of their capabilities. We've been taught a model that says education and change is about filling heads with facts, information, and skills. We've lost the original Greek sense of education, which was to draw out that which is within. This company seemed to be using this older model and people embraced change more willingly and deeply.

This seemed to create a whole different kind of energy that was larger than the job and the company. Other employees told me similar stories. Particularly revealing was a pattern of the changes at work spreading into people's personal lives. Sixty percent of employees reported that they could see that work changes had affected them at home. People told how they were using their improved communication skills with their spouse and children or on the town council. Others felt their confidence had increased and they were doing new things in community volunteer programs or in their churches. When we undertake change efforts like this company's, we have the potential of significant mirroring into our communities. Our companies can become prisms of positive change. Our employees may become the prisms that change our world.

Sandy Miller's Story: Prisms for the Greater Good

"I live in a rural area where there aren't many job opportunities, so I was glad to get a job in a manufacturing plant. I have worked in Schott Corporation's lead setting and soldering terminations area for over 10 years. That's what I was hired for and that's what I did day after day after day until three years ago. It was a very dictatorial place. There was only one way to do anything and that was that.

I had a negative attitude in the old system because whenever I would bring in a new idea, the managers would say, "No. This is how we do it here." They never encouraged us to share ideas. I like to try new things, so I had a bad attitude. Even though I learned to keep my mouth shut most of the time, I wasn't easy to get along with because I was frustrated and angry. I would go home and complain about work. Today I'm a different person.

I remember rumors that a change was coming. I was apprehensive, but I was excited, too. They started changing to a more empowered and team-oriented way of doing things. So many things changed! The first thing they did was to take the time clocks away. Wow! That sent a message they trusted us to be at work on time. That was just one way of showing they trusted us. Over the last $2\frac{1}{2}$ years, absenteeism and tardiness have gone way down. There's very little abuse of that and when there is, the person answers to the team. That has really worked well.

The line flow of the products is not what it was. We worked in a department and probably did the same job every hour for the whole day all year. No variety. Now we start a project and we follow it from start to finish. We're taking a lot more pride in our work. For instance, we never knew that some parts went into medical devices, like pacemakers. That is important to know and it makes a difference.

My foreman couldn't handle the change, so she quit. We were without a team leader for several months. Her boss told me, "We're just going to watch and see who blossoms, see who takes the bull by the horns." Evidently they thought I was doing that because, about six months later, they asked me if I would be interested in being a team leader. I jumped at the opportunity.

I've grown a lot from this change. I've learned more about myself and dealing with people. I have a long way to go, but I have a much better feeling about myself. I know people are listening to me now. Whether my idea is accepted or not, at least I'm being heard.

I'm easier to get along with. I don't know how to explain that. We've had classes on how to communicate with people and I've had an excellent group leader. She's really helped us grow. I feel great when I come to work and great when I go home now. I like working here. My husband remarks about the difference it has made. He thinks it has helped me and that I communicate better in our marriage. I'm more open. I could never get in front of a group before and talk. Then I was asked to be part of a team presentation to another company that was interested in what we were doing. I did it and it was a lot of fun. That gave me great inner satisfaction. I have a deep feeling of gratitude that I've had this chance.

I'm less fearful when I hear a new rumor now because I know I'll adapt to whatever the situation is. I'm learning that I can handle just about anything that comes along. I might need help, but people are willing to help each other if we aren't afraid to ask. Some people that I had never worked with before have become good friends to confide in and to support me. I feel like a flower that has been allowed to blossom.

It isn't just me. Most people have blossomed. I can see it on their faces and in how they talk. There are so many things to learn, but people are willing to learn. We never had that before. Sometimes our patience is a little thin as we try to do so many things, but it's about 90 percent greater than it was. The change is like night and day.

I'm proud of our perseverance. We don't give up. We believe in the change and we're willing to adapt. Sometimes it isn't easy and it seems to take a long time. When we started reaping some of the rewards and success from even small things, we celebrated. It takes patience, understanding, and lots of communicating. That's the biggest thing. Don't ever shut down the communications.

I have been able to share many of the things I have learned beyond the plant. Within the past year, my husband and I purchased a business: constructing and manufacturing wood trusses. I tell my husband what I have learned in Schott over the last three years and he's sharing that learning with his employees so they will benefit. It has been fun.

Looking back to where we have been and to where we are now, I wonder why it took us so long to figure this out. I wouldn't want to go back to the other way. What I've gained from this experience can never be taken away from me."

Bob Suelflow's Story: Prisms for the Greater Good, Continued

"For me, the change at Schott was a financial disaster. We had had an outstanding profit sharing plan for managers and I lost about 50 percent of my income with the change. At the same time, I knew what was happening was right for people reasons. I also think that eight to ten years from now the company might not have existed, if we hadn't gone through this change. But it was hard, at first, not to have an offended attitude. I had managed companies for 30 years and I'd never had a month when I lost money. I had to communicate with the Lord regularly to keep myself on an even keel; otherwise, I'd have gone over the hill. Today, I'm delighted that I didn't bail out.

We had used a hard-nosed management style and we had a very successful production machine. Instead of developing people, we were developing cash. That was the only goal. It wasn't a real neat place to work. We lacked cross-training; people had no pride in themselves, no contact or knowledge of customers, no involvement. The old type of thinking prevailed.

Today, communication flows freely from individual to individual and great learning takes place. The flexibility of the organization is significantly greater to respond to a customer who wants things more quickly and who places many smaller orders. Schott is aligning itself for that type of business because that's where the market will be.

We worked unlimited hours, as plant managers, to cover all the bases in the old system. We were doing it for money and, really, at a cost to our families because we were gone so much. As a result, some of us had ulcers and other problems. When our goal is not correct, that's going to stress our spiritual sides, too. In my mind, the change was spiritually correct. When we're spiritually correct, our physical body is going to become correct and our head is just better.

Schott has had an important impact on my community and we need the business to continue growing for the sake of the whole community. So even though I was hurting, I could see that for our area and the people of Schott, this was right. I believe things will work out for me.

You see, 20 years ago, this area was destitute. I helped bring Schott into our community. It was the only major employer. I felt really good creating a couple hundred jobs that had been nonexistent and that have meant a lot to our families. Schott is not as critical today as it was then, particularly in Marshall, but it's still important. The college has developed, Rhienhart Foods has gotten bigger, Schwans is growing. There's a lot of employment in the area now, but 20 years ago there was nothing. We were strictly a farming community. Schott expanded from here to two nearby towns and is critical to them today, the way it used to be to us.

Many of the people in these communities have never had health insurance, and that is critical for farmers. A lot of these families would go without having their teeth fixed. Now they can have a checkup and it's covered. In many cases, it's the wife who works here and gets that benefit for the family. Also, in order to make ends meet, most of us need two wage earners. People in this company are able to do things with their family now, able to take vacations, and do things for their kids they couldn't do before.

Before the change, I probably would have said everything was great and that I was satisfied, even though I was living with too much stress. I think that's where many managers kill themselves. We get caught up going after the almighty dollar and that becomes our god. We end up with heart attacks and maybe even lose our families. I think I was borderline on physical stress. So I am benefiting in other ways from the change. I'm learning to listen, I'm learning to give up some of the big "I" and become part of the "we." The macho "I" needs to die. That was good for my marriage. Thank God my wife was so understanding. Most of all, I'm trying to live more unselfishly. It's in giving that we receive and whatever I give, whether it is knowledge, words, or money, I know I will be blessed. That kept me going."

5

The Road to One World

When we try to pick out anything by itself, we find it hitched to everything else in the universe.

JOHN MUIR

We're slowly coming to comprehend the fact that we're part of a global community, and just learning how to behave as one. Ever since the first manned space flight, this understanding has been awakening in all of us in more ways and at deeper levels. We had an opportunity then to see the earth in all of its beauty and isolation. Edgar Mitchell, one of the early astronauts, says that the first few times they circled the earth, they saw the United States, Europe, Africa, and the Soviet Union, but as they moved further into space, those imaginary lines began to disappear and they saw that we were one. That profoundly affected the astronauts and many of us on earth who witnessed this revelation through television. Science will never be the same because we came to see that the earth is one complex, living organism.

Over the last decade, we've been hit over the head, personally and organizationally, with an economic two-by-four telling us we're in a world economy. Conflicts in Iraq, Kuwait, Somalia, and the former Yugoslavia appear in our own living rooms and at the office, covered moment-by-moment on CNN. A volcanic eruption in Asia affects the weather and crops in the United States and the fallout of a nuclear explosion in Chernobyl spreads around the world. The starvation of children faces us over the dinner table. We have begun to realize that poverty, violence, environmental degradation, and depletion of natural resources really do get in the way of business goals, not just social goals. So many of our problems and our opportunities seem to have global dimensions.

Global is an interesting word, as is its mate, *the world*. They can mean the earth, the heavens, the universe, and all creation under the sun, according to my thesaurus. They also refer to a sphere, even the personal sphere of one's life, business, community, country—as in "my world." We need to keep both dimensions in mind and the fact that each reflects the other. Otherwise, we slip into thinking these issues belong to someone else.

Before we can learn to act like a global community, we must be able to grasp who else is in this community and what their lives are like. Sometimes we understand the whole better when it is smaller and local. Joe Miller of Moab, Utah illustrates this in the following poem:

> If the Earth were only a
> few feet in diameter, floating a few
> feet above a field somewhere, people would
> come from everywhere to marvel at it . . . The people
> would declare it as sacred because it was the only one,
> and they would protect it so that it would not be hurt.
> The ball would be the greatest wonder known, and people
> would come to pray to it, to be healed, to gain knowledge,
> to know beauty and to wonder how it could be. People
> would love it and defend it with their lives because
> they would somehow know that their lives
> could be nothing without it. If the Earth
> were only a few feet in diameter.

Edgar Mitchell said, "Amidst all the beauty was the profound realization that all was not right with the earth." Perhaps a way to grasp the state of the world community we're in is to imagine the world as very small. What if it were the size of a city? Data for a world profile of diversity, provided by the Ligget-Stashower Public Relations firm, is insightful: "If the world were a town of 1,000 people, there would be 564 Asians, 210 Europeans, 86 Africans, 80 South Americans, and 60 North Americans. Seven hundred people would be illiterate, and 500 would be hungry."

Playing out a partial description of this global city seems as though it could be helpful. If we increase our understanding of the situation, we can examine what the role of business and individuals can be. There are lots of numbers with many discrepancies between them, so these are not represented as precise. The point is to develop a conceptual model. The different estimates will give us a beginning sense of dimension. For example, some sources describe the Southern hemisphere's standard of living as using 10 percent of the world resources but having 90 percent of the world's population. Others use a $\frac{1}{6}$ to $\frac{5}{6}$ ratio, or 17 percent to 83 percent. I have used the most conservative 25 percent to 75 percent split to be consistent with the Ligget-Stashower numbers.

In this hypothetical city, there are 340 people under the age of 15, 600 people between 15 and 64 years old, and 60 people over 65 years of age. About 150 babies are born every year, so within a short period of time, the population under 15 will be closer to 420. About 25 of the babies will live in the northern part of the city and 125 will live in the southern part. The percentage of those over 65 is increasing rapidly. There are numerous languages, religions, and cultures. About 240 people are employed in the military and 500 in agricultural positions. The largest industries, in terms of dollars, involve the sale of illegal drugs and weapons.

There is enormous disparity in this community. About 250 people are consuming the vast percentage of everything—70 percent of the energy, 75 percent of all metals, and 85 percent of the wood. These people live in the northern part of town. There is great variation in this part of town in terms of wealth, but some basics are pretty common. They all have running water, sanitary conditions, and many conveniences. Their children are fed, clothed, and attend various schools. An average of four people live in at least a three- to five-room dwelling. A few people have 10 rooms in their homes. Almost everyone has a telephone, a significant percentage have radios or televisions, and most people have cars.

There is a river that runs through this city separating the north and south, and it's entirely navigable. The two communities do intermingle on both sides of the river for trade, developmental and humanitarian assistance, travel, and occasional town meetings when there is a crisis. The main discussions have to do with gang warfare between the various parts of the city and with environmental degradation. The northern part of town consists of much pavement and many industrial plants that are sending pollution into the river, the ground water, and the air.

The southern part of the city is split between magnificent forests, agricultural and semi-arid land. These are being harmed by the city pollution and the burdens of a large and exponentially growing population's need for food and fuel. Seventy-five percent of the populace lives in this southern portion of the city. The word *city* even seems like a misnomer. This portion of town is more like a rural area. Housing generally takes the form of shacks and huts with numerous people per room. Most people are engaged in agriculture or living off the land. Children are malnourished and education is sporadic. Some enclaves have their own small, poorly equipped schools. There are about 200 telephones among the 750 people, a handful of radios, and a couple of television sets. The number of radios and TVs is increasing as villages share a common unit. Some smaller groups within this town are dying off, along with their unique knowledge—history, medicinal knowledge, and unique perceptions about the nature of life. This description is hypothetical only in terms of the use of the smaller city dimension. The picture to be painted is the reality of our global system.

We can build a major new skill to help our own lives, our organizations, and the dynamics of the global description we've just seen by widespread use of *systems thinking*. It is estimated that only about 8 percent of us naturally think this way. Systems thinking has several characteristics. One is to be able to see inter-relationships among many factors that then lead to certain results. In health, for example, it is understanding the interrelationships of mind, body, spirit, and heart that manifest in health or disease, rather than only seeing a diseased organ that needs replacement.

A second characteristic is the ability to identify root causes of positive and negative results, rather than focusing on symptoms. Using the health analogy again, in systems thinking one would look for a root cause of migraines, such as a life-style pattern of high stress and the beliefs that lead to that, and try to modify those causes, rather than treat only the symptom. A nonsystems approach would focus on the symptoms and alleviation of them.

Another characteristic is the capacity to look at all the possible effects of a given action, considering secondary and even tertiary consequences, rather than using the linear approach of "If I do this then this happens." New computer-based decision trees are coming on-line to help cancer patients review options, consequences, and quality of life factors in selecting treatment, in a mode somewhat consistent with systems thinking.

When we learn to think this way, we can significantly increase our capacity to deal not only with narrow organizational issues but also with global issues such as the following. We need to do this for its own sake and because our organizations, as parts of the global system, cannot continue to think they are separate from these issues.

- The daily struggle for survival of so many people must be addressed. By that I mean food, water, and shelter fit for survival, and life-saving health care. We seek survival first out of all our needs. When survival is threatened we have fear, often coupled with anger that can lead to violence. So we need to create a sustainable life-style for each person.
- The potential instability caused by such a disparity between the haves and have nots is threatening. If we have enough to survive but see huge discrepancies between what we have and what others have, anger and hatred surface. Life seems

unjust. It creates good guys and bad guys and can lead to violence. So justice and fairness are at the root of creating peace. Otherwise, the best we can have is a temporary truce.

- The community at large is in danger from the environmental degradation. We are destroying our foundation—air, water, land—and depleting natural resources at an incredible rate. Destroying our environment is destroying that which sustains us. It's the values and consumption patterns of the northern part of our global "city" that drives part of the environmental degradation. In the southern portion, it's the cumulative effects of population.

- The tremendous diversity could be an asset or a source of constant conflict endangering the total community. We notice differences between people and many assume that what is different is bad. We remember previous grievances. This can lead to fear, discrimination, hatred, and violence. The community needs a process to come together and dialogue about issues that could separate it. We need to share our understanding of justice, fairness, forgiveness, freedom, and the balance of rights and responsibilities. We could learn from each other and be enriched.

- One of the core issues is the wealth of the smaller part of the population and their consumption patterns. The ideal shift would be for this group to reappraise their needs versus wants and voluntarily simplify their material life.

Focusing on these goals one by one is self-defeating. We often end up with contradictory actions and investments. These issues are part of a system and need to be thought through as a system. We also should keep in front of us the fact that a system includes emotions. They are our drivers. Let's keep asking, "How would I feel, if I were in the other person's situation?"

All of us need to learn about the world as a system with interconnections. This is the same internal agenda that many businesses have in order to solve their own problems. We must develop a curriculum for lifelong holistic education. It's inspiring to observe the number of schools that are teaching children of all ages to be peacemakers/dispute mediators. I wonder if this isn't part of our education for the next millennium.

Is there hope we could think like this on a global scale and act locally? I believe the answer is yes. In fact, it's already underway. It requires the assistance of more of us.

The following stories illustrate things already going on in the business community that are teaching us skills and giving us experience to help shape a global community. Many of the same issues we saw in our "global city" surface as business leaders discuss their concerns, experiences, and activities. We'll also look for further elaboration of other systems thinking elements.

A fundamental question about any system is "Who is it supposed to serve?" David Koch is chairman and CEO of Graco, Inc., a $300 million–plus company engaged in fluid-handling technology. He addresses this question by exploring the purpose of business and its authorizing body. I was particularly interested in his message about the evolution of business's purpose in light of global change. He raises issues of serving society in a global economy and of our competitive ability to do that. He asks a critical and penetrating question about how well equipped we are to serve the world.

This question has several levels to it, all of which need our reflection. One layer addresses our ability to serve others while in our position as competitors to other companies and countries. Another level deals with the growing global awareness of the differences in standards of living and how we can respond with limited resources. I wonder how well equipped we are, individually, to deal with the issue of resource disparity within our own communities and throughout the world. We have much more than we need and others have nothing. Can the world survive with this state of affairs?

As companies take ownership of their community roots and responsibilities, we may see even more fundamental changes. These could enhance and diversify the private enterprise system we have had thus far. Capitalism will fail if it forgets that the individual was made to serve society. Communism and socialism will fail if they forget that society was made to serve the individual. If humanity fails, I wonder whether it will be because we forgot we had to walk between the two, living in balance.

David Koch's Story: Business—Servant of Many Publics

"My story has to do with the purpose of business. Whether we're planning for 1996 or the year 2000, we come back to the question "What are we trying to do?" What's our objective? Too many companies' objective is to make a lot of money, to enhance shareholder value. I don't think that's the purpose of corporations. If we manage our business well, that's one of the results. Historically, when elected officials decided they would allow corporations to be formed, I don't think they had in mind enhancing shareholder value as the objective. I don't think they decided to set a process in place to allow a few people to make a lot of money. Their objective was to serve people and increase the general standard of living.

The reason that this country, in over 200 years, has reached the standard of living it has, and the amount of personal freedom it has, is because of the economic system of private ownership and the market system. It exists to serve people and it has done so very well. That should be the objective of all societies and organizations. That's the driving force behind the mission of Graco: to be of service to people.

Many people, or publics, benefit. The employees are provided jobs, holidays, vacation, retirement pay, and medical benefits. That's the good news when somebody creates jobs. The products we have, our houses, food, transportation, and the entertainment we enjoy are a function of some company developing a product or service and competing in an open market. So the second public, the customer, has benefited tremendously by the process as well. The shareholder invests money, expects to get a return, and expects the value of that share to appreciate. Shareholders receive a balance between the risk they take and the potential reward.

The fourth major public is government. The government wants corporations to comply with all the rules and, on average, to pay half of what we earn in taxes. So government has prospered as a result of corporations doing well. In addition, when corporations provide jobs, employees, in turn, also pay taxes. The community is a participant in the business system as well. I believe that a company should share its resources with the community that gives it a franchise. We can share the talents of our people. We can share our products and services and we can share our financial resources, especially with those in need.

We set aside 5 percent of our pretax income for community contributions. The government allows us to deduct half of that as a business expense. We then use our best judgment to invest those funds in community projects that the government says qualify as charitable organizations, whether they relate to human services, education, medicine, or the arts. I feel strongly that corporations exist to serve those five publics, as well as suppliers, bankers, and other people who somehow are positively affected when a company does well.

Given the collapse of communism and the existence of an extensive world communications system, we now have an enormous chance to serve the rest of the world. The world knows that there's a better way to live. There are millions of people who are going to want to improve their standards of living, whether it's in Eastern Europe or Asia or the former Soviet Union or China. It's scary to imagine what's going to happen all at one time, and the demand on the global system to respond within the constraints of scarce resources.

As a society, we have an opportunity to be of service in producing competitive goods and services to meet those needs. We need to make the proper investments in people, education, processes, quality systems, and empowerment. Doing this will enhance the standard of living for most of the people in the country and the world, but it's not an automatic. It's not going to happen easily. It's a painful process to go through. The question is "How well equipped are we to do that?"

I have a concern. As we have gone away from a society of small shops and farmers, from a personal involvement and understanding of business, there are fewer people who know how business is run and why it exists. Therefore, there's antagonism and anger toward businesses and business people. I hear politicians who try to promote jobs while talking about being antibusiness. I get the feeling that they think jobs just appear magically. I'm concerned that the economy is going to be run more by the government than by this private enterprise system that has been so good to so many people.

My other concern, after 38 years at Graco and interfacing with a lot of other companies and customers, is whether we can be competitive from the standpoints of people, cost, and quality. Relative to people, it's clear our education system hasn't kept up. Our K–12 system isn't as good as it needs to be for us to compete around the world. Our work force isn't as well trained, because we haven't had an apprenticeship system like Germany's. Our school year is too short, in comparison to other countries. We have too many youngsters who drop out of school. We need to adjust the subjects that are covered; in particular, we need more math and science.

This last issue is critical and not enough people understand why. Ten or fifteen years ago, there was a move toward a service economy, but the problem with that is it doesn't generate enough value-added jobs. We need to be designing, fabricating, and manufacturing something and adding value, whether it's to TVs, computers, airplanes, or cars. For people to have meaningful jobs, we must have innovators, designers, engineers, and scientists in this country who make things that people want. And the nonscientists and nonengineers will have to understand more math and science and technology than ever before to work in those companies. Given world developments and environmental issues, we need more math and science just to be good citizens.

We also have cost and quality issues. Business was too easy in the sixties and seventies before Germany and Japan entered world markets with quality products. We took customers for granted. We gave salary and wage increases without productivity improvements, and passed the costs on to customers. Our quality also decreased and we lost our customers. They aren't gong to come back until we have decent products at reasonable prices. It's as simple as that. We have to earn them back as a country. We'd like to believe it's somebody else's fault. Finding that other person or country who is at fault is always a tough thing to do. They don't exist. We are at fault.

My primary job is to make sure that our business continues to grow and prosper. These are the issues that influence our ability to do that. When I came to Graco in 1956, it was about a $5 million business. Through a death and a retirement, I became the head of the company in 1962 when we were a $12 million business. My job and my aspiration at that time was to promote the growth of the company to a $100 million business. When we set that goal, I thought that would be a career's worth of work and then I would be finished. I had no idea how we were going to do it, except I believed we had some good products, good people, and good customers. In 1978, we got to $100 million almost magically.

We couldn't stop there. So time has gone by and we are over $300 million, and part of our planning process is to determine where the company is going to be in the year 2000. So my primary job is to grow the business and to make it a decent place to work. I want to have good jobs that are well paying and that utilize people's skills and allow them to develop to the extent of their capabilities. With those capabilities, we will serve as many people as we can. At $300 million, we're able to serve more people than when we were at $12 million.

Our goal is to get to a billion dollars. That's a fun and exciting job because we do more than half of our business outside the United States now. It causes many of us to be involved in the economy and the society of many other places. We see how people live and act in other parts of the world. We have associates and friends in many interesting places that we otherwise wouldn't have."

There is a fascinating prototype available to us of a cooperative in Spain that is an example of living in the balance between individualism and community. It's called the Association of Mondragon Cooperatives and is described in some detail in the *World Business Academy Perspectives*. The association includes more than 160 cooperatives with over 23,000 employee/owners, producing a wide range of consumer and industrial products. Terry Mollner, the article's author, states, "In terms of productivity, technological sophistication and competitiveness, the Mondragon Cooperatives are fully the equal of the best capitalistic enterprises. In addition, they create social benefits that tempt one to think of the Mondragon free-enterprise model as significantly superior to the usual capitalistic model."

He goes on to explain that the single guiding principle behind the enterprise is "How can we do this (business) in a way that serves equally both those in the enterprise and those in the community, rather than serving one at the expense of the other?" This leads to such things as an association-owned bank that assumes every new business will succeed and therefore commits to support its enterprises until they do succeed. It also grants loans on the basis that the riskier the business, the lower the interest rates should be. (That sets a paradigm on its head.) The community nurtures its start-ups until they can go on their own.

An interesting corollary is that owners and employees should be the same person. So every employee must lend the cooperative about $10,000. When a new employee starts, he or she signs a note, and over time that amount is withheld from their salary without any interest charges. Thus everyone is invested in their own business, sharing the risks and rewards and building a stronger community of shared purpose. This model suggests to me that we have more options open to us than we may realize.

There's a major shift happening consistent with this. In the article, "Executives of the World Unite," Craig Cox and Sally Power point out, "A 'Third Wave' of the environmental movement is upon us, lead by some of the most unlikely activists you can imagine: corporate executives. And it's not regulations that are driving them, it's their own values. Something profoundly new is at work here: a social movement, beginning not at the fringes of power, but at its very center." They quote Dupont's manager of corporate environmental affairs, who says, "Most people can talk about saving the earth, but business can innovate. We are the ones who can do it."

Others giving themselves license to push the business envelope on a global scale include a group of business leaders in conjunction with the Minnesota Center for Corporate Responsibility. They have created a document recommending a common set of moral principles for the global business community. About five months ago, I saw an article in the *Minneapolis Star Tribune*, "Minnesota Principles: Draft of State Guidelines Received Enthusiastically at International Meeting in Switzerland." As John J. Oslund, staff writer, put it, "Light beams emanating from Japan and Minnesota recently converged in Caux, Switzerland, where some of the world's most powerful business executives embraced the so-called 'Minnesota Principles' of corporate conduct as well as the similar sounding Japanese tenets of 'Kyosei' which have long been espoused by Ryuzaburo Kaku, Chairman of Canon Corp."

The document lays out some general principles dealing with fairness, honesty, promise keeping, and respect for human dignity and the environment. It then looks at stakeholder principles for employees, owners/investors, customers, suppliers, communities, and competitors. Who would have ever thought that a document called "Toward a Moral Basis for Global Business" would be drafted voluntarily and approved by such a broad range of executives? A new world is dawning.

Herbert Johnson has been an entrepreneur his entire life and has tried to apply all these types of practices, especially the environmentally sound ones, in his companies, which include MTS Systems and DataMyte. He has also been one of the founders of the Minnesota High Technology Council, the Minnesota Technology Corridor, and the Friends of the Boundary Waters. Technologists are often regarded as the enemies of the environment, but Johnson has been one of the pioneers in integrating his love of nature with his love of technology and innovation. He is very concerned about environmental degradation. His story is about having it all. He is a concrete example of integrative thinking, rather than the either/or thinking Anne Wilson Schaef discusses in *Women's Reality* (see Chapter 4). This story also demonstrates the systems thinking need for process knowledge and improvement.

Herb Johnson's Story: The Business of the Planet

"Environmental issues pervade my life, regardless of what hat I'm wearing. The business of the planet is integral to all we do. It's part of being a businessperson. It's part of my personal life, social activities, and how I spend my volunteer hours. It has been a source of learning for me and the source of a new venture in my recent retirement. A great side benefit for me is the quality of friends I've met and worked with on environmental issues.

My father was a great fisherman. He loved to fish standing up in the boat with a fly rod and he'd bring me along to row. There were some other young boys my age and we used to roam through the fields next to the Mississippi River. I developed a sense of nature at a very early age that kept being reinforced my whole life. When I was in the Navy, I saw some of the islands in the South Pacific that were as close to virgin land as you could find in those days. I appreciated that. I heard about the Boundary Waters and went there after I got out of the Navy. I loved it. I learned to appreciate pure nature, nature as God made it.

My interest in nature probably influenced the way I managed. I like to delegate fully and give people a chance to be responsible. That's the way a camping trip works. Someone would say, "I'll get the firewood," and another would say, "I'll get the tent up," and so on. So we'd look at our corporate goals and different people would take on different tasks, based on their expertise. I think my companies tended to be more free-form than traditional companies.

I would take my managers on canoe trips into the Boundary Waters as a bonding experience. It was a wonderful way to get to know people and find out how they react under different circumstances. Sometimes we'd bring our sales representatives from other parts of the country and they loved it. Many had never experienced wilderness, never seen the Northern Lights. These were canoeing, tenting, and camping trips that would last four or five days to a week. We'd just be together. Sometimes when we did long-range planning sessions, we might go to a resort on a lake, but that was work; we didn't go there to play. The Boundary Waters trips were to play, to have fun in the woods.

Since I was involved in a number of environmental organizations and received their publications, I became aware of air pollution and acid rain. I helped create one of the first professional slide-show presentations on acid rain. Even though we know more now, the basics haven't changed much since 1980. I was concerned because in my companies we produced waste. Very early on, I wanted to have good environmental practices.

At MTS, we did machining of steel, brass, and aluminum, and we kept the different kinds of waste separate and sold it back to the salvage people. We made circuit boards and they had to be washed. We used water-soluble solvents rather than the CVC stuff that's destroying the ozone layer. We could stand over those tanks and smell that stuff and we knew it wasn't good. This was long before there was any public awareness that there was anything wrong with it.

In my last company, DataMyte, we took a lot of pride in segregating our wastes and taking the lead out of our soldering machines and recycling it. There was a clear sense that this was the right thing to do. Our total quality program helped us produce sound products and contribute to the environment.

Total quality can have a positive effect on the environment. We produced less scrap, monitored our processes for harmful effects, came to understand systems, and looked for all manner of waste. I think the quality consciousness extended beyond what we were producing, to our lives and to the way we wanted to live. That affected people's political stances. If people demand clean environments, politicians will have to pay attention.

I'm afraid that if we continue to foul our water and air, cut our last forests, plow up our last prairies, and destroy our last wetlands, we will lose something very valuable that I had as a child. We see this hunger in adults and children when we look at the number of people visiting the Boundary Waters Canoe Area each year. It has increased so much that for the last five years the Forest Service has had to set quotas on entry.

I get angry when I hear that companies are less competitive when they adhere to government regulations for the environment. There are businesses that regard the sky as their air dump, the ocean as their water dump, and the land as their land dump. If they don't have to be responsible for keeping those dumps clean, they think it makes them more competitive. We need to seek out ways to use our inventiveness to protect the environment.

It's an entrepreneur's dream. We're becoming more and more conscious of the fact that pollution products have values of their own, if we can just figure out what they are. One company I know of has done a lot of work on that and, even though it is a major polluter, it is not nearly as big a polluter as it used to be. I see my entrepreneurial activities and environmental concerns as all part of the same thing.

Sometimes, like the CVC example I mentioned at MTS, it's just clear that there is a problem and all we need is our eyes and nose to know it. The Boundary Waters area issue was clear-cut. Back in 1975, a legislator put a bill in Congress that would have fundamentally destroyed the Boundary Waters Canoe area. It would have changed it to a recreation area with only a couple little nuggets of wilderness left. I heard about it and was outraged. I decided I wasn't going to sit by passively and let that happen. With some other people we founded the Friends of the Boundary Waters and we were able to block that bill. I probably worked harder at that than anything I have ever done in my life. Whenever I wasn't at work or with my family, I was working on the Boundary Waters issue.

I am persuaded that we don't have much time to address the broader issues of pollution. We have to realize that it's not a matter of a city or state or even a nation. It's a world problem and we have to deal with it as such. The first attempt to do that was at the Earth Summit in Rio de Janeiro. I talked with some people who were there and they said there was manifest anger at the United States for the positions enunciated by our government.

On a more quantitative basis, a woman named Meadows from MIT wrote a book called the *Limits to Growth* that impressed me. It's based on a very detailed computer analysis of our earth's finite limits in terms of water, air, and natural resources. I'm sure it wasn't perfect. People picked at it, but it mainly established that there are finite limits. I see us pushing up against those limits in a relatively short time.

Sometimes technology jumps in and saves us, pushes our limit out a little further here and there. I see technology helping us in more efficient use of energy and materials so that we don't consume as much per person. I like to listen to Amory Lovins, who is president of the Rocky Mountain Institute. Lovins has a huge house on top of a mountain in Snowmass, Colorado. Despite raising bananas inside his place, he says his electric heating bill is only $50 a year because he uses solar techniques.

Through use of new manufacturing technologies and new products, we can cut our electrical and transportation fuel consumption down to the point where we wouldn't be importing oil and we wouldn't be putting this junk in the sky. There are all kinds of things that are coming along, and I think if we use them intelligently we can conserve a great deal of our resources and energy. Part of the problem is that some older companies don't want to change, aren't looking for the opportunities and forging ahead.

There are all kinds of things that people could be making that would be good for the environment and the economy. Phillips is making these wonderful fluorescent light bulbs that consume about one-sixth the electricity that an incandescent light bulb uses. I recently heard a speech by Lovins, in which he said that the Pacific Gas and Electric Company is giving these light bulbs away because it's cheaper to give them away than it is to build new generating capacity. There are all kinds of things like this that we could be doing. Think of the number of jobs we could create if we made a national resolve to get all the old clunkers off the roads that consume high amounts of gasoline and put out high amounts of pollution. It could be a manufacturing bonanza.

If the federal government had invested in renewable resources to the extent they did in nuclear energy, we wouldn't have any kind of an energy problem today. We'd have new industries. What are we going to do with those nuclear plants, once the metals in those things reach their fatigue limits? Nobody knows. It's going to cost unbelievable amounts of money.

For another example, it wouldn't be difficult to manufacture cars that could get at least 50 miles to the gallon right now. There are experimental cars now that get 100 miles to the gallon. I have a friend with a car that has a special carburetor that gets 50 miles per gallon without any sacrifice in performance. He puts far less pollution out of his tail pipe because he burns all his fuel. I would like to see much better long-range thinking on the part of our managing executives. Conventional thinking, short-term profit needs, and greed are holding us back. We entrepreneurs are moving ahead, but we don't usually control the really large companies.

I'd like to set some corporate goals for more efficient use of materials and energy, and then empower people to work toward accomplishing those goals. I'd set a relatively tight time period on it so people could accomplish them during their career periods. I would give very high rewards to people who did great things. One company does that to a degree, but not anywhere near the degree that it could. The end result would be more prosperous companies.

The biggest thing I have learned about change is that it's important to embrace it and set goals for getting things done. Then have a commitment to goals rather than just letting things happen to you. The companies and individuals who have the most trouble are those who have resisted change. It's amazing what we can do with a few plans, moderate experience, and little resources when we make a commitment.

For example, I didn't have any idea what to do to save the Boundary Waters. I just started calling people. The Friends of the Boundary Water Wilderness group had a very common goal, a lot of trust in the group, and a sense of urgency. People just did what fit for them and what they saw would contribute to the larger goal. Nobody was directing it; there was no big action plan. We had an executive committee. If you wanted to be on the executive committee you just said so and you were there. Nobody ever got pushed off anything. It was a very fluid organization. The executive committee would identify things that had to get done and someone would say, "I'll do that."

We maintained a high energy level throughout the whole campaign. If people needed to get off and take a breather, they just did and it seemed there was always someone else ready to fill in. Some of the professionals in the major environmental organizations in Washington, D.C., told us, after it was over, that we had the best organized, most effective campaign they had ever seen. This was with a very informal fluid structure, with people from all walks of life. Recently I read a book called the *Age of Unreason*. The author, Charles Handy, says future organizations are going to function like we did. I never tried that in a business, but I think he is right.

Fear often holds us back from change; it's a basic human emotion. We just have to face the fear and change anyway. All we have to face fear is our internal reserves. I've always run scared because it seemed that the things I did were continually growing faster than I was capable of growing. I had to run hard just to keep up with what I had created. For example, I became a president of a separate, publicly held corporation at a relatively tender age and then I had to learn many new skills. As a society, too, we are being challenged to grow faster to keep up with what we've created.

We have many changes to make. We're going to need all the creativity we can get out of people. If you want to talk about change, just think that 20 years ago there was no such thing as a microcomputer and hand-held calculators were just coming into being. A lot of people have cellular phones today and don't think anything about it. The next thing will be video phones, and computers will be as common as TV sets in homes. There will continue to be all kinds of changes and we will adapt to them in work styles just as we have in the past; but the rate of change will be greater than it has been. "

All of us are being called upon to help shift system paradigms. One of the biggest shifts is in creating a new role and sense of personal responsibility for whole organizations. Every organization I work with is trying to break down barriers of all types, barriers that separate people and therefore lead to underperformance. These barriers come in many shapes: functional, divisional, hierarchical, departmental. All forms of discrimination and stereotyping get in the way. Too many rules do, too.

The emerging organization needs people committed to the well-being of the whole, rather than to some narrow portion of the whole. We want people committed to the spirit of serving customers, not implementers of 1,001 rules. Doing this means each of us must become a responsible intrapreneur (internal entrepreneurs.) Our "product" is cooperation and collaboration in every job element we perform. No one can do this except each individual.

If we approached this consciously, we could also leverage our efforts at the global level. We'd realize that, as we break down the barriers in our businesses, we have two significant opportunities for leverage. We could do community building at work, which would increase our cost effectiveness and quality results. As we taught this to people in our organizations, they might take it back into the broader community. We might realize that many of the things that create separation at work are the same root causes of global strife. So while improving our businesses, we would be improving the world's chance for community.

We are clearly becoming connected globally:

- More and more people have friends and associates all over the world because of business dealings.
- English is the primary language of only 15 percent of the world, yet accounts for 70 percent of international mail, 80 percent of computer-stored text, and 60 percent of radio broadcasts.

- We are linked globally by 3 million air passengers per day and by millions of miles of fiber-optics, coaxial cable, and satellite hookups. We can share global events in a way never imagined.
- Businesses have a growing multinational structure for change.
- There are more and more global agreements being made beyond arms and trade, including environmental ones like the Valdez Principles, and others like the Kyosei and Minnesota Moral Principles. There are also more and more global business organizations, conferences, and trade shows.

What concerns me is the extent to which a common culture is being developed unconsciously. If it were conscious and operating out of high principles, we could really do some good. When it is unconscious, we can do harm. We destroy cultures and lose diversity. We could become too much of a one-size-fits-all culture. Not all the things that industrialized society has to offer are particularly admirable or useful—for example, junk food, junk TV, and an overly materialistic way of life.

The skills we need to look at improving have to do with meeting the needs of a diverse set of people and balancing those needs to benefit the whole, not just a part. Paul Halvorson spends part of his time consulting and assisting companies with computer and software problems. More fundamentally, he identifies himself as an economist and a *social entrepreneur*. His definition of this term represents a major undertaking in systems change.

Paul Halvorson's Story: The Evolving Business of Business

"I'm an economist and a social entrepreneur. Social entrepreneurs are people who are bridging the old and the emerging paradigms in business. Much of the current economic paradigm is framed in terms of tradeoffs. For example, either we hold the line down on labor cost to keep the bottom line up, or we sacrifice our bottom line to increase wages. We either make money or we do something good. The belief is that for every gain, there's a loss. By reframing or reconceptualizing the problem, we can get outside that negative sum thinking and turn the experience into a win-win situation.

Social entrepreneurship has an orientation that says we're creating a venture that is economically viable using good business sense, and we're doing good. At the outset, we design a company that seeks to raise the quality of life in some area. Before we start to sell a service or a product, we deal with potential environmental and community concerns. And then we also make a profit. We are demonstrating how business can take a leadership role in making a positive difference for the planet.

I am involved, peripherally, in the soda industry. As consumers, we spend money and muscle lugging soda home for the luxury of having a cold, sugary, carbonated drink and create waste in the process. We know recycling the cans and bottles helps, but what we really need is to reduce waste at the source. A social entrepreneurial approach is to deliver the same kind of carbonated beverage and at the same time deal with the environmental concerns of having so many disposable containers. There's a machine called the Drink Maker that's like a home soda jerk. It carbonates water and mixes it with syrup in your own glass, so it eliminates the cans and glass, and there's no cleanup. Not only does this save the consumer money and help the environment, but we've added the value of convenience through home delivery.

There's another element that's different from the traditional image of an entrepreneur. We have usually thought of this person as the rugged individual who does it all, largely on his or her own. With social entrepreneurship, there's more of a sense of partnership and collaboration. Everyone is shaping the outcome. Fifteen years ago, my mother and I cofounded ARC, a retreat center. Our collaboration was such that the end product exceeded our dreams. For me that's the benefit of collaboration: when the net result surpasses what you thought was possible and could have done alone. Without that synergistic element, it's not a true collaboration.

Part of that dynamic is commitment and belief in the other people with no attempt to undermine others. The challenge is to work through the conflicts in a way that doesn't blame someone, make them wrong, or invalidate yourself. Another part of the dynamic is that once you commit to this relationship, there is no back door. For me, that means listening in a fundamentally different way. It's a kind of deep listening we all yearn for, but don't often experience. The other person really feels heard and understood, whether we agree or not.

This kind of listening affects both people. It's important to acknowledge what others have shared or taught me that has made a difference in my life. That validates another person. We all want to know that what we shared with another has made them a different person or has made the business a different place. It's this combination of listening and acknowledging, or validating, that builds and maintains partnership. And it gets done over and over again.

Another quality of social entrepreneurship is giving people the space to express their dreams and desires, independent of what needs to happen in the particular moment. I think this creates the energy it takes to start something new and grow it. There is a difference between the two words *work* and *job*. A job is what we have to do to earn a living. Many of us have jobs we don't like, but we don't see any other choice. Work is a labor of love. It's where our passion lies. It's connected to our dreams and purpose. It's the stuff that feeds us: it's the artist painting, it's the teacher teaching, it's the dancer dancing.

As I see it, most people's experience is that we spend 40 hours on the job, or 50 hours if we're managers. At the end of the week, we expect to be drained. Thus, we can justify salaries and escapist things in the evening and the weekend. My commitment as a social entrepreneur is to have work be such that, at the end of the workday or the workweek, as much energy as we have expended has also been fed back to us by the relationships, the processes, and the projects in which we've been engaged. I continue to learn how to do this. I have a new opportunity emerging to assist my learning.

We're in the planning stages for a start-up that will be a retail store. It's a holistic retail concept and, simultaneously, a community center. We'll be purchasing an existing store that provides materials for people in chemical dependency recovery and, over time, shift the emphasis from rehabilitation to wellness. To do that, we'll offer an array of goods and services that reach mind, body, and spirit. You might describe the store as the Wal-Mart of Wellness. We will be introducing people in the mainstream to healthy, holistic products and services that are aimed at enhancing the quality of life, whether it's physical, emotional, or mental health. We'll also be trying to create a better sense of well-being in the community.

We're in a brainstorming stage, looking at possibilities. In the next century, malls will have to come up with new ways to bring people into their stores, other than gimmicks of antique cars or amusement parks. We're suggesting that one way would be for the malls of the next century to become community centers. They could be places where people network, interact, and meet one another. Even now, retired people use the malls as places to get exercise, and there are walking clubs. What would it be like to have a retail store or a mall that was also a community center? What would we have to do to help people meet people of like mind and invite them to help strengthen their community?

Wellness doesn't exist just at an individual level; it also exists at a community and corporate level. So every month we could have a different school design a display around a particular theme. Maybe we could even have a day-care center where a parent could drop off his or her children for a structured or unstructured program. Maybe senior citizens could help out, providing a link between old and young, for the purposes of mentoring and providing a sense of community. In return, they could receive products from the store. We could have corporate sponsors whose employees could participate in programs on a variety of wellness and holistic issues, not only affecting family and the workplace, but also extending to the community. And the list of ideas goes on.

People often ask me how an economist could be interested in this kind of activity. What I've learned in my life is that everything is connected; I just have to follow the connections. So I've done that in my life and I'm doing the same thing with the store. How it works is like this: I was led to economics through the back door. In college, my majors were things like psychology and communications and my program was peace studies. My mission in college was global peace and my fundamental goal was to learn how to take an idea and turn it into reality. So I created and designed a student-led course called "Human Perspectives in a Corporate World," which looked at economic aspects of social issues. We used a textbook that looked at pollution, poverty, and transportation, and had speakers from the economics department.

When I graduated, I was asked to work for the National Lutheran Church on these issues. So I focused on economics in the church. The intent was to educate North Americans about the increasing gap between rich and poor and the degradation of the environment. Much of my effort was on economic development and the structural changes we were facing on the home front. When 6 percent of the world population is consuming 40 percent of world resources, we need to learn to live with less material resources without sacrificing a quality life.

The job involved teaching and international travel, connected with my involvement on several committees. In the process of doing that, I'd be challenged by corporate executives who lived in third world countries. I was intimidated by that because I wasn't a business person, nor had I been a corporate executive in a third world country. I don't like to be intimidated, so I decided that I would get more direct business experience and learn economics, because that's the basis on which business is built. I ended up getting a Ph.D. at American University with a focus on economic development and the study of economic methods. So by following my interests and connecting them one by one, I've become a social entrepreneur. I'm following a similar process with the retail store planning. I let one idea connect to another and another.

That can create a lot of tensions. I believe social entrepreneurs manage their creative tension this way and out of that creative tension come new kinds of programs, services, or products. So when I followed my need to connect to something new, I created more tension. I like this because without it, I am in danger of feeling knowledgeable or successful and that tends to ossify and destroy spirit, and possibly kills it. I want to continue to exercise my mind, body, and spirit, no matter what.

Organizations also need creative tensions. In our society, we're too prone to coming out on one side or the other. I think it's better to stay in the tension, to maintain that natural balance. It's like learning how to be balanced naturally on a piece of rope. We are prone to wanting to go left or right and then we fall off. We need to stay in the tension and to be comfortable there. When the tension goes away, we'll no longer be a socially entrepreneurial company. We'll become another ordinary place and eventually that will affect our bottom line. So I am creating new tensions."

After people and companies have finally accepted a change and come to value it, I frequently hear a similar sets of questions: "Why did I (we) have to be told something three, five, ten, twenty times? Why did it take so long to grasp it and to act?" In hindsight, it frequently looks obvious. When the insight comes, we feel as though we're surrounded and we can't imagine how we could have missed it for so long. Often, we notice that there are friends and colleagues who have already understood for quite some time, some who are just waking up and others who are still asleep. I'd summarize the issue as "How do we wake up faster to change?"

We need support when we're exploring any change. Being a heavy-duty, independent, solo type, myself, that was a hard lesson to learn. We need a place to discuss ideas and get new information and explore old beliefs where we don't feel attacked and where we have a reason to listen. That usually means an emotional tie or an atmosphere of exploration rather than evaluation. Facts alone don't seem to work. When we have a group like this it seems to provide a place for early learners to share what they know and wonder. I think we're very hard on those who are only beginning to challenge the current paradigms.

One of my friends, Anne, was on the leading edge in "getting it" when it came to the environment. She was frustrated with the rest of us. We were frustrated with her and sometimes embarrassed by her suggestions, like taking our plastic stuff back to our favorite Chinese takeout. Now we respond much faster to her latest ideas and honor her for them. She has speeded up our evolution. It wasn't easy for her, though.

It would be wonderful if we had more ability to work through these times with more awareness and better tools. There are five things I find to be simple and helpful:

- We need to become aware of our patterns of not hearing and how we block out views that are different from those we hold. Awareness is much of the solution.
- We can seek safe places within which we can explore new ideas and, in fact, will be encouraged to do so. We seldom change alone and we need help to stretch our edges.
- We could learn the Dialogue process David Bohm has written about in his books and article, "On Dialogue." This creates a better environment for exploration and safety.

- When someone challenges us, asking hard questions, offering unheard-of suggestions and observations, making astounding remarks, we can remind ourselves that he or she might be one of the early learners who is one step ahead of us. We should learn to respect and honor them. They are serving us well.
- When I am overwhelmed with the magnitude of global transformation, I remember to bring my focus back to who I want to be and how I need to act to be a responsible, caring part of a global community.

Barbara Shipka is an example of how to do this, as is the organization she describes. She is a corporate consultant, a member of the board of directors of the World Business Academy (WBA) and founder of the Minnesota chapter of the WBA. She works with many systems issues, including global, interdepartmental, interteam and interpersonal ones, helping to further an organization's vision through the creativity, innovation, and experimentation of its employees. She's also a contributing author in several anthologies including *When the Canary Stops Singing: Women's Perspectives on Transforming Business, Community Building,* and others.

Her experience with learning to see systems is extensive and stems from living in Eastern and Western Europe, the Middle East, Africa, South America, Asia, and the Caribbean. Her story illustrates the human and emotional sides of systems change as well as the need to look for root causes, instead of treating symptoms.

Barbara Shipka's Story: A Quiet Change of Mind

"My experiences have led me to understand that we are in the midst of a desperately needed global transformation. I have been an educator and a corporate consultant for over 20 years. That includes three years of work in Somalia, the Sudan, and Ethiopia, under the auspices of the United Nation's High Commission for Refugees. As I worked with refugees, I began to realize that we provided temporary relief, but we didn't change anything in the big picture—nothing systemic. We were saving lives as long as food continued to arrive from the outside. While people perhaps became physically stronger, they also tended to become psychologically weaker. I began to realize that many of the ways we try to "fix" problems lead us deeper into symptoms and/or create more of them.

With that awareness, I decided I wanted to work with whole system change rather than treating symptoms. An example of working on a symptom is encouraging recycling. That helps with the short-term symptom of waste. On the other hand, eliminating waste generation would be closer to creating fundamental systemic change. Nonetheless, it's important to work with both symptoms and systemic change. As symptoms are managed, it increases the time we have to understand better how to change the whole system. But again, focusing on symptoms isn't enough.

I wanted a place to share hope and support for my own change process, to explore the meaning of a global transformation and my role in it. I decided business had the greatest capacity to respond to this, so I left international work and returned to my business practice. I eventually became a member of a global organization called the World Business Academy and an organizer of one of fifteen local chapters in locations from Bombay to London to Chicago to Seoul.

A person who has influenced my thinking tremendously and at times has articulated things I was already thinking is Willis Harman, one of the founders of the WBA. He sees two response paths to our global crisis. The first path, which can be represented by organizations like Businesses for Social Responsibility and the Business Council for Sustainable Development, is focused on trying to change the current system through policy, advocacy, and legislation.

The World Business Academy is on a second path. This is one of exploration of the transformation and sharing of this knowledge with others. The focus is on learning about fundamental change in the system at the level of cause. We have much to learn about what this really means. One part of our process is to provide a safe harbor for members to engage in this learning and explore what the role of business is in relationship to that. For many of us, looking into both the large, apparently unanswerable questions—as well as the personal, vulnerable questions—is easier when we find a safe place to do it. The idea of a harbor brings to mind protection from the weather: a place to get nourished, to rest, and to take on new stores so we can return to our purpose, our ocean passage. Local chapter groups meet periodically to develop a bond that can facilitate personal change.

When we come together, it's as a group of learners. Because, by definition, transformation means something we've never seen or experienced, it's like going to first grade in a way. It's a classroom, but it doesn't have a teacher. Some students can read a little better than others, have thought more about the issues, and have been around a little longer. We go to this classroom to learn and to play together. We're making up the curriculum together and it's a continuous learning experience. We take our learnings back home with us, to our organizations.

I've begun to learn signs that tell me when we are focusing on a symptom instead of a cause. One is when we apply great energy and resources and the problem gets worse. Unfortunately, we are responding this way to almost every social problem I can think of. The war on drugs and the effort to reduce teen pregnancies are two examples.

Another big example is unemployment and the poverty it creates. Our assumption is that everything would be OK in the United States if we could create more jobs. The first fallacy in this assumption is the belief that we can separate ourselves from the rest of the world. A second fallacy is the assumption that we will have less unemployment through creating new jobs. Many of the people who have lost their jobs in the last few years may never work in a traditional job again. In addition, we're adding 250,000 people to the planet every day. Can we really create that many jobs? What would they be? And if we were able to create that many jobs, what would that do to the environment? So believing in more jobs as a solution to our current ills is a myth.

We need to explore new alternatives that allow everyone to make a contribution and, in return, receive a way to live decently. Creating a system based on meaningful contribution may mean that our current ways of employment totally disappear because they represent an insufficient idea. "Contribution" is a much larger framework.

Another assumption that I think needs challenging is the idea that expansion equals progress. As a culture, we're like a teenager who is at a point in a cycle of life where the growth and development of the body is the main focus. We need to move into maturity and develop an understanding that progress may mean lessening quantitative growth and increasing qualitative growth. What qualitative growth of business and society could look like is part of the mystery we are encountering.

I believe that transformation happens inside each individual and in the world simultaneously. Our individual beliefs create our values and behaviors. These, in turn, create our organizations and our world. "Systemic" means we can't easily break things into parts as a means of understanding them better. I have come to realize that global transformation is underway, regardless of whether we choose to see it or whether we want it. To the extent we can align ourselves with it, we can develop attitudes that reduce the suffering that tends to go with transformative times. We have to change ourselves, one by one, rather than trying to solve individual symptoms one by one. In *Global Mind Change*, Willis Harman says something to the effect that, when historians look back on the 21st century they will say that the most significant change was the change of the mind, a quiet, but pervasive change of the mind.

I suspect that dialogue and relationships will help stimulate this change of mind. Dialogue is about creating a place where we can explore the unanswerable questions. This includes acknowledging we aren't in a debate or even a discussion. We do a different kind of listening and we look more deeply. Dialogue means "with the word" or "with spirit" so it is a reverent conversation. True dialogue may allow the creative process to bring us something new, something transformative. Therefore, I believe this kind of dialogue is very important in the business setting. Business has become the most powerful institution on the planet and, therefore, it has a significant role and responsibility in the world today and tomorrow.

Inseparable from my intellectual thoughts is spirituality. My experience is that as I grasp what's really going on in the world, I deepen my spiritual journey. When I look at some of the external reality, it can be scary. There's no choice but to draw upon Spirit and to look inward. When I'm in touch with my spiritual path, what's happening isn't quite so scary. I'm not talking about religion per se. I'm talking about a sense of connectedness with each other, a sense of something larger than we are, recognition of the miracle of life on earth and the preciousness of that. It's a humbling experience to realize we can't easily think our way out of our global dilemmas. They aren't rational problems. The depth of who we are, our spiritual essence, is a primary human resource that we can draw on wherever we go—including the workplace.

I feel like I am in a partnership where I support change in myself and in the world. I feel tremendous hope because I'm in first grade with people who are captured by the opportunity for innovation and creativity beyond our dreams."

Another critical element to systems change is measurement, and extension and standardization of practices proven to have achieved higher performance and quality than the previously used practices. This is happening inside manufacturing organizations, but it would also be tremendously helpful for the improvements to become the basic new operating practices for all organizations.

The next story illustrates an existing company successfully operating within much of the model that Paul Halvorson described, and grappling with many of the issues raised in that story. This organization has been able to standardize practices within the company and are trying to promote them beyond the company.

Horst Rechelbacher is the founder and chairman of Aveda Corporation, which he incorporated in 1978. *Aveda* is derived from the term *ayurvedic*, the science of longevity. The company specializes in products that are made from pure flower and plant essences. Rechelbacher was introduced to the benefits of plant-derived ingredients by his mother, an herbalist, in his native Austria. I liked his subtle sense of humor, as exemplified on a label covered with green plants: "The ingredients in our products are manufactured in plants all over the world."

Initially, Rechelbacher was an internationally known hair designer. During the sixties, he became dissatisfied with the petroleum-based hair, skin, and beauty products, so he traveled the world and consulted with doctors and scientists to create something different. Starting in his kitchen, the company has grown to 350 people and a 272,000-square-foot headquarters. This company works globally and seeks to do the right thing simultaneously for people, the earth, and profits. They're not alone. Rechelbacher is one of the cofounders of Businesses for Social Responsibility, an association of like-minded businesses.

I also had a chance to talk with Nan Upin, director of public communications, who spends much of her time with the Businesses for Social Responsibility organization and the Give to the Earth Foundation, which was created by Rechelbacher. An interesting part of that conversation was a side discussion about what it's like to work at Aveda. Upin's comments are an example of how a company can influence employees to have a personal sense of responsibility for the whole.

Upin said, "Before I started working for Aveda I never said 'Where does this moisturizer come from?' or 'How do they make my lipstick?' They just existed. It's really a shift to come to a company that says 'What is this made from, and how is it made, and how does that affect the person and the planet we live on?' It really made me see the world differently. It's a wonderful experience to work for a company that can also help me grow personally."

Horst Rechelbacher's Story: Living in the Twenty-first Century

"Our mission at Aveda is to care for the world we live in, from the products we make to the way we sustain people, to the ways in which we give back to society and the earth. In a sense, my most important personal product is environmentalism—that is, creating ways to live in a sustainable twenty-first century. All of us at Aveda try to live that way, in every aspect of what we do. We hope the rest of the world will follow that example.

I think Bill Norris was way ahead of his time in helping small companies to organize themselves. I enrolled in that training and it was great. They gave us examples of a mission statement, a five-year plan and many other things. There's something, though, that precedes a mission statement. It's what motivates and excites people, what raises our spirits. For me, that's making sure I and the corporation are good citizens of the earth. That involves a spiritual search for daily activities to support all the living organisms of the earth, rather than being a predator. These goals become a mission when we write them down for others. All businesses, from my point of view, have a choice to be or not to be a predator in something as simple as recycling a can and reducing waste.

In our most concrete form, Aveda is a manufacturer of beauty products with a vision of beauty that incorporates environmental balance. We're concerned with making the best products possible, products that will make you smell great or make your hair look wonderful or your house shining clean. The backbone of who and what Aveda is, though, is in making those products from plants and flowers, from renewable resources. This approach helps protect and preserve the planet rather than deplete it. These two purposes are so entwined that we really can't separate them.

You can see this in everything we do. For example, we're a very science-intense company. Twenty-two years ago the first lab was in my kitchen. Today, we have about 25,000 square feet of R&D laboratories with many chemists, pure-fumers™ and botanical technicians. Pure-fumes™ is a word we have trademarked, meaning aromas blended from the highest quality pure plant and flower essences. Our scientists are challenged to design a wide range of products we feel serve people well and are made from natural, renewable resources. We also are totally against animal testing.

We're open to exploring many areas of products because we are about total living. While we began in the haircare field, we expanded into skincare, pure-fumes™, natural cosmetics, and today we also have work- and home-cleaning products. We don't do a lot of market research. We're customers, too, so we just see a need and respond to it. I used to go home after a housecleaner had been there and it would smell like chemicals. I would get a headache. That led us to come out with the home care line. We'll be coming out with an oral care line of toothpaste, mouthwash, and a breath freshener next. Again, all of these are made from healthy, natural, and renewable resources.

Our raw materials come from around the world. We're currently using about 1,500 flowers and plants, primarily from Nepal and

India. We also have plants coming from France, China, Kenya, Hawaii, Peru, and many other places. We are constantly expanding. Organic plants are important to us. By organic I mean grown without petrochemical pesticides, herbicides, and insecticides that cause pollution to air, water, and soil. We're trying to get to the point where 100 percent of our resources are grown organically.

When it comes to people and our internal company practices, we also focus on beauty and a sustainable life-style for the twenty-first century. When we work with our suppliers around the world, we are careful to help indigenous cultures preserve their wisdom, their way of life, and their intellectual property rights. We seek a mutually healthy relationship. At the same time we try to provide our employees with a healthy environment and relationship. We have a wonderful facility on 65 acres of beautiful grounds, exercise rooms, racquetball and basketball courts, walking trails, and bicycles. We have natural sunlight in every work area, including the factory.

We have a cafeteria called Organica. It's a natural foods restaurant, featuring a wide selection of delicious, healthy foods. Most restaurants of its size produce about 50 pounds of waste per day, but Organica only generates about 5 pounds per day. This is accomplished through smart menu planning, bulk purchasing, and using silverware and plates, rather than throwaway items. We also send food waste to a pig farmer. This is how sustainable living pervades everything.

We strive to get better and better at what we do, so we create an environment that is healthy without harmful waste. All of our materials are printed on recycled paper or recycled content paper. We use soy inks, double siding everything, and recycle throughout the facility. We also have a recycling program for our plastics through our 25,000 salons, schools, esthetiques, and spas. We're trying to minimize waste in every possible sense so we reduce, reduce, reuse, reuse, and recycle. Recycling is really the last option.

Aveda has been committed to enhancing the life-style of the employee. Child care is a huge issue. We're a company of about 60 percent women. Although child care has been considered a woman's issue, it's really a family issue, a human issue. It's a global concept about humanity. One of the reasons that we have felt so strongly about opening an on-site child-care center is that it gives employees the opportunity to more easily blend work and family. That's an issue of balance. Without balance, we don't have a sustainable life. When we make such decisions, we examine how to do them in a way that is compatible with who we are and our mission.

We have been told that only about 150 companies provide on-site day care for preschool children in this country. Most companies choose not to, for a host of reasons. But when we looked at the data on employment, productivity, cost, the return to the company, and our values, it was obvious that we should go ahead. We are about excellence in everything we do, so we didn't just want a child-care center, but to have one that really gave the child and the parents something special.

I'm from Austria and I am familiar with the international Waldorf School association. Rudolf Steiner, who was from Austria, started the Waldorf movement there in the early 1900s. I have studied many different philosophies and approaches and I really felt that the Waldorf educational approach best fitted what we wanted to do because it's just so in line with who and what Aveda is. Its philosophy is based on the total child. It does not separate the child's head from his or her hands, heart, or soul. It's about nourishing and balancing those. Since we are about planetary and personal balance, that really seems to fit. It's also a team-oriented, noncompetitive approach, which matches our management style. Waldorf's excellence is suggested by its success rate. It's one of the fastest growing private systems in our country and in the world. And it's even being explored by public schools. We're able to draw on the expertise of the two Waldorf Schools in the Twin Cities.

We've created happier children, loyalty to the company, and more productive employees who don't have to be on the phone all day worrying about child care, trying to get in touch with their kids. They can just go down and have lunch with their children. What we are looking at next is a form of elder care or some kind of assistance program. We're also looking into programs for after school and summer programs for older children.

The third way that Aveda works consistently through the whole system is through giving back to society. We have created the Give to the Earth Foundation, which provides money to local organizations to clean something up or to change something directly. Aveda has donated thousands and thousands of dollars each year to different environmental organizations and groups, especially to those who generally don't have a voice or a chance.

We give back by trying to assist in the creation of a broader agenda for change throughout business and beyond. We helped initiate the Businesses for Social Responsibility organization, and I am on its board of directors. It's a business alliance created to revolutionize how businesses operate in America. We believe our organizations demonstrate that doing good is also good for business. We're engaged in political advocacy and education on many issues, including the environment, family leave, encouraging investment in job creation in low-income areas, and much more. We also encourage employees to volunteer in the community and beyond.

I travel extensively for R&D reasons, for environmental purposes, and to keep learning. I met some phenomenal people in the Global Forum at the United Nation's Earth Summit meetings who are doing things to make the world better. In all these ways, we try to share what we have learned, learn from others, and give back to the world."

Some things that impressed me about Aveda were their preschool and their efforts to start addressing the family/work balance issues. The need for lifelong, global education is absolutely critical. The Waldorf education system Rechelbacher describes goes a long way toward addressing that need at the Pre-K–12 level. It provides a good start on a global curriculum, emphasizes a holistic approach to learning, and is paced according to the child's natural development pattern. It would be exciting to explore the implication of using that model beyond high school.

The issue is even larger. Our children are still often treated as a low priority in our society. A major reframing is underway in how we raise children, not just here, but around the world. This one is more complex than many strictly business issues. I'm more afraid about what is happening to children and the implications of that for our future than about any other issue. I've often commented to business leaders that it seems absurd for them to invest so much money and time in education and then have such backward work policies and norms that affect parents in the workplace. It's like shooting ourselves in the foot (or the heart).

Every issue about how we raise healthy children belongs in the workplace with us. Here is an issue that affects many, many people and one that business has a vested interest in. It dramatically affects who we can be. Education in particular has local, regional, national, and global aspects. It has many dimensions of diversity: racial, sexual, religious, and philosophical, to name a few. What if we approached this issue as not only an issue in its own right but as an opportunity to learn more about creating unity out of diversity, about working through conflict, about peacemaking? It presents an opportunity to try the dialogue method Barbara Shipka mentioned and the kind of listening Paul Halvorson discussed. Many of the unconstructive dynamics that I will describe below are apparent and perhaps could be overcome using these methods.

The dimensions of this issue are huge, even if we confine the discussion to just education in this country. The issues range from educational reform of many types to questions about the integration of all child-related social services in the schools. We debate the length of the school year and requirements for math, science, language arts, foreign languages, and geography, just to name a few. A recent report documented that there was little difference in the finances of families who send their children to public as opposed to private colleges. This blew a lot of stereotypes out of the water. Questions are being raised regarding shifting to vouchers and letting the money follow the students, regardless of institution and religious affiliations. Counterpoints are that the disenfranchised children will get lost in this system and we will increase the split between rich and poor.

Several experiences have given me a little clarity on the next step forward in this area. One was reading a thought-provoking article, "How Public Are Our Public Schools?" by John Taylor Gatto, a former New York State Teacher of the Year. I invest quite a bit of time in educational issues and read extensively. Yet he explained a lot of history and raised points I haven't seen raised. One issue was an exploration of what makes a public school public, which was far from clear. Another was whether it is appropriate in a democracy to have a compulsory monopoly in education that can be overcome only by buying your freedom in the form of a second tuition payment for a "private" school, taxes having paid for the public schools.

We get excited in different ways when someone raises these basic philosophical and structural issues; they aren't tinkering at the edges. And so our conversation immediately degenerates into a fight. Yet I think the vast majority of people feel that change is necessary. A major element of what is in the way is that we seldom have a chance to explore new options and the hard questions associated with them. There are serious questions about every proposal for change that deserve attention. Rather than explore how we could implement the alternative and reduce the potential harm that could come about, we end up in a debate about whether the potential harm is real or not. Accusations and defensiveness run high. Relative to the voucher discussion, we never get to explore how to protect the disenfranchised child if vouchers were put in place. We end up arguing over who will benefit and lose.

I have a lot of compassion, in particular, for the teachers, parents, and children caught in this chaos. I think it's critical we walk through it with less animosity and closed minds and more compassion, community, and openness. We need to have the second form of discussion. We need to practice peacemaking and community building. Work is a good place to do it. Our children need it.

6

Going Through the Pain

I am convinced that it is not the fear of death, of our lives
ending, that haunts our sleep so much as the fear that our lives
will not have mattered, that as far as the world is concerned, we
might as well never have lived.

HAROLD KUSHNER

We often avoid change in our personal and organizational lives
out of fear of the pain we believe goes with it. Often this change
is critical to our health and well-being, but we still choose to avoid
it. Why would we do such a harmful thing to ourselves and our
organizations? I think we've programmed ourselves to believe
change has to take forever and be very painful. Organizational
pain is usually in one of three categories: "I'm going to lose something," "I'll be punished for this," or "I might fail." This last one
might be because we don't know how to create the change or we
don't think we have the resources to make the change happen. All
these categories have their roots in fear of pain.

What is "pain," and why are we so afraid of it? Between the
dictionary and my thesaurus, I found there are many more definitions and synonyms for pain than for pleasure. I also found that
many of the words for pain are depressing and frightening, like

torture, misery, despair, mental suffering, desolation. Others aren't quite so bad—like *discontent, weariness, burden,* and *hurt*—but they don't exactly make a person feel warm and encouraged.

Along with those definitions and synonyms, there are the frequent connotations that wrap around these words, carrying a sense of punishment. If we have pain, it seems to imply that we did something wrong and that we deserve it. Even the word *pain* comes from the Latin *poena,* as do the words *punish* and *penalty.* This is what our culture focuses on when thinking of pain. No wonder we feel the way we do.

We can't escape pain, but we try very hard to do so. Perhaps it's one of the reasons why, more so than other cultures, we try to design feelings out of large parts of our lives, like the workplace. Some of the other ways we deal with emotions are to drown them through addictions or to move into a state of depression and melancholy, as Jim Bowe described in Chapter 2. Others have written about this and suggest that our emphasis on materialism is related to a sense of emptiness caused by the absence of feelings. Yet I wasn't satisfied that this was the only side of pain.

High school was a painful period for me. When one of my teachers gave me the book *The Prophet,* by Kahlil Gibran, I found great solace in the section on "Joy and Sorrow." I have returned to it many times in my life.

> The deeper the sorrow carves into your being, the more joy you can contain. . . . When you are sorrowful look again in your heart, and you shall see that in truth you are weeping for that which has been your delight.

I wanted to understand more about pain and explore this other side of it. I found insight in Stephen Levine's book, *A Gradual Awakening,* and Rabbi Harold Kushner's book, *When Bad Things Happen to Good People.* Kushner talks about how dangerous it would be if we couldn't feel pain. He describes a child with a rare disease called familial dysautonomia, a disease that prevents the child from feeling any pain. Such a child can experience cuts, burns, broken bones, stomach aches, and fevers and never feel them. And the child's parents may not know he is sick until it's too late. Kushner says, "Pain is nature's way of telling us that we are overexerting ourselves, that some part of our body is not functioning as it was meant to, or is being asked to do more than it was intended to."

When we ban emotions from the place where we spend a huge percentage of our lives, it's almost like we are creating organizational familial dysautonomia. So we don't see the warning signals of burnout, lost creativity and capacity for growth, lost market share, the lost energy of truth and commitment. We rationalize the personal and organizational pain away. In severe cases, we even create enough fear about "shooting messengers" so that no one will identify the pain when they do see it. And in our personal lives, we decide this is the way it has to be, and a piece of us dies.

Levine explores mental suffering, which he defines as "wishing we were elsewhere." He then observes, "Wanting things to be otherwise is the very essence of suffering." Referring to physical pain, he explains, "Most of what we call pain is actually our experience of resistance to that phenomenon. . . . And the resistance is usually a good deal more painful than the original sensation." Some of what Levine describes was similar to a section in a PBS Bill Moyer special on a clinic that uses meditation to deal with chronic severe physical pain. The meditation coach said we must focus on the pain instead of evading it. He described how, in the process of relaxing and concentrating on a total awareness of what it is that we feel, we discover multiple sensations and less pain. More importantly, the pain loses some of its power over us.

So pain is a gift to be welcomed and used as a sign that something needs to be addressed before things become much worse. And the first lesson in how to reduce the pain is to become aware of it and explore it, rather than deny it or run from it. The second lesson is to add meaning to it. Kushner's example is drawn from research into various degrees of pain, and how much different things hurt. He explains that two of the most painful things a person can experience physically are the passing of kidney stones and giving birth. From a physical perspective, these two events are nearly identical in pain and intensity. But we experience them very differently because birth is meaningful and kidney stones are not.

This approach is just as valid with mental and emotional pain. The first year after my mother's death was a time of settling into a new life with relatives, changing schools, and getting through the initial shock. After that a different kind of pain developed. It was associated with realizing this was going to be a life-long experience of loss. At some point, I remember deciding that somehow I was going to be better and stronger for this. There had to be some good that could come out of this or I had nothing to hold on to. I needed to let myself believe there was a reason, even if I didn't understand it. I certainly didn't know what I was doing in this process; it just seemed like the right thing to do. It allowed me to stop resisting what had happened, to go into the pain, to make it meaningful. The pain did decrease and I did learn lessons from that experience that have affected my whole life. It became such a valuable life lesson that, if there were such a thing as choosing, I would choose it again because I couldn't be who I am without those lessons . . . despite the pain. That was liberating in a way I cannot describe.

Other related thoughts from Richelle Pearl-Koller come to mind. Chapter 2 gives her description of the hermit crab's sense of fear and vulnerability when it was time to choose to stay or leave, to resist reality or to respond to it. She elaborated,

> There is a great art to allowing yourself to dwell on the beach, vulnerable. If you don't do that, you miss the opportunity of this dying/birthing moment. It's true in work situations, true in religious situations, that the in-between time is like a threshold moment: it's an opportunity to the new. Those I counsel see it as a spiritual opportunity because they have come to recognize that if God isn't in these moments, She isn't anywhere. It is a search for meaning. . . .
>
> I wonder if the empowerment to make a change comes from the recognition of a deep sense of discontent, often a gut sense.

It's as though we have to hit the bottom of the pit or get to that point where we say, "I am drowning." We have to be willing to see and experience the pain, the darkness. Robert Frost says "the only way out is through." We can't bypass it; we can't jump over it; we can't go around it or under it. We have to go through it and to do that we have to hit that feeling level. It's probably at that feeling level, that it becomes so tangible that we have to do something. But we often don't know what to do.

If we were to use that idea in terms of a physical death, that is the angst of death. We have no idea what is beyond, if anything. No matter what faith we have, that doesn't take away the feeling that "I don't really know what is over there." All the biblical thought in the world and all the belief does not take that away. In this process of pain and dying at work, the other side isn't clear to us. That's what the trick is: to be willing to walk through, even though we don't know what is on the other side. Then the realization can begin that we have made moves before and have been able to survive them. We have to go back and do some looking at the other transitions we have made in life and remember that we have survived. Maybe it's like swimming: we have to believe that the water will hold us and that we won't sink. I don't think we can swim if we don't believe that.

So we come to an act of faith and trust that we can go through the pain and come out better for it. As we make choices about that, we might also reflect on and challenge the basic assumptions that go with change efforts. Do they really have to take so long? I don't think we can afford change cycles of seven to ten years. Most markets won't give us that long. Do they have to be all pain? Might there be some fun, pleasure, satisfaction in them? Let's stop focusing on one side of things. Everything comes to us more whole than that.

All these thoughts can help an organization undertake change. But they don't help an individual or organization that denies it needs to change. I know many people and organizations that insist things aren't changing and that life can go on much as before, if we just wait it out. It's as if our whole life surroundings are being dismissed as a global program of the month. Let's wait out pollution and hazardous wastes. Let's wait out violence and increasing poverty. Let's wait out quality and competitiveness. Most organizations spend a lot of time just convincing people that there's a need to change. Others have to get in serious financial trouble before admitting that change is necessary. One step up from this approach is deciding do what we always have done, but faster. Often the fear of pain is underneath these behaviors, but not always.

Occasionally there are other causes. I'm just beginning to understand one of them. The only way I can describe it is that it looks like a philosophical view of life that says we are at the culmination of history. People don't use these words, but this seems to be the underlying meaning. I know it is there when I see and hear about how good things are.

This pattern of statements is always a reaction to someone else's comments about the need to change: "But look how much we've already improved." "Compared to so-and-so, we're so much better." "They've been asking for that for years, and it's not necessary. What do they know about it anyway?" "We are the best _____." (Fill in the blank—producer, country, department ...) "We should maximize what we already do." "Be grateful for what we've got." "Hold on to what we've achieved."

Denial drives me nuts. As I dig under it, I see it more as a world view that we are the ultimate in the development of human history and so, suddenly—except for new technology—everything can stop. All we need to do now is tweak things. Every high school student has studied changes throughout history, century by century, but in this world view, the mindset seems to be that our century won't follow that pattern. Sometimes we get through denial best by getting to this core. After we have dealt with it, people may be more able to see and hear the data about current changes and what they mean.

Once we get past the denial and fear of pain, things can begin to happen more quickly if there is some sense of direction and excitement as to what to do next, or at least how to come together to plan what is next. In other words, we need to create a shared sense of purpose, as previously discussed. If we don't, we backslide into denial or move into anger, frustration, and blaming. We can get stuck there for a long time. This is very painful and can lead to becoming numb, which keeps us stuck even longer. We cannot *not* choose pain. We *can* choose which *kind* of pain to face.

This matters in the workplace. We like to think we don't bring our "stuff" with us to work, but we do. It's important to realize that every one of us takes our whole history to work with us. We also take our denial of it or our healing of it. This affects other people and the organization. Only we and the people around us can answer whether that is positive or negative in our own case. Will we take responsibility for healing ourselves so that we don't harm others and so that, possibly, we can heal others?

There are many forms of pain. There are probably four to five million Vietnam veterans in business who are in their forties and fifties and in leadership positions like the person we will hear from next. Those who have learned how to cope with and build on their painful wartime experiences are bringing benefits to the workplace. Those who are still struggling with it often bring inappropriate anger and distrust into their relationships at work. The bottom line is that we can't go to work and leave behind some of our most formative experiences, either positive or negative.

Addictions of all types are also prevalent and a source of pain and lost productivity, as well as poor judgment. In the books *When Society Becomes an Addict* and *The Addictive Organization*, Anne Wilson Schaef and Diane Fassel make a thought-provoking case that addiction covers a broader range of dysfunctional behaviors than generally acknowledged. Using this broader definition means that it would be pretty hard for any of us to claim we are totally healthy. Organizations seem to be taking more responsibility for working with these issues since the trend toward teams has developed and relationship issues have become more predominant. All forms of discrimination and diversity conflicts at work (a major source of pain for those on the receiving end) are closely related.

Robert Carlson is a former sales and marketing executive who is now a management consultant. He received his undergraduate education at West Point, his MBA at Wharton School of Business;

he spent time in the military in Germany and Vietnam. He has worked for four diverse companies including IBM, a smaller ($50 million) organization, and two companies in between those sizes. He has worked his way up from a sales rep to vice president of sales and marketing in these companies. I heard about him from one of his former employees, who described him as "one of the best bosses ever." When I connected with him, he had just been laid off in what he described as a massive cost-cutting effort. Pain and work relationship issues were on his mind.

This story gives us a chance to learn more about going through pain and to get a glimpse of what it's like to get at least part way on the other side of it. Carlson seems well into the process of carving out a new and better life. As he does so, he has every intent of creating a new workplace that will be much healthier and happier for everyone associated with it.

Bob Carlson's Story: On the Other Side of Pain

"It's sad to say, but I have a very jaundiced view of how most corporations manage the human side of the business. I've had some painful experiences in my professional life. The most recent was a layoff from a company in the midst of a major turnaround effort. The owners felt they needed to cut costs dramatically because of short-term financial issues. I was surprised by the layoff. I didn't see it coming. In fact, they had implied lifetime employment. I had been laid off once before, so as a result of the first experience, I felt like more of a veteran this time. I was even congratulating myself on how well I was handling it. As time went on, I realized I had gone numb for several weeks without knowing it, so then I got in touch with a lot of anger at the injustice of it all.

The expectations of owners for rapid short-term returns is a critical issue in maintaining change efforts. We can have everything going right at the management level, which was the case at the company I just left. Unfortunately, there were a lot of things that needed to be fixed in the company and the owners didn't understand that. They just looked at it as an expense and didn't provide the support and the time to develop better products, better customer service, and better systems for delivering those things.

We have so many owners that have never run a business in their lives. Frequently, they are people with financial backgrounds who don't understand the fundamentals of designing, manufacturing, and marketing. Consequently, they drive people away who are good at those kinds of things because they don't know how to support those people. The focus with so many of these owners is "Just make money. I don't care how you do it. Just go out there and make money." They don't understand short-term versus long-term tradeoffs.

For most companies, the result of downsizing and layoffs is that they are then inadequately staffed to do a decent job. So things have become worse for many people. Companies are expecting 60-, 70-, 80-hour workweeks, especially from managers. People can't work at those levels for long periods of time without burning out; in some cases without having very serious health problems, even death. The other very stressful issue that gets exacerbated by the downsizing fear is truth telling. I worked at companies where it wasn't safe to express opinions that were contrary to the company line. By doing so, we could put our jobs or futures with the company on the line. The cost reduction may help in the short run, but it's debilitating in the long run.

I'm a little like the person who got jilted one too many times. I am a little reluctant to "date" right now, in the sense of going back to another corporate job. I've had other painful experiences and my experience is fairly common. There are thousands of people out there who are dying inside. I heard something a couple of Sundays ago that really stuck with me. It was "Hurt people—hurt people and healed people—heal people."

One of the most destructive situations I've experienced in the workplace was an alcoholic boss. That's a problem I believe is bigger than the business world is willing to admit. He lied to me, was abusive, and managed through intimidation and fear. By abusive, I mean he was threatening and very demeaning. He didn't focus on what I did or didn't do. He just seemed to suggest I had an inherent defect that wasn't very definable. For my part, I erred in just writing him off. That caused the first layoff experience. I had never had a problem with a boss and I didn't know how to respond. I went through the motions and did what had to be done, but without any passion or sense of satisfaction. I knew I would be part of the next general layoff, because we were in constant conflict. I was fortunate and found a good job quickly.

Unfortunately, there's a double standard with alcoholism. I've seen executives force the treatment issue with middle managers, but God help us if one of the executives has a problem. I've known about a number of situations at the executive level and I've never seen one dealt with. At the least, this will make the company an undesirable place to work, but even worse, it can bring companies to financial ruin. Untreated alcoholics or drug users bring all their bad behaviors to the workplace. It isn't that they necessarily drink or "use" on the job. They cause damage through their lies, lack of trust, and because they're incapable of having healthy business relationships with people.

The biggest thing I've learned and come to appreciate is that relationships really matter. We can't separate the intellectual and the emotional sides of ourselves in the workplace. We can't come to work and say, "We're going to be robots today. We're not going to be emotional. We're not going to be human beings." I think a lot of companies implicitly expect that. It's not OK to be angry. It's not OK to grieve the loss of a fellow worker. It's not OK to have fun or be excited about something. What inspires individuals and makes companies soar is to capitalize on what makes human beings unique, which is our spiritual and emotional sides.

I've completely flip-flopped on that. I always thought I should be cold and analytical. Now I know that when emotions get expressed in the workplace in an appropriate way, something constructive invariably comes out of that. If somebody is angry, perhaps the issue that brought about the anger in the first place will be dealt with. Or take the case where somebody who was very popular retired or left or died. If that doesn't get appropriately grieved over and acknowledged, there will be something unspoken present for months. It will detract from the job. On the positive side, creativity, excitement, and energy are related to our inner selves, to our emotional and spiritual selves. By allowing and encouraging people to be who they are and to express themselves emotionally and spiritually, creativity, energy, and productivity soar.

Six years ago, I had a crisis that taught me to appreciate the relationship side of work. I was carrying around a lot from my Vietnam experience. I ended up in therapy and it's probably the best thing that could have happened to me. I had dealt with the bad memories by suppressing all emotion. Life was blah. I didn't feel anything. There wasn't any joy, there wasn't any anger. Life was in black and white and not in Technicolor. I had to learn to discover the emotional side of myself. The things I learned from this experience I've brought to the workplace. The results have astounded me. People enjoy their work more, do a better job, and get more done.

My purpose now is to blend what I've learned from the painful experiences. In my next position, I want to achieve something very special and fulfilling for the employees of the company, the owners, suppliers, customers, and me. I have to turn the pain into a positive experience. I wouldn't choose to repeat my Vietnam experience, but despite all that was negative, there were positive things I learned from that. I believe we give meaning to negative experiences by learning from them and applying what we have learned wherever we can.

I'm learning more about taking responsibility. Life is unfair in some ways, but I have a choice in how I react to it. I can slowly destroy myself on the inside by focusing on the negative things that have happened to me, the unfairness and the injustice of it all. In looking back, I can go to extremes in trying to find fault. I could say it had nothing to do with me or get real down about it and blame myself totally. I think the truth is somewhere in between. It's important to own the mistakes I did make. And then it's better to move on.

I'm also learning more about my values and clarifying what's most important to me. It's important to have the courage to walk away from an unhealthy situation. This has always been hard for me to do. I believe that when we're in a work situation that is incongruent with our values, we die inside a little each day. And as we die, we don't bring our best to our job, our family, or our friends. Looking at it analytically, it doesn't make sense to stay in a self-destructive situation.

Fears about finances and insecurity as to whether or not we can do anything else hamper us from leaving these places. I ignored what was wrong, perhaps hoping that things would get better, which they rarely do. Being unemployed wasn't nearly as scary when it happened as it seemed when I was anticipating it. The prospect of losing my job was absolutely terrifying. Actually getting into it, I found ways to survive. I am not sure why, but my self-confidence has actually increased. If I ever get into a situation again that isn't good for me, I will probably react more quickly.

Much of what I want in the future is captured in the word empowerment. We have two kinds of cultures in companies. We have cultures that trust people and believe in the goodness of people. They believe people are honest, want to do a good job, and are hardworking. Then we have cultures that are the opposite. I'd like to create an empowering place where people can be fully alive, that encourages people to bring their humanness to the workplace. It would be a thrill to bring people into such a company and give them an alternative to what's generally available. That's a personal mission for me. I have no doubts that it will serve customers, suppliers, the community, and profits very well."

We sometimes have the feeling that we can't be unhappy or in pain because we have done or are doing what everyone says we should have or should want to do. That's the first big breakthrough: to say I have what others define as "the good life" and I'm not happy with it. The next, even bigger hurdle is to say I can do something about it. That requires taking responsibility for my own life.

There's an unproductive pattern that's easy to fall into—the victim trap. "Life is hard, unfair, _____, and my parents, boss, spouse, God, _____ are the cause, and there isn't anything I can do" (fill in the blanks). In the case of a company, it's "Business is tough . . . and if the government, competition, customers, employees would just _____, everything would be fine" (fill in the blank). We often are part of the cause of our own pain. That's hard to stomach at first. Anger is a frequent response to this, and under the anger is fear and guilt. Throw away the guilt. It's not helpful.

We can choose to receive responsibility differently. We can see it as liberating and invigorating. If the cause of my pain is outside myself and controlled by others, I might be able to try to change things, but I really have no control. I'm at the mercy of someone else. I'm a victim. If, however, much of my pain arises out of me, unknowingly and unintentionally, than I'm more in control and there's much more hope. I need to awaken the heroic in myself to create a change.

How to do this has much to do with the next story. It's about identifying our own most significant beliefs and choosing to own them and/or replace them. Anita Ryan is an owner of the St. Paul Brass and Aluminum Foundry, president of C. McFarlane Associates, and director of the Leaders Alliance.

In 1981, Ryan left her career in the Wisconsin public school system as a speech and language therapist to join her brothers in managing the family business, as head of its human resource function. Subsequently, she also became the total quality facilitator and worked on safety and environmental issues for the company. In 1987, her older brother, who was president at that time, was involved in a severe motorcycle accident. Ryan assumed his position, while her other brother continued in his role as head of production.

Anita Ryan's story is about accepting that she was unhappy and could do something about it. Many people can accept that they are unhappy; but don't believe they can do anything about it. "Doing something" often involves disappointing others, at least in the short term, and being willing to endure the pain of self-exploration, of what Ryan calls the myths in our lives. These are the beliefs we have somehow acquired from our families, culture, and life. These beliefs create walls that hem in our lives. My experience with them is that they frequently are framed as "shoulds": I should do this, be this, get this, act this way, dress that way, think like them, live here, buy that . . . . These beliefs don't force us into anything. Instead, at a subtle level, I think they start clouding our ability to see other options.

Anita Ryan's Story: Struggling with Walls

"About two to three years into my five years as president of a family-owned business, it became clear to me that I was not very happy. In March of 1992, I left the company to pursue my own dreams and turned over the running of the business to my younger brother. That decision was hard, long, and painful. I felt I was letting the family down, letting the employees down, and walking out on the way I was supposed to be.

My father was wonderful in the business community. People loved and adored him, especially the employees. He achieved so much. He took the foundry from a tiny operation with six or seven employees, and built it up so that at the time of his death, it was a solid, midsize manufacturing operation. I had felt that I needed to carry on the family torch. It was also hard to quit because so many people have given me positive feedback about running a manufacturing company well and congratulated me for being a woman who could do that. So the feedback loop said to stay.

On a practical level, I am leaving the top position in a family-owned, heavy manufacturing company. In a more philosophical sense, I am leaving a set of myths to which I no longer feel bound. I am leaving a pattern of doing things to satisfy other people's expectations, rather than my own. While my father was a wonderful businessman, he was also an alcoholic and I realized that had created a lot of beliefs to which I no longer subscribed.

I think we all grow up with a set of beliefs or myths that lead us down various paths in life. Often, we don't even know we have these beliefs. We haven't chosen them. They're like unseen walls that hem us in. In my case, those beliefs were tied in with family and work. Perhaps the relationship between beliefs, family, and work is easier to see in a family-owned business. But I think those elements are there for all of us. So many of our fundamental expectations, needs, and beliefs about who we are and who we are supposed to be come from our families. They go with us into the workplace. I have come to realize that I took the expectations that came out of my family myths and built my career out of them.

The first myth was that I came from the best of all possible families. The second myth that came out of that was that we thought we had to achieve in the same way the head of our family did. So I felt I had to live up to that expectation. Also, being the first born out of an alcoholic system, there is a tendency to want to overachieve.

To some extent, my response to my environmental responsibility is an example of this. When I started out, I was enthusiastic about being able to do positive things from an environmental point of view. I felt that having the will to solve environmental issues would allow me to achieve great results. One of the things that has been very disillusioning was to realize that it was a difficult job that had little to do with my will. I felt that no matter how hard I worked in a small, heavy manufacturing business, it never made a difference. I couldn't fulfill my expectations, nor could I overachieve.

There were so many regulations that we could never get to dealing with them all. If we did get to dealing with them, it didn't make any difference in terms of the way we were viewed by the media and the community. I could work very hard, 10 to 12 hours a day, bringing our company into compliance, but no matter what I did, the feedback loop still said we were undesirable. That was very difficult, very painful.

Another major myth in my life has been that everything I did was supposed to be very altruistic. When my father ran the business, we tried to intervene whenever an employee had a problem. The way we intervened was by giving people more and more chances when they were doing things that were detrimental to themselves: giving people money if they didn't handle their finances or getting them out of jail if they drank and got in trouble. I now see that we took so much responsibility for their lives; they never got a chance to do it themselves. When they finally did have to take responsibility, it was much more painful. They would end up in much more trouble than if they would have had to take care of things earlier. We had a history of doing that for people.

I felt that what I needed to do, in any role I had with the business, was to take absolute care of any of the people who worked for us. The unwritten, unspoken part of that thinking was that I needed to do it at my own expense. I was always supposed to consider others first, without considering who and what I was and what I needed. So when I realized I wasn't happy as president, it didn't occur to me that I could have any alternative. It's frightening how we get caught in those kinds of myth systems.

I finally discovered that if I didn't start to follow my own path and look for what was true for me, no matter what I did to take care of other people would not work out in their best interest. Taking care of ourselves is much more important than I had ever realized. I am now moving forward toward understanding who I am, what I want, and what I am passionate about.

My process of change is still in the early stage. I started looking at why I wasn't happy. I examined the kinds of things that came out of my earlier life that got me set in patterns and ways of thinking, that put me into boxes, and I identified what the boxes were. That didn't make me any happier. It just made me able to say, "Yes. That's what I have been doing."

What has been most helpful to me came out of the Empowerment Workshop conducted by David Gershon and Gail Straub. The first one I went to was helpful in providing a format for looking at where I wanted to go, not so much in terms of absolute destination, but in terms of a general direction. It also allowed me to realize I must look at some visions for myself in all kinds of life areas. That helped me shift my perspective to something of my own creation. It also helped me look at those boxes that hemmed me in and say to myself, "How can I remove the walls?" That's where I am now in my personal journey.

I have had some real surprises. I have realized that most of what I've done throughout my life has been left-brain kinds of things. When I look at particular areas of my life where I have derived joy, they've been right-brain activities—music, theater, literature, creative writing. If you ask people who have known me for years, they would describe me as being an entirely left-brained kind of person and very outgoing. I am starting to understand more and more that there is a portion of my life that is very right-brained and very introspective. For me, this is a huge adventure. The way I struggle with the walls is kind of like walking into them and bouncing off. I almost think that I need a good whack between the eyes with a two-by-four and then the light will go on.

The same thing must happen in organizations. Everyone needs to have a shift in perspective. Let's go back to my example of environmental issues. We need a shared vision of what it really is that we want to accomplish for our planet. I often felt I was supposed to choose between a pollution-free planet and the livelihood of my employees. I don't think there are many people who are going to say that their vision for the world is to have a completely pollution-free planet with everyone living in poverty. A pollution-free planet is part of the vision, but the other part of the vision is to have quality lives at the same time. Once we have that vision, we can come to different kinds of solutions.

The walls, or boxes, are like the adversarial roles we believe we have to have. That's another myth. We can choose new roles. Everybody needs to put their minds and their souls in one direction.

From the legislative and the regulation point of view, rather than taking—an adversarial perspective based on how to punish companies into compliance—we'd look up to the vision and say, "What is it that we, as a nation, have to do to achieve that? How can we help get all the people together to get to the vision?" From a business perspective, it means looking at the vision and asking, "How can we get there using all the human potential we have?" We waste so much time and energy when we fight.

I am now a member of the advisory board for a group called GAP, the Global Action Plan, that is operating in more of this mode. It allows me to continue my personal interest in environmental issues, but in a manner that's fulfilling to me and free of the old myths about how I was supposed to do things. In GAP, we have a shared vision of reducing global waste by 20 percent through corporate, individual, and neighborhood efforts. There's no focus on guilt or mandatory requirements. It's a system for self-education and change through what we call EcoTeams. In addition, though, we have a global reporting system so each can see how his or her individual contribution helps the whole. We have about 300 EcoTeams going in this country and 700 internationally. I'm making a contribution I feel good about.

I still want to do things, like this, that contribute to life and the world. I'm coming to understand, however, that I cannot be a Mother Teresa unless I know myself, like what I am doing, and know I am doing it for myself, as well as for others. That voice, that motivation has to come from inside me and then I can do well."

It's hard to choose pain, even when it's clear we have to. Companies that are in financial trouble still keep holding on to the old familiar ways, sometimes until they die. It's even harder to choose pain when you're succeeding by everyone else's criteria. When profits are very good, it's tempting to say, "Don't fix what isn't broken." The next story is about a company that set about implementing radical change when things were going well.

Schott Corporation is a privately held, family-owned business. You have already been indirectly introduced to this organization through the stories of two employees in Chapter 4's section,

"Prisms for the Greater Good." The company has 300 employees, sales of about $12 million, and manufactures custom magnetic components and power supplies. It has a metropolitan head-quarters and three rural manufacturing plants, Marshall, Canby, and Minneota, about 150 miles away. I was allowed to interview people throughout the organization, to observe several key plan-ning sessions, and to survey all the employees who were involved in a major change.

Owen Schott, the president, CEO, and an owner, chose to bring in Robert Brattlund and James Meyer as change agents in 1988 and to implement a drastic change, rather than an incremental one. He wanted to move from a rigid hierarchy to empowered teams. Employees told me the experience was like turning an ap-plecart upside down and letting the apples roll.

I interviewed Owen Schott, to try to understand why a com-pany would do this and how he justified it to himself and his board of directors. You'll read his answer. I believe him. But my perception is that there is another dimension to that answer, based on what I observed and from what employees told me. I believe that the more fundamental impulse was his own spiri-tual core about what was right and wrong with the way people were managed.

The Voices of Schott Corporation: Revolution, Not Evolution

Donna Larsen (front line team member): Schott was a male-dominated, top-down organization. The employees had nothing to say. We were there to work and that was it. We came and punched in and did the same job, day after day after day. If we had an idea, we could say something to the male management, but they seldom did anything about it. If it was a really good idea, they took the credit. All that has changed.

Yvonne Caron (front line team member): We keep our customers happy and that's our main object now. Before, we didn't really care, as long as we got paid. The customer wasn't our number-one priority. Our bosses had never given us the feeling that they thought the customer was important. We have that priority now, because we make our own commitments. Customers aren't just names on a piece of paper anymore. They are people I've met or spoken to on the phone and I want to satisfy them. I feel really good about that.

And we get recognized for doing this. We had a customer who sent us money to buy coffee and rolls for all three plants because they were so happy with the product we had sent them. The check came with a big banner that said "Congratulations! Have coffee and rolls on us."

Rose Eggleston (quote coordinator): I was a production worker. They gave me my own corner of the world and kept me there. If I had a good idea, I'd share it. I seldom got the credit and I burned inside. I thought, "Someday, my day is going to come." I feel like I've been set free now. There are more workers and fewer bosses. We don't feel like there's a big boss watching us all the time who will cut us down for making a mistake. If you have people, you have human error. When people make mistakes, they usually know they did it. They need an uplift, not a kick in the seat of the pants.

Shirley Gawerecki (front line team member): I used to be deathly afraid to come in this room. This was the manager's office. I wasn't afraid of losing my job because I knew I was good. I was afraid of getting yelled at. It was part of the normal jacking up he did.

Sandy Verschelde (continuing engineering team member): I grew when the change came. I went from just working in testing to being team leader of inspection. I went to the Canby plant for a year as team leader of production support. Then I decided I wanted to be back in Minneota, a little closer to home and the kids, so they brought me back. It's nice they don't put us down for deciding to change, whether we just don't like it or feel we can't do it well enough.

Bob Brattlund and Jim Meyer let us grow. I noticed that right away. I grabbed it and it gave me a lot of self-confidence. The old structure didn't let us grow. They liked us in one little corner and that's what we did. Especially as a woman, it was very difficult. Males had more advantages in the old system.

Brenda Alley (front line team member): I definitely have had to change. We do a lot of cross-training. I was worried whether the product would go out the door correctly. I had the feeling that nobody else could do it as well as I could. It took a long time for me to get over that, but I did. Now I am more than happy to teach others. Then I can go do something else.

I tell people to give it a shot; it's a lot less boring when you learn to do more things. It makes the day go by faster and you feel better. Learning new things is scary at first. You may think that you can't do them, but if I can do them, anybody can. Don't be afraid that it's going to threaten your job because that's just not the way it works here.

Judy Orren (interface manager): I was the assistant supervisor in the old system and I was a very hard person. If we were supposed to do 300 units an hour, we'd better do 300 an hour. If we were supposed to ship something to the customer today, then we'd better ship it today, not tomorrow. If I went into a scheduling meeting and said something hadn't shipped, I was the one who got chewed out, so I chewed out my workers.

I had to turn myself around totally. I told myself, "You're not going to have a job if you keep screaming and hollering at them." I've mellowed out. I'm more of a team player and more supportive. That made a big change in my life at home as well as at work. I am much happier!

In the old system, I lost many nights of sleep. I used to work almost all night in my mind. I would think, "OK, now if we could do this, and this and this, then we can get this and this and this done." Now, it seems like it just falls in place and we're all in it together.

Shirley Gawerecki: We couldn't have handled today's product and customer mix with the old system and managers. We used to be good at what we did, but we were experts at only one thing. I just worked through my break to get some parts done so I could get them to varnish today. In the old system, the plant manager would have been pacing back and forth making me nervous. Today, I was doing it on my own.

Don Full (launch coordinator): The culture change was awfully hard for most people, because they grew up working for a boss. That's been our background. We grew up knowing that we had to report to somebody. That person told us what to do and we reported back and forth. Now, I feel as though we have responsibilities, but nobody is telling us what to do. I have mixed feelings about that.

I was raised to have a lot of ambition. That makes it harder to know that I can work and work and work and I'm still going to be at the same level. It leads me to wonder if I would be better off finding something else on my own. Here I can do a good job, I can get recognition, but I can't fulfill my true ambitions. As far as job knowledge and satisfaction, I think I've gained. The satisfaction with this system can be that I'm helping people work through problems, and we're working together as a team. It's a tough decision.

Barbara Warlop (prototypes team leader): I've learned how to get to the root of the problem and to eliminate finger pointing. I've developed a lot more patience. When you're team building and letting others grow, you can't do everything for them. I always used to be the doer. "Here, let me do that for you." So I've had to learn to back off and let people do things themselves. I was criticized for this approach when I was trying to turn Minneota around. I knew I had support, so I kept going. I felt that Bob Brattlund was a guardian angel and he would come down on anyone who interfered. For a year, it didn't seem like things were going very well. We were behind everybody else and then, all of a sudden, we started jumping ahead. A lot of things came together, but the biggest factor was that we let people grow.

Jim Meyer (manufacturing vice president and change agent): The hardest part has been dealing with the people who don't want to change. We have had people who have fit all ranges of the spectrum; from those who say, "All right, let's go for it," to "No way, I'm absolutely not going to change," to "I'm not going to change. In fact, I am going to be vocally against it." Some people left on their own.

First, we tried to bring everyone along. We offered support, training, and help. There were a lot of tough times, sitting in Owen's office talking about people who had been employees for 10 or 15 years and about the contributions they had made in the past. The only humane thing we could do was look them straight in the eye and tell them, "We appreciate the things you've done in the past, but you're not helping us for the future and this is what we have to do." If they were not willing to change, I gave them the ultimatum that after a certain period of time, they wouldn't have jobs.

I find that one person in a key position who is really dead set against the change can destroy a whole plant. We can't afford to let those people control us. It's important to remove those who are fighting the change to protect the rest of the organization. It's more important to me to have 200 people feel good about the future than to worry about one or two who are willing to destroy it.

The emotional impact is still very hard, though. Letting people go has a significant effect on them, their families, and their short-term livelihood. It gets real tough. There were many sleepless nights for a lot of people, including me. I believe that most people are good enough to go out and find another job and probably be better off in the long run. But in the short term, it's going to be tough.

I feel like I've been on an emotional roller coaster. There were days when it just felt like everything was going wrong, everything was a bad decision. It looked like failure. Then, the next day, I'd see some shining lights and I'd feel good. We had a lot of tummy aches when things weren't right and we had a lot of up days when all the customers were happy.

At first, I felt isolated. As change agents, Bob and I were out there leading it. Everybody looked at us as though we were crazy. We talked to each other a lot because we knew we had to keep each other pumped up. There were many times when it would have been so easy to quit. We had to hang in there. That first year was the toughest. Then the second year wasn't too easy, either, because halfway through, Bob was gone.

At that point, things were starting to make a little more sense to people, so I had followers who helped me. We started seeing more and more people come to say, "Hey, this is right, this is good." Now I have more change agents inside the organization helping to lead. It has come to a point where I find myself spending more time looking at the future.

Owen Schott (CEO, president, and owner): Many people have asked me why we did this. The answer is that I realized the world was changing. The business was changing fundamentally. Customers expected more, our product mix was changing, and technology changes were occurring. We had gone on for a long time as a successful organization, but there comes a point when you look into the future and ask yourself, "If we keep on doing things the way we are currently doing them, will we be successful?" The answer was "No."

I feel strongly that people are the dynamic, energetic force that really propels an organization and makes it possible for any entity to change. I was impressed with the power of people in some of the early Tom Peters videos. I can recall thinking, "Wow that's really neat," then being troubled by the thought, "I don't think that can happen here." I concluded we had to start with people and go through a dramatic change.

I went through some questioning: "What is my role? If people are going to be the dynamic force, then what do I need to do?" I read about Johnsonville Sausage and Ralph Stayer and I realized that he didn't exactly know, either, and that he went through a period when he totally backed off and tried to let the business take its own momentum and find its right way. I think I did that for a while. Then I came to realize that there still has to be some overall direction. Someone has to be responsible to say, "OK, we're going to go northeast."

Next, I learned more about how to envision and how to involve other people in it. My responsibilities became things like, "How can I help people take on new responsibility? How can I remove the roadblocks that come into their way so they can be successful?" My role, also, was to hold a steady course. This is an important quality during a transition because there gets to be a lot of questioning as to whether this is really the right way or not. If I'm wavering back and forth, people don't know what's going on.

Change takes a certain amount of courage. It's not easy. There have been times when I really struggle. There were times when things weren't going the way we wanted. Certainly, some of the results weren't what we wanted. We have lost a lot of money, some of which was related to the internal change, some of which would have happened anyway due to market changes. I continue to feel that we are on the right track. We're moving in the right direction, doing the right things, making positive progress.

I think of employees as volunteers. It seems to me that for the amount of time we spend at work, our jobs should be rewarding and gratifying. I can't remember where I heard the story about someone who is just cutting stone verses someone else who is building a cathedral. At work we should be building cathedrals rather than just doing drudgery kind of stuff."

Sometimes we start down a new path and find it incredibly difficult to keep going. It takes courage, stamina, and faith. If we are on the right path and can be tenacious and patient when change begins to take hold inside us, we start making new connections. We get a multiplier effect, rather than an additive one. Physiologically, we actually create new connections in our brains when we have major new learning. Intellectually, we start seeing how things all fit together. We see the connections in the system.

Spiritually and emotionally, we begin to create healthier relationships at work, with each other and between functions or departments. We might even have a new insight into our personal and organizational purpose. We develop new insights on how to deal with what appeared to be multiple issues but now seems like one.

Only when more of us begin to see these connections will we be able to identify those critical changes that will have profound leverage on the problems of our total system. Then we can look with fresh eyes at the many organizational, social, and global problems that are part of our pain. We might take the problems we have and think of them as painful symptoms of a disease. If we medicate the pain, doing short-term cost cutting, tranquilizing ourselves with rationalizations and blaming, or ignoring the problems, we are turning our backs on the gift of health to which the pain could lead us.

If we recognize physical pain and treat each symptom separately, we will spend a lot of money on many pills and treatments, and we may temporarily solve the pain, but still have the disease. If we look at the interrelatedness of the painful symptoms, we will identify the disease and focus on that. Then we increase our chances to restore health faster and for less money. Likewise, with our business and social ills, if we continue to see each of them as separate and in need of different funding and programs, we will never have enough resources to do what needs to be done and we will never really deal with the pain.

Frederick Green is president and CEO of Ault Incorporated, a $23 million manufacturer of power supplies. His story speaks strongly to this part of the journey. He has been leading the change effort at Ault Incorporated, and has seen incredible progress and new interrelationships by going through the pain.

Fred Green's Story: Staying the Course

"On a pragmatic basis, I'm helping people take responsibility and become accountable for making the company and their personal lives more successful. Part of that is trying to get a common set of values so that people are as consistent as possible when they make decisions or take action. This is the cornerstone for our total quality efforts, people development, and product and market development. They're all connected.

Our personal lives and work are connected, too. I don't separate my work from the rest of my life. If I'm successful in what I do in the business, then those same things will make the rest of my life successful. If I learn things that make my personal life better, then that is reflected in the business. You can't talk about empowerment, responsibility, and accountability at work and then go home and say, "It's five o'clock now, so I'm no longer empowered, accountable, and responsible." It just doesn't work that way. If the change comes about at work, it will at home, too.

If I had young children now, I think I'd teach them to be more empowered. My children are adults and they're products of who I was. I'm older now and know a little more about life. I've worked hard enough and in lots of places, and I know the old way isn't very effective. I know those results and I've done it the old way long enough. I've seen enough glimmers of hope from going a new way to know that the power of it is so much greater than the other way.

It's very hard, though. It's a tough process and agonizingly slow. It's much harder than I thought it would be. The hardest part is staying the course. I'm impatient to get things done. It's especially hard when I'm trying to be the change agent and I have a vision of where I want to be. I see how the results will be so much different and better. That drives me to be even more impatient to get there. In the process, the rest of the organization probably thinks I'm crazy. Facing that every day, I have to say to myself, "It's going to happen." Then I have to move back from my impatience and help everyone come along. The most important thing I've learned about change is how hard it is.

It's a blind leap of faith when people don't really understand what I'm talking about. And it's frustrating when I can't articulate it in a way they can understand because I don't have anything to show them. It's getting a little easier now because there are more companies who can show what the change has done for them. A few years ago, that wasn't true. I couldn't send employees off to see concrete examples. One trip to Zytec is worth 10 months of my talking.

I don't think people really believe we need to change yet. There's a lot of talk about it, but the vast majority of American businesses and people still don't believe or understand the rationale for it. Some people hide from it. Some see disaster and others see opportunity. I remember visiting two prospective rep firms a number of years ago to determine who we wanted to carry our products. They were in the same market and product area, even right down the street from each other. But there was a world of difference in how they saw the market changes. One saw great opportunity and had lots of ideas, and the other saw hard times and belt tightening.

Even people who are into the change process aren't in it as deep as they think they are or perhaps want to be. I heard the CEO of a major company explain why they have two quality systems. They manage both a total quality process and a traditional system of quality control. They have a major customer whose slogan relates to quality, but they can't sell that customer's field people on total quality practices, so they have to maintain both. ISO 9000 is the same way. I must have spent three hours with the ISO 9000 team leader during the site visit explaining why we didn't have a quality department like he wanted to see—in other words, a traditional quality assurance department. Many are doing quality practices both ways, so they're doing twice the work. Progress is, therefore, slow and very difficult.

It's been a process of 15 years of learning, listening, reading, experimenting for me. It didn't happen overnight. I got started when I visited a couple of Hewlett Packard plants that were pioneers. Just seeing somebody do something different and talk about it started me exploring a new reality. A few years later, on the personal side, I went through a divorce and received some counseling. It allowed me to see myself as others saw me, instead of how I saw myself. I realized I had to bring those two pieces together. In both cases, I found the more we explore, the more we think about change, the more we start acting differently.

We can't continue to take this long to change. I think we're reaching the point where the change process becomes much faster. This happens as the body of knowledge and experience grows. It starts feeding on itself and people cross over the line. I have seen individuals physically cross over; you see it in their energy and excitement. As it builds, we reach a critical mass. Those who don't come naturally will be dragged along or forced out of the organization. Then the rate of change is exponential. It may have taken us 10 years to get to that point, but from there on, it isn't 10 more years to get the same distance. It's more like in one year, we've changed more than we did in 10, and the next year we're changing the same degree in three months.

There's a funny thing about change, though. We don't see ourselves as others do. The change begins to seem natural to us, but doesn't look at all normal to other people. I see this on factory tours all the time. So we don't see how much or how fast we have changed. We need to look for this. It helps us keep going, to have faith.

I'm not sure if that process works for all types of change. I don't know if we will ever solve the issues of diversity. Being Black, I used to say that when a purple Martian comes to the United States, then Blacks will be seen as better than somebody. At its heart, discrimination is the same whether the differences are racial, religious, or conflicts between business functions. It floors me every time I hear the Irish Catholics and Protestants. The same stereotypes and rationales are used there as are used racially.

The same thing happens inside companies, between manufacturing, finance, engineering, and other functions. Each wants to take care of itself, even if it's to the disadvantage of another function, and that's to the detriment of the company. Individual group goals become more important than the company as a whole. This is counterproductive to total group success. The company deteriorates and fails, as do all the subgroups. The same thing holds in races, religions, cultures, and countries.

We have a lot of diversity in this company. We try to face conflict and get people to verbalize what they're thinking. We try to get them to ask if that stereotype is true or not. As human beings, we identify with our group, whatever that definition is. What I try to do is to change the identification of the group. Once we do that, the biases and territorial fighting change. We try to make the group identity focus on Ault Company. Then we need to identify with all Ault members, regardless of differences. That's very powerful. Personally, one of the driving things in my life as a Black person is to affect whatever people thought and felt before they met me. I hope they cannot leave me with the same impression or stereotype that they came in with.

Clearly, the world is going through a great transition and change because of communication and mobility. People from cultures that never saw and touched each other are now doing so, so we're going through a learning process. White America, in particular, needs to learn that the issue is that people are just different, not bad or wrong. That's the only judgment we should make, that someone else is different, not wrong. Once we understand that, with no value judgments, then we can do any number of things.

In some respects, the same thing is going on in world markets. We have a plant in Korea and we spend a lot of time in Asia. As a businessman and a member of the American culture, it appalls me that we have ignored that part of the world to our long-term detriment. We're so European-focused. In terms of potential, Asia has so much more to offer us in growth and revitalization of our economy. How do we break out of this thing, that the world is white European?

Boeing and Coke are two of the few companies who have taken the blinders off and said the world is the world and it is different, but that's all—not good or bad—so we should be doing what we do in the whole world. South American and African markets will follow right behind. They will come. They don't have the money right now. But we may miss them when they come.

So I keep trying to swim upstream on all these change issues. I'm working with a consultant, Rob LeBeau. His research suggests there are some universal values that we can tap into that cross all cultures. Some of them are that people want to be told the truth, to be trusted, to have the opportunity to help each other. I take some solace in that. It gives me hope. We have something in common to build from.

If you believe LeBeau's research, people are inherently risk takers and are receptive to new ideas. We have taught adults to be something other than that. Unfortunately, we still spend our time trying to change our youngsters, to reduce their curiosity and risk-taking attributes. We do this personally as well as in the schools. This weekend, I took my grandchildren on a driving trip. I spent most of my time trying to get them to sit down and be quiet and stop asking questions. We have been conditioned that it's better to keep them quiet. Of course, we adults were also conditioned this way.

If you try to explain everything to them and satisfy all their curiosity, that's hard work. Half the time I'm not sure if they understand what I'm telling them, so that's frustrating. I can't see if they are getting value. Yet we know that everything we tell the mind, it keeps. But how it goes in, how it is used, when it comes out, and how it comes out we don't know. It's an act of faith. We can't point to it or see it. Riding from here to Columbus, Ohio, it's hard to see what value explaining some things has, but it does. It's hard, though.

The same thing is true when we're trying to give people new responsibility at work. They can't take responsibility without asking a thousand questions and so we have to answer. The other way—just telling them what to do—is a lot easier. That's what's so difficult about this method. We have to shift from our role as a teller to a role of answering questions and helping others. It's more work on the front end. We need to trust that it makes a difference.

I think we all have had experiences where someone may not have even known they were changing our lives. Looking back, we recognize turning points that may have seemed insignificant at the time. My parents always made an effort to take us on vacations as much as possible, just to see the country. We went to Washington, D.C., one time. I remember seeing the Capitol, going to the Lincoln Memorial and reading the Gettysburg Address. It gave me a feeling of what could be—the power and awe of all that. At the time, I probably was a pain in the butt to my parents. I'm sure they had no master plan, just exposure, but I soaked it all in. It's all a part of who I am, what I aspire to be, and what I want to do with my life. So we have to have faith and believe in what we cannot see."

7

Getting Started When We Don't Know How

We are all the architects of the future. When you have an
inspiration, take note. It may only come through once.

JACQUELINE SMALL

Endings really are beginnings. This chapter is about how to start
creating changes we want in our lives, our organizations, and the
world. I will offer an iterative process, the Transformation Web,
containing four "power points" for transforming our own lives
and areas of organizational influence. This isn't the typical magic
six-, eight-, or ten-point plan arranged in sequential steps. That's
not reality. The insights I have, the process I offer, and the following stories share a much less orderly and precise structure and
are organic in development. They are more complex and, simultaneously, simpler. They share at least one other common element:
They are based in great respect, even awe, for the capacity of the
human spirit to keep growing.

Most of us have not had much training in how to change ourselves, let alone organizations or the world. If we know we aren't

satisfied and need to do something different that we've never done before, how do we get started? Those who have had training in change management know there's something in addition to all the available knowledge. That's what the stories in this chapter address. Some of what I've learned is that we must dream often and well, learn new skills in exploring what is inside ourselves, ask clearly for support, commit to personal growth, and seek out new models of who and what we want to be. One of my dreams was to write this book. But I asked myself, "Where does such a book start?"

We all grow up learning certain patterns of behavior that work for us. Our experiences and the feedback from many sources teach us a set of beliefs and behavior patterns. Because we have been successful with those patterns, we tend to use them again and again. I had been taught that answers come from experts. I grew up learning that research and writing involved constructing an outline; telling the reader the message in the beginning, middle, and end; providing the appropriate testimonials and data; and following the rules of formal, professional writing. So to write this book, I set about my new task using my proven methods.

It fell dead.

Every time I tried to write something using this approach, it felt as though it had already been said. I'd try again. Again, nothing. I was willing to explore my beliefs that were locking me into this process. I realized I needed to look at my system of gathering data and insights. I had been ignoring evidence and answers that might be inside me and my prospective readers, so I shifted gears. I tried some changes in my system. Then I was off and running. That had life.

When I examined the microcosm of my process and that of the people and companies in this book, I found some hidden commonalities in process and in major intervention points that seem to be the source of power for the shift. I've chosen the image of the spiderweb (see Figure 7-1), because it comes from the wisest and most enduring of teachers—Nature. She teaches us to remember the constant interactive, relational, and patterning laws of all life.

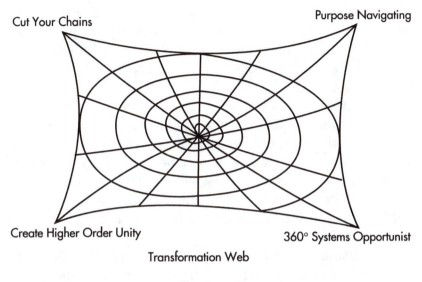

Cut Your Chains

Purpose Navigating

Create Higher Order Unity

360° Systems Opportunist

Transformation Web

Figure 7-1

Models and processes are instructive when they provide enough shape to help us move into focus on an issue and take action. They can be wasteful when they create a set of hurdles to jump and the correctness of the jumping becomes our goal. I have seen quality efforts get derailed because of a focus on correct use of all the tools, rather than on improvement for the customer. Anything involving life is not controllable and reducible this way. I encourage you to think of this process as a web with multiple choices open at any point in time unique to your needs, but offering you some navigation along the way.

The process can start at any of the four power points: Cut Your Chains, Practice Purpose Navigation, Become a 360° Systems Opportunist, and Create Higher-Order Unity. Find the one that has the most energy for or affinity with you. It will eventually lead to the others in the right sequence to serve you. I'll begin with Cutting Your Chains because that's what happened in my writing example.

One way to recognize we need to start here is if we are relatively clear about our dreams and purpose, but are feeling stuck. We begin to get excited about the possibilities, but our fears start undermining the ideas before they have a chance to form. It's all the "Yes, but," "I wish, but I can't," and "Get real" messages we give ourselves and receive from others. Or it's when we try something and it doesn't work and we begin to lose our courage.

These beliefs, messages, and fears are chains that bind us as individuals, teams, neighbors, or organizations. They chain our thinking and behavior to the past and present, and threaten our ability to forge a new future. They are the beliefs we acquired as children and young adults. We need to review them to see if they really are still serving us.

Chains is a strong word. It is the exact image I get, though, when I coach many people about pursuing their dreams. Their beliefs are so strong that they might as well be chained to a tree with the dream 10 feet beyond the chain length. The biggest problem is they don't see these as chains that can be cut. They see them as some ultimate, unchangeable reality. To cut our chains, we first have to be able to see them, name them, and know we can choose to keep or let go of them.

Richard Leider and David Shapiro discuss one version of this point in their book, *Repacking Your Bags: Lightening Your Load for the Rest of Your Life.* Leider describes a trek through the Serengeti Plains of East Africa. After walking for miles with a new, high-tech, and very heavy backpack, he noticed his African guide's interest in it. Leider proceeded to take the whole backpack apart and show the guide all the amazing stuff he brought along.

After reviewing it, the guide turned to him and asked, "Does all this make you happy?" Leider says this question spurred some serious review and reassessment that led to a much lighter pack. More than this, he carried the question into a review of his own life.

Leider had to spread out all his stuff to see it. We need to spread our beliefs out, as well as the material accumulation that goes with them. There are many ways to do this. Some people can just sit down and start reflecting and writing. Other people need to ask friends and support groups for help and involve themselves in discussion. Many good books and articles provide food for thought and exercises. Workshops, retreats, and resource people also offer information and a structure for exploration.

Various tests on styles, personalities, and preferences can be an external, objective source of data about ourselves to generate new insights, as long as we don't start thinking they provide a complete picture of us. And there are many types of counseling available. At some point, though, it has to be just you going inside yourself, because that's where the answers are. No one else has the keys that you have to do that.

This isn't a process of throwing everything away and starting over. It is a review and opening-up process. If you know the answer to your sense of purpose and your dreams, look at what is in the way of pursuing them. Keep looking for the fundamental root cause beliefs around these blocks and you'll find one or two core chains.

The process just described is fairly intellectual. In reality, emotions play a heavy role in this. To move forward often requires us to let go of something, let it die, or let it sit on the sidelines for a while. At the same time I was looking at my research and writing process, I had to admit my normal approach wasn't working and deal with my frustration and sense of inadequacy about that. I had to let go of it.

As John Schaaf from American Paging pointed out in Chapter 4, we need to take responsibility for having contributed to the situation we are in. This is true of everyone and almost everything. Some of the habits and skills that have brought us to our current jobs may not help us to do a new job, or may even undermine us. There are deep feelings tied in with taking this kind of responsibility and doing this sort of self-assessment. It takes humility and courage.

I've seen quite a few articles about how we are becoming a nation of victims interested in blaming someone or something other than ourselves for whatever isn't working. I fear there is truth in this. We won't have the breakthroughs I am discussing if we stay stuck in that mode. Only when we simultaneously deal with the emotions can we let go of the old beliefs and behaviors. Sometimes we want to throw away the old patterns and we should. Other times, we don't need to throw them away. We need to learn there are other alternatives for different situations.

Once we accept having to let go, the other piece of the launching pad is to see something familiar we can hold on to through the change. It makes it easier. Research on how people learn suggests that we learn most easily and retain what we learn when we can connect the new with the old. This is based in the physiological and biochemical reality of how information is stored in the brain. Emotionally, we often need a link to the familiar as well. It makes us feel grounded.

Both Tony Andersen and Bill George, in Chapters 3 and 4, discussed how important it is to have stability while going through change. One of the main reasons so much training doesn't "take" or last is that learners have become too passive. We expect the teacher, expert, trainer, facilitator to do it for us. If we don't learn, we assume it was their fault. Yet no one can do this crucial step of connecting to the familiar except the learner, because the familiar is unique to each of us.

This is a benefit of clarity about our sense of purpose. It can give us the sense of stability and constancy we need. Purpose Navigation has to do with cultivating not only the conviction that we have purpose but also inner navigational tools called values, virtues, or gut feelings that we can go back to again and again. I emphasize conviction even more than articulation because many of us will never have the perfect written statement, but we will have the inner sense of it.

I have written extensively about purpose in previous chapters. What I emphasize here is that purpose is very real, powerful, and connected to the well-being of others. It is fitting for authors or speakers to be challenged about the source of their data. Someone once asked me if I could prove my assertion about purpose. The answer of course is "No"—at least not the way he meant. He then went on to ask me, "What if, at the end of your life, you find out you were wrong? There is no purpose. There is no God."

My answer was and is, "I think I would have lived a better life and come closer to my sense of a good life than to have lived out of the other option." From a totally practical perspective, I look at the consequences of the alternative beliefs. If we were to choose to live out of the belief that there is no purpose, that we are a molecular accident, that life is meaningless, we may as well act out of selfishness and get it while the getting is good. We'd have a really sorry world ready to self-destruct. We're close enough to that now.

Theologian Andrew Greenley has said it well:

> It seems to me that in the last analysis there are only two choices: Macbeth's contention that life is a tale told by an idiot, full of sound and fury and signifying nothing and Pierre Teilhard's "something is afoot in the universe, something that looks like gestation and birth." Either there is a plan and purpose—and that plan and purpose can best be expressed by the words "life" and "love"—or we live in a cruel, arbitrary, and deceptive cosmos in which our lives are a brief transition between two oblivions.

We do get to choose.

The second question I hear about purpose is, "Does this mean we are cogs in a machine, that we have no free will, that we are predestined?" No, I don't think so. It's one of those mysteries and paradoxes of life. It's like our political system. We simultaneously have freedom and responsibilities. There are no rights without corresponding responsibility. And we have tons of choices daily to prove this out. More and more people, for example, are intrigued with the idea of meaningful coincidence, which is a manifestation of this paradox. The sense of meaning and a higher presence in life is there, but there is no coercion implied.

These first two power points are interrelated and are feedback loops to each other. They work with and reinforce each other. The more you cut your chains, the more free you are to fulfill your purpose. The more you get excited about your purpose, the more the motivation to cut your chains.

The third power point is developing skills as a 360° Systems Opportunist. The idea here is to learn to look full circle, from many vantage points and perspectives. We tend to put on blinders and look down tunnels. When we do this, we block out the most creative possibilities that are often exactly what we need. Susan James talked about this phenomenon in Chapter 3: "I notice that when I am feeling fear, it affects my thinking. I start thinking broadly and then it gets narrower and narrower. It's hard for me to keep the walls from closing in."

The application comes when we want to make some change in our lives or in our organization. We tend to want to attack the problem head on. Often we want to do about a dozen things at once and we can be overwhelmed by the magnitude of it all. Then we start running into the chains of time, money, and other constraints.

We need the skill to look for common solutions to diverse problems and needs instead of separate solutions to every problem. This requires a sensitivity to the larger system and a broad awareness of diverse areas. It means recognizing the unifying potential in a diversity of needs and perspectives. Being an opportunist means taking the initiative to start this on your own.

In our greatest successes, this often happens by accident, that is, without forethought. It's that sense that a whole bunch of things came together as if by magic or that one act brought many more benefits than anticipated. I see it operating in the story of Sandy Miller and Schott Corporation in Chapters 4 and 6. I've experienced it in my role as a marketing manager and team leader for a major customer improvement. We found a way to increase customer satisfaction, increase market share, cut costs, and improve employee satisfaction with one action.

I've also applied it in my personal life by making one major decision that allowed me to be a better and more available mother, while cutting costs for myself and my clients and increasing my flexibility and satisfaction. Anne Morrow Lindbergh describes this as a feeling of "living in grace . . . where one seems to carry all one's tasks before one lightly."

Power point four is Creating Higher-Order Unity out of diversity and conflict. This is going beyond conflict resolution. Steve Wikstrom's and Fred Green's stories in Chapters 1 and 6 illustrate elements of what this means. It's the ability to realize that many perspectives can be right at the same time, even when they seem to be in opposition to each other. What is needed is a shift from the battlefield approach and either/or thinking that says we have to pick which perspective, person, or group is right. There is great opportunity through the integration of opposites to create something totally new. Nature teaches this; fire and water create steam.

There are some powerful practices in the Native American tradition that are instructive on how to do this. They involve taking the power of the circle and recognizing or assigning different perspectives around it, all of which must be honored. In this tradition, people assume the voice of each perspective and try to speak from within that larger context, rather than just from their personal views.

A superficial form of this can be found within our management training and development programs. There are role-plays on wearing different hats, or eye perception exercises where people see different images in a picture. I do not say "superficial" in a derogatory way. I have used these methods myself and they are helpful, but they do not engage the whole person the way the tribal practices do. In particular, they leave out the heart and spirit.

Points 3 and 4 are very synergistic. The more you look at systems from a 360° perspective, the more you see the opposing sides and the need for an integrative higher-order question and solution. It works the other way as well. If we are within conflict, it is imperative that we learn to look out at the larger system and circle of perspectives and needs.

The intangible work we do in Purpose Navigation and Cutting Our Chains creates energy that needs to be focused and used or it dissipates. Seeing from a 360° perspective provides the opportunities, focus, and discipline for point 1, and point 3 does the same for point 2. The full-system effect is inspiration, energy, empowerment, commitment, challenge, and innovation. With that, you begin to draw others to you with a powerful force.

The following stories are about individual and organizational processes for change that are consistent with being more whole human beings and demonstrate aspects of the Transformation Web. Several stories are about the unique experiences of an individual or a company. Others are the reflections of people who have assisted many individuals and many companies through change or growth processes.

Gail Straub and David Gershon are cofounders of the Empowerment Workshop, as well as husband and wife. They have used and worked with the concept and reality of empowerment at its profound levels for almost 15 years, long before it was on the top-10 list of organizational topics. At this deeper level, empowerment is about taking responsibility for the creation of our own lives in the way I have been discussing.

Straub and Gershon have two different roles to play in this book. One is that their own lives model many of the areas we have explored. Gail Straub describes how a personal action, their marriage, resulted in the creation of the Empowerment Workshop, which has touched people all over the world. We have discussed vision and the ability to make vision become real. In 1986, their shared vision and teamwork resulted in the founding and organizing of the First Earth Run, under the banner of the United Nation's Year of Peace. A lighted torch was passed around the world with more than 25 million people and 45 heads of state in 62 countries participating in an expression of harmony. I was deeply touched by a videotape of this run, because it reminded me of the power of individuals with a dream. David Gershon is also the visionary behind the Global Action Plan described by Anita Ryan in Chapter 6.

Their second role in this book is to share their learning about how to help people get started in creating the changes they desire. They've seen and supported thousands of individual change efforts, and have worked with organizations as well. Their work adds depth to my discussion of Navigational Purpose and Cutting Your Chains.

In their workshops and their book, *Empowerment: The Art of Creating Your Life As You Want It*, Gershon and Straub discuss our "inner soil." They use the metaphor of soil and plants. We are the plants and have new growing edges continually emerging, which are our growth and change issues. Our inner soil consists of the core beliefs that shape the way we live. That soil may or may not nourish us, because we acquired our beliefs before we had "developed filters that allow us to discriminate between helpful and unhelpful beliefs."

It strikes me that throughout history, all those who have given thought to how to live a "good life" have been exploring some form of our inner soil, regardless of what they called it. The Greeks used the terminology, the "Good Life." For Socrates, life was about "Knowing Thyself" in relationship to the good city—that is, our community. He explored that and the virtues associated with it. There are other versions of the good life. There are the Ten Commandments, the Beatitudes, and the seven gifts of the Holy Spirit from the Bible. Some visionaries have looked, instead, at what takes away from the good life; Mahatma Gandhi described these things as the Seven Deadly Sins.

The Buddha teaches a path of salvation, the Noble Eightfold Path: right views, right aspiration, right speech, right conduct, right means to livelihood, right endeavor, right mindfulness, and right meditation. The *Tao Te Ching* is often called the *Book of Integrity* and *The Way*. Benjamin Franklin never finished his book, *The Art of Virtue*. It was to be his formula for successful living. In Native American culture, the Medicine Wheel explained much about the path of life. More recently, Steven Covey has explored the issue of principles and character in his books, *Seven Habits of Highly Effective People* and *Principle Centered Leadership*.

Under these diverse names and interwoven with our beliefs are some common, very basic things like trust, integrity, justice, humility, and self-responsibility, to name a few. The simplest word I know to denote things like these is the word *virtue*. Virtue has to do with goodness, ethics, integrity, excellence, quality. Other words that come to mind are value, worth, meaning. We speak of a virtuous person as the "salt of the earth," "one in a million," a "jewel." As I understand life, I see part of our inner soil to be a set of virtues. We are born with sparks for many virtues. Which ones we choose to ignite and to what degree affects the quality of our lives and the lives of all those around us. It's on this bedrock that we have created our current life and organization. And it is through tilling this soil that we can create more of who we could be. Change rises out of who we are, rather than what we do.

Gail Straub and David Gershon's Story: The Art of Empowerment

---

David Gershon: In a personal sense, what empowerment means is helping an individual realize that they have the power to take responsibility for their life. We help people see that they have more choices than they give themselves credit for. We work with the seven areas of life: emotions, relationships, sexuality, body, money, work, and spirituality. We help people explore their choices and give them skills for moving toward the vision they create.

Gail Straub: There is never a training session in which I am not greatly moved by the courage of people to change incredibly difficult things in their work, family, and spiritual life, as well as issues related to all the seven different areas we work with. When I hear their stories and see their progress, I know we are providing a true service. I know that the human spirit is indomitable.

Thousands of people have gone through the Empowerment Workshop. In the first several years we offered it in the United States and Canada. Then there was an invitation to present it in Europe, Russia, Singapore, and other parts of Asia. Now I am doing a lot of work in China with the model. About a year and a half ago, we published a book based on the workshop, called *Empowerment: The Art of Creating Your Life As You Want It*. It is translated in seven languages now, including Russian and Chinese. We began doing the workshop in the Soviet Union before the changes there, and it was a marvelous experience to help open that country up.

We see incredible changes going on in people and we receive hundreds of letters telling us what has been achieved. I guess the number of people who come back for a second session or who move on to our other offerings, like the Art of Empowerment, Advanced Empowerment, Empowerment in Organizations, and Fire in the Soul, is a form of testimonial. Several of these workshops were developed at the request of our attendees.

David Gershon: What we do first, in a variety of ways, is suggest that people ask themselves, "What do I want?" Then they start opening up options. Once that happens, we begin to develop a process to deal with what comes up when people start to go for their visions. People often have barriers or limiting beliefs that get in the way of moving forward. These need to be dealt with, so we help people develop the tools to do that.

There is often an assumption that growth always has to be painful, but it doesn't. Growth has many emotional textures. Sometimes dislocation causes pain, but it can also cause a sense of exhilaration, a sense of delight and joy, a sense of newfound energy in creativity. We use the image of the growing edge in our workshops. We see each person having ever more new growing edges. When a seed comes through the earth, it can encounter a root or a rock, or it can go straight up and see the light of day for the first time. You can have a variety of emotions on the path of growth. Pain is one of them, sometimes. We aren't limited to that response.

My definition of empowerment for organizations is to create an environment that will enable its people to be more productive, creative, and fulfilled. There are many more levels of complexity in an organization because it already has a set of strong beliefs and expectations about what's possible. We need to work more strategically to pull this off and we have to start with those who are responsible for the corporate belief systems about what is possible. It doesn't always have to be initiated at the senior management or the CEO level, but it does have to evolve to that level. It can be initiated at middle management, but then it has to work its way up and get that buy-in to be corporate-wide. On the other hand, it can be done divisionally or departmentally.

The real shift is in managers. Their primary identity can't be based on controlling and having power. It has to be shifted to the satisfaction of helping others in growing, expanding, and being fulfilled. Through their personal empowerment efforts, there develops enough sense of self, generosity, and self-esteem, so there is the willingness to do this for others. I have come to appreciate how superficially the concept of empowerment is used in organizations. At the same time, I know how vital it is and how challenging it is to pull off in an organization.

Gail Straub: A key to pulling it off is that it must be done from a multidimensional perspective. Our workshop is based on this. The fun part of that story is that David and I met in 1980, fell madly in love, got married, and what we knew immediately was that our common purpose was empowerment. So we spent the first year of our being together developing the training. We came from very different backgrounds. David had a strong background in business and finance. His spiritual path had been mostly in the Eastern tradition.

I had a strong background in relationship and sexuality counseling. My spiritual path had been more Western. So we merged our skills and talents, which were very different, but which made a whole. We created a double marriage, in a sense, and created our first child, the Empowerment Workshop. What's interesting is that we didn't realize how powerful the vehicle was until years and years later.

One of our philosophies is that if we have a multidimensional, eclectic way of learning, then someone who learns through a mental framework can really have a wonderful time. But the person who sits next to him or her, who changes through the physical, can also have a good experience. In other words, there are modes that are mental and intellectual, modes that are emotional and feeling, modes that are physical and kinesthetic and modes that are spiritual or what I call "interior." The more multidimensional the learning process, the more inspired people are to change.

When you look at business, all this holds true and goes further. Many of the most effective vehicles for change involve balancing the masculine and feminine archetypes. The American culture is a very masculine culture. We are brilliant analytically, we are product oriented, efficient, and timely. We need these skills to function as a human family.

We also need the feminine, which is the heart. In a business setting, you could call it the process. So a humane process is one in which the workers are in clear communication; they feel cared for, nurtured, and valued, all qualities of the feminine. This allows for a product to be created with great passion, clarity, efficiency, and intellectual brilliance. So we have this incredible opportunity to learn within our businesses, within our own personal lives, how to honor that partnership. It's a big agenda. We're talking about becoming whole.

Given the right support and the right skills, I deeply believe that there is a primordial impulse to change, to grow, to find more meaning, to understand, to have quality. I have seen this in our Russian and Chinese friends who have grown up in a Communist system, and in our friends here in the West. Our backgrounds are very different, but if we are alive, if the spark is still ignited, if we haven't gone to sleep or sold out spiritually, people are much alike and can do incredible things."

Guy Schoenecker is founder, president, and CEO of BI Inc., formerly known as Business Incentives. BI Inc. is a service business focused on assisting companies to improve their people's performance. They won the Minnesota Quality Award in 1994. It's a story about finding purpose, growing with it, and keeping a sense of constancy within that growth. It illustrates Navigational Purpose at work and the ability to look in the 360° Opportunistic fashion I have suggested.

It's also a spiritual story. This is one of the newer sets of ditches we will have to learn to walk between, to use Steve Wikstrom's metaphor from Chapter 1. We need to learn how to talk about spirituality publicly, while respecting the boundaries of privacy and the separate issue of religion. Few of us have had much experience doing this. Tom Peters, Bill George, and others have traded thoughts in newspapers and magazines on the appropriateness of spirituality being brought into business.

In my mind, it isn't an issue of whether it should be in business. It's part of who we are and it's already in business in some form. The issue is to communicate more fully and clearly who we are because that affects everything. I have begun to talk about virtues when I speak of spirituality. That is a larger framework than a specific religion.

I think Guy Schoenecker's story is particularly important to illustrate the meaning and implementation of constancy of purpose in our personal lives and in the life of a company. Here, in the microcosm of one person's life, we can see some of the essential dynamics of what happens in a company. Many of our companies struggle with constancy of purpose. I recall the example in Steve Wikstrom's story in Chapter 1 about someone asking an executive from another company if he really believed his company would hold on to their purpose once the going got tough. The answer was, "Probably not." Our employees don't trust us and many leaders aren't sure if, in a changing competitive world, they can promise that anything will stay the same. What does it really mean to have constancy of purpose? Does it make a difference? What does it take to do it? We struggle with this.

A number of insights came to my mind as I listened to Schoenecker. I intend to mull over several thoughts about purpose and its relationship to virtues. Faith, hope and trust are very close kin. They give birth to courage. A poem that captures some of the wholeness of this for me is "Desiderata":

> . . . You are a child of the universe, no less than the trees and
> the stars; you have a right to be here. And whether or not
> it is clear to you, no doubt the universe is unfolding as it should.
> Therefore be at peace with God, whatever you conceive Him to
> be, and whatever your labors and aspirations, in the noisy
> confusion of life keep peace with your soul. With all its sham,
> drudgery and broken dreams, it is still a beautiful world.
> Be careful. Strive to be happy.
>
> ST. PAUL'S CHURCH 1692

Purpose and constancy are also commitments. They are commitments to the spirit of an agreement rather than the concrete specifics. People are much more flexible and forgiving when they sense the spirit of an agreement is continuing, even when the specifics have to change. We need this in a rapidly changing world, or we lose trust and the ability to adapt. Schoenecker's company has changed dramatically in products, services, customers, and size, but has been very constant about spirit. This kind of behavior is the living out of the virtue of integrity. In biblical times, it was thought of as purity.

Commitment also implies exercising the virtue of responsibility in relationship to ourselves and to others. It's not a taking-care-of type responsibility, it's more the sense of a quote I read once: "The greatest good we can do for others is not just to share our riches with them but to reveal theirs to themselves." This is what seems to go on in BI Inc.

Purpose comes full circle. We need to give a return for what we have received. Tithing happened to be the process for Schoenecker, but beneath that are the virtues of generosity and mercy in many forms. Intricately bound up with those is the virtue of poverty. We often take that to mean we are supposed to be materially poor. As a virtue, the meaning is much broader. It means not to be controlled by, owned by, or dependent on material possessions. In this sense, we can live very comfortably and yet be free of possessions. Then we are more free to share, to have a generous spirit. We don't live in fear of losing things.

Guy Schoenecker's Story: Constancy in Purpose

"We continue to work on defining our purpose as the company changes. We searched for the root word that would give us meaning and substance and we have found it in the word *performance*. We came to the conclusion that to communicate, to learn, to measure, and to reward were the four core drivers that affect behavior and invite good performance. We bring techniques, knowledge, tools, and skills to companies to help their people improve their performance through those four drivers. And we bring incredible creativity and energy to that.

Performance is a very meaningful word to me. Ever since Adam and Eve, the issue has been performance. In a sense, it's the output of our lives, the final act. I love what this company does. It gives me a great sense of deep purpose. There's not another one that is identical to it. We have come a long way, though, from our origins. I started by selling diamonds to returning GIs at the University of St. Thomas so I could put myself through college.

I studied political science and philosophy as an undergraduate and then received a Bachelor of Science in Law degree from the University of Minnesota. When I was in the middle of pre-law, I couldn't decide if I should finish law school and get my doctor of jurisprudence or not. I really loved the mental discipline that went with law, as I loved philosophy and speculation, but I didn't want to practice law. I went into a real zonk and said, "What the hell is my purpose? What am I doing? What do I want to do?" It was undefinable.

I was living in Ireland Hall, and I went over to the chapel at the college and sat in the back pew. I remember it very well. It was quite dark in there. As I sat there, I said some of the normal, learned prayers but . . . no miracles happened. So I sat. I remember thinking, "This doesn't make sense to me. I don't know where to go. I'm in no-man's-land. I don't have a vocation. I know that I don't want to be a lawyer. I don't think I should go home and work in Dad's business with him. I don't want to go work for a big corporation. I just don't know what to do."

As I just began to freewheel my thoughts, I realized that I had not had much control over any of the big issues in my life. For instance, I didn't have any control over my birth. I had no input into it, but all of a sudden, I was. Another issue I have no control over is my life. In me is a flame or an essence called life, that I can't understand worth a darn. I have never seen it, I only see the result of it, but it's there. The third issue is death. I didn't choose to be born, I don't really understand life, and I have to die, and I have no control over that. So it seemed like the three biggest things in my life, I had no control over.

So then I said to myself, "It's kind of dumb for me to be sitting here asking what will I do with my life when I have no control over the most fundamental issues." So I said, "OK, Lord, you did the other three, so I am going to give this one to you, too. I don't know what I should be, I don't know where you want me, but I am going to go along totally with giving it to you. But you can't be subtle with me because I don't pick up subtle signals. I'm intuitive, but my awareness level will miss it for sure." That was kind of the essence of what took place that day.

From there, it seemed to me that things began to happen. I believe deeply that no prayer is ever unanswered. I have no doubt about that. They aren't always answered the way we would like to see them answered, but in some way, that's sometimes a mystery to all of us, they are answered. I would bump into people that I shouldn't have bumped into and didn't know but who really came to matter. I would get into situations that were clearly different and would change the direction of the things that I was doing. This company is now about 43 years old and has grown and changed significantly through this process.

I don't think I expected a clear picture. I expected direction and a natural evolution. Natural Theology was probably the most interesting course I took in college. It taught me that things evolve naturally. It made the existence of the Creator a reality that I could accept by natural reason, not just by faith alone, and that happened to be good for me. I knew that my purpose would evolve. I wasn't looking for a fixed deal. I wasn't saying "I'll join the Army and that will be it."

When I look back on my business career, I think that experience in the chapel gave me purpose. Today I ask myself, "Do I like this business? Do I really want to continue coming to work in the morning and dealing with these thousand people and their problems and my concerns for them? Do I want to continue to pay the price to lead?" And I can answer that very clearly; I can say, "Yes." I feel God planted me here, this is where I'm supposed to be. When I'm supposed to be somewhere else, I will be somewhere else. There have been many difficult times, as there are in all lives and in all businesses, because life ebbs and flows. When things are looking troublesome, then I remember that this is where I was planted, so I'd better work my way through it. So this whole experience for me has continuity; it gave me a real sense of purpose on the career side.

My priorities in life are also clear. They are God, Family, and Career, in that order. That is plastered in my briefcase as a reminder, and I make sure that my activities fit those priorities. I'm not a good joiner anymore, because of that. I have belonged to many organizations in my life. I made a list of all of them at one point and decided that they did not fit my goals, so I resigned from most of them. I said I was not going to participate; it was wearing me out for nothing. When I am focused, my performance is better and I am more satisfied.

I like the people I work with. I like the problem solving that takes place between groups of people, so that no one has to carry a problem around alone. We like to sit down and talk about problems with whoever wants to talk about them. In a sense, the business is my extended family. It is an extension of my ministry in life to be in this business. I was given a very creative mind and this is where I am supposed to be, to exercise whatever talents I can.

I think helping people to grow is very important. I don't mean that in a light sense. The biggest impact I can have on people is through this environment. They bring with them all the baggage from their past life and all of today's problems. Each one of them has a load of some kind or another. So when they come here, I want them to have a collaborative, supportive environment that makes this portion of life a good thing.

So many of the ways we behave in business, churches, and other institutions is not at all the way a functional family would behave. We also are affected by our legal system and the definitions of employer and employee rights, which are often antagonistic. All these things become institutionalized and the systems begin to run the show. What we're trying to do here is let the people and their needs run the show. Working toward that is a special accomplishment.

I believe very strongly in the concept that this is a community of people. When we invite people to join this community called BI, there's a certain set of values that are part of that. Unless the person who joins us can line up with those values and feel comfortable with them, either the group will force them out or they will force themselves out. I think that just happens. We see that happen in schools, organizations, and churches. If we don't fit, we don't fit and we all know it.

My role in this community is to be one of the responsible leaders. To be a leader is to be a human being who appreciates other human beings and accepts the responsibility of having to set a mission, a vision and direction. I am talking about the whole concept of leadership, whether you are an informal or a formal leader. The concept of a CEO as the only leader really irks me. I have watched too many CEOs of major corporations become absolute egomaniacs. I consider that nonleadership. There's too much self-aggrandizement with corporate jets and compensation and things like that. I have seen some executives make a decision in a flick that could affect half the company, and then they walk away and look for a job with another company. That is not responsible leadership.

Sadly, there's a difference between the law and justice and sometimes it's a big space. Justice exists out there and the law is always trying to catch up, and it never seems to get there. What happens with all these situations is that they offend our sense of justice and fair play. That is hurtful. The same is true in business. Sometimes there is a big gap between power and responsible leadership. That, also, is very hurtful.

I continue to learn about responsibility, too. I had started making retreats when I was in college and I have continued for 40 years. Some time ago, while I was on retreat, I was thinking about how well things were going. I have a big family and they're being well supported. The business was growing and fun. I have been responsible. I know what is right and what is wrong. I don't always do what's right but, generally speaking, I do. I have worked at being a good father and husband. But, I realized, I haven't given back. I began being bothered by the idea of tithing. I don't know why tithing and I don't know where it came from.

I had mortgages and I owed the bank a ton of money and I had all kinds of reasons for not doing it. I had a selfish struggle. I didn't want to do it. I wanted to see that money in the bank or use it to pay the loan down or whatever. This thing just hounded me. It was like the hound of heaven. I had to ask, "Can I really trust all the way?" Finally I said, "I've got to take a leap of faith. Life is a constant leap of faith, so just do it and that's it. I am going to give my whole life, not just my career, to the Lord and reinforce the fact that my life does have purpose and that I am where I'm supposed to be."

We started tithing personally and for the business, and that seemed to complete the circle. Before that, it was kind of a curve and it needed to come about. There needed to be a payback because we had been so blessed. The business tithes back to the University of St. Thomas, where we have had the privilege of providing scholarships for 350 or more students. We also tithe to a Lutheran Home in Wisconsin that houses 1,000 retarded children, and to the Hospitality House that works in the Black community, and to the Salvation Army. The payback to us has been tremendous, emotionally and intellectually.*"*

Magaly Rodriguez is the founder and president of Rapid Change Technologies, Inc. She speaks about the paradox of change. Like Gershon and Straub, she has two roles to play here—the learning we may share through her own life, and her experience working with change in a wide range of environments. She has encountered global change and world diversity from the time she was a child. Her work speaks strongly to the power points of Higher-Level Unity and Becoming a 360° Systems Opportunist.

Rodriguez's learnings in life began in Havana, Cuba: her family fled that country after the revolution. She has been a resident of Germany, Panama, the Dominican Republic, and the United States. She has been a consultant on organizational change to some of the largest corporations in America. She has also worked with people suffering from violence, poverty, drugs, and the slave-like life of migrant laborers. I learned that the needs of people in corporate America aren't that distinct from these other groups. The change process is very similar.

Rodriguez's life provides a model of another set of virtues that is critical in our time. In the last story about Guy Schoenecker, we looked at the virtue of poverty as freedom from being owned by our material possessions. The other side of this virtue has to do with caring for those who are suffering or disadvantaged. We usually think of this in a material or physical sense. We think of the poor, abuse victims, teenage mothers, or the physically handicapped. But it's much broader. We're all suffering in some way, some of us less observably than others. When we support a friend through a painful divorce, treatment for cancer, or a layoff, we're caring for the suffering. There is much suffering in corporate America that's hidden inside the individuals who work there.

Rodriguez works with corporations suffering from what I'd call the poverty of spiritlessness and addiction to the logical. Both these forms of suffering have been described throughout this book. The symptoms range from a lack of meaning in work, to deprivation of emotions and spirit, to the squelching of creativity, to a belief that everything is logical and sequential. Magaly Rodriguez works with this through paradox, which, according to the dictionary, is a true statement that seems to contradict itself.

This is another virtue we need to rediscover—a sense of wonder and awe. We need to relearn how to make the ordinary extraordinary, how to be filled with awe at a sunrise, to see the world in the face of every child, and to see wisdom in every wrinkle. Children are this way naturally. They often reawaken this in their parents, if the parents allow it. I remember a cartoon of a child looking at a sunbeam and seeing an angel's robe, a magical slide, and other wonders. The parent commented something like, "Wow! A moment ago, all I saw was dust."

This type of simple shift reawakens love for all life and can provide the fuel for the more difficult behavior shifts. Because the world is not three feet in diameter and, therefore, not recognized for its wonder (see the poem in Chapter 5), we need to see the world in our daily lives and find awe and wonder there. Every one of us needs to be appreciated as extraordinary, if we are to exert ourselves to be extraordinary. And that is what is needed at this time. Then the journey is filled with more possibility and joy.

Part of what Rapid Change Technologies is about is helping people learn to delight in themselves, to delight in each other, and to challenge themselves to be more. It is also about helping people find enough humility to be able to listen to each other and learn new things. When we are filled with ourselves, our ego, our needs, and our ideas, it's pretty hard for anything else to break through. Humility really means creating space for learning and growth. Rodriguez does this with a gentleness and patience that's inspiring.

I'm reminded of an archetypal story that I've modified to fit here. There was an Expert who had great experience and knowledge. Now, it came to pass that the Expert heard of a Great Teacher in the land. He was torn as to whether to visit this Teacher or to decide it would be a waste of time. Finally, with the urging of colleagues, he journeyed to see her. He talked to her and the assembled group of other learners. After even the shortest comment from the Teacher, the Expert became very animated expressing his observations. After a day of this, he stopped and in disappointment observed, "I have enjoyed this day, but I have not learned anything new. I have been sharing my wisdom with you." The Teacher gave him a glass full of water and picked up a pitcher. She began to fill the overflowing glass, spilling on his hand and the table. The Expert dropped the glass and exclaimed, "What do you think you're doing?" The Teacher said, "It's hard to give anything new to a glass that is already full."

How do we become more gentle, inspiring, humble? Where do these virtues come from? My experience is that they are developed in two ways—by practice and by insight. The spark for each virtue is there, a gift from the day we were born. Our task is to practice it, to ask ourselves, "How would I look if I were gentle in the process of doing my work?" Most often, we have some idea of that and we can just do it. We can enhance that practice by gaining more of the insight that comes from exploration and from asking for feedback. We need a safe harbor to dialogue with others about their understanding of not just the concept of these virtues, but of the ways to live them. Given the multitude of support groups, salons, and other group formations, the opportunity is available to us to create such a place. We could find all we need to know in ourselves and the diversity in each other.

Magaly Rodriguez's Story: The Paradox of Change

"Much of our work is a paradox. We find that that which is personal drives the business, that what is known as the right (receptive) brain drives the left (active) brain, the metaphorical drives logic, and that which may seem nonproductive drives productivity. Basically, we have discovered that the intangibles drive the tangibles. In our western paradigm, we think that action is the only important thing there is, so we don't pay attention to listening, resting, receptivity, and relationships. Business relies heavily on words to generate actions, and that mode only works a fraction of the time. That's why we have learned to rely on many right-brained technologies or tools to improve relationships, which generates actions rapidly, spontaneously, and more creatively.

Our work is based on brain research undertaken by Paul McLean, which has shown that only 7 percent of the impact on the brain in any interaction is from the words that are used. Ninety-three percent of an interaction and message is nonword vocals and body language. Business ignores the 93 percent to a large extent, whereas we focus on that 93 percent. So we get results that others don't get, and we get them through means that are hard for business to accept.

Very often, companies try our approach because they have no other place to go. They have tried it all and nothing has worked. They have tried training, business consultants, cost cutting, and layoffs. They have tried quality, incentive systems, and other approaches. None of them have worked well enough. In many places, we have been the last resort. They don't have anything to lose and this is the last shot. They find, within a very short period of time, that things turn around and there's new energy. Where there was no hope, there is new hope. Then they begin to believe in paradox.

In some places, we have had to try to change the organization without even being allowed to talk about the business issues. We recently had this situation with a client. They were manufacturing a daily average of nine units when we came in. They needed a significant increase in that number, as well as quality improvements. Within a six-month period, they were averaging 14 units. We worked with their operators and could never discuss the business at all because of a hostile union. That change was driven by getting people to understand who they were as individuals and who they could be.

If that happened a couple of times, one could say it was a coincidence, but when it happens time after time, it's clear there is a relationship that hasn't been recognized about how to create change. Our fundamental assumption is that people either hinder or help any type of organizational change, so we start with people. We speed change through the indirect route. The direct route of driving exclusively through business-related tasks may seem faster, but there are often swamps and quicksand in the middle of the direct path of action. By contrast, the indirect path of people contains the key to change. People will create the safest, fastest path when they feel valued.

That's the big key. The personal makes the business. If people don't feel like valued human beings, they don't contribute to a business the way they can. Our job is to help people to be compassionate with themselves, to like themselves, to have greater expectations of themselves, to let go of some of the past, to dream of a new future. We take people through a five-step process for rapid change. The result is that people become more flexible, creative, and more positive toward change. In a sense, we remove the barriers to change and light the fires for forward movement.

We introduce people to their own brains and the talents they haven't uncovered yet. In the process of being introduced to the brain, people begin to understand their own reactions to other people and situations. They can begin to find their untapped potential and unshackle themselves from old paradigms that are no longer serving them well. There is also a piece of the heroic inside us that begins to wonder, "How strong can I be? How courageous? How creative can I be? How high can I reach? What can I dream? What can I accomplish?"

Then they are ready for an opportunity, as a group, to experience what it's like to be part of a supportive team, to feel a true sense of empowerment, to be treated with respect as full human beings, and to understand themselves and others in a new way. We help people understand buzzwords like empowerment, creativity, and diversity at a deep, personal level. On the surface, many people say they don't need anything like that, that they're fine. Part of what has happened is that these people don't really know what's possible. Their capacity to imagine another way is limited by the past and present. When they get a taste of a new environment, suddenly they thirst for it, they want it. With that comes a level of understanding compassion for themselves and for each other that's very valuable. It makes team building much easier.

We believe that there is a learner in all of us who may be asleep as a result of education and life experiences. When people awaken that learner within, the business experiences a new burst of energy, spirit, and the capacity to solve complex problems. That speeds up organizational change tremendously.

We usually start with the people at the top because they are the final gatekeepers who will keep change and creativity out or let it in. They're likely to need to make the most change in themselves and that's scary for them. To create change takes courage, commitment, vision, humility, and a good bit of willingness to listen to people who differ from ourselves. It's hard to face the fact that we make such a big difference. When something goes wrong, it's hard to accept that we can point the finger at ourselves and ask how we contributed to it.

I do believe that change can be driven from any place in the organization and be successful, within certain bounds. If someone wants to create change, and cannot get top management support, they must recognize their own area of influence, as Steven Covey describes it. I support people in doing what they know is right. I tell them to let their hero come out and ask what they can do—given the restrictions—that's absolutely magical, majestic, and in which they can take pride. I suggest they take care not to put too much stress on a system that may not have much strength.

Creativity is not being able to use every color in the spectrum. It's about having only two colors and making miracles with them. Art is discovered by restrictions. Use restrictions as an impulse to creativity."

The issue of community has surfaced repeatedly throughout this book, especially in reference to a global community. It is also a critical part of individual change. Most of us don't change in isolation. There are pieces of change we can begin alone, but for the larger changes that most of us want to occur in our family, workplace, and world, we need to be in greater communion with others and to work out our changes with others. Some of us are looking for a new community. Others feel their lives are full of people, family, groups, clubs, and other organizations. But I think many of us share a longing for there to be a different way to be when we are with others. We know there is an even better way to be together. It's time to define that more precisely and to ask what virtues would be needed to support community.

Jeanne Borei is the director of human resources at Tel-A-Train, Inc. The company is an international training organization. It produces training videotapes and other support materials, as well as conducting seminars for industry and education regarding safety, industrial hygiene, technical and environmental topics. Tel-A-Train's story illustrates the power point Higher-Order Unity through community building in organizations and in communities. It also suggests the number of chains we may need to cut in order to achieve that.

Those in Borei's organization have exercised courage in committing themselves to a pioneering effort in a total-community-building process. Despite a quality reputation, they were beginning to have serious problems. They looked for an alternative to the traditional approach of cost cutting. Tel-A-Train is among the first private companies in the United States to undertake this journey. Hearing Borei's story firsthand was powerful. Her personal testimonial left me wanting to know more and to experience what she had experienced.

I pledged to myself that I would read M. Scott Peck's books, *The Different Drum: Community Making and Peace* and *A World Waiting to Be Born: Civility Rediscovered*, which seemed to be the underpinning to what she and her company had experienced. I followed though and was also moved by these great writings. Peck says in *The Different Drum*,

> In and through community lies the salvation of the world. . . . If we are going to use the word [community] meaningfully, we must restrict it to a group of individuals who have learned how to communicate honestly with each other, whose relationships go deeper than their masks of composure, and who have developed some significant commitment to "rejoice together, mourn together," and to "delight in each other, make other's conditions our own."

He goes on to state that some of the characteristics of community are its inclusivity through which all people are accepted, the group's commitment to coexistence, and the development of a pattern that transcends democracy through the ability to create genuine consensus.

How Peck and others help people work through this process is described in these books and in an article Borei has written for the World Business Academy's journal. I could not do that process justice here. What I can do is discuss the virtues that seem to be particularly important to community building as I understand it. I preface this story with things to think about:

- The journey to community and peace requires practice of the virtues of honesty and authenticity, which takes us into new levels of intimacy, of closeness, than we have had at work. It might create a place of mature affection, regard, warmth, and kindness even when we are in conflict. What would that be like? That has been called love and caring.
- Part of the community-building process is creating space for something new to emerge. It requires an emptying process similar to the story of the Expert with the full glass as discussed before the last story. I wonder if in that new space we could discover the virtues of deeper understanding and wisdom so we could create a sustainable life for all of us. Perhaps a piece of it would be like a portion of the Apache Wedding Blessing:

Now you will feel no rain,
For each of you will be shelter to the other.
Now you will feel no cold,
For each of you will be warmth for the other . . .

- Could practicing skills for peacemaking at work in our corporations have an impact on nations? Could experiencing this at work reduce violence in our homes, schools, and streets? Could we finally break through the other barriers that separate us, like sex, race, and creed? Could we actualize virtues at a community level? Could we create justice and truth for all? From the ancient Greeks, through our own Founding Parents, philosophers have sought the road to the just or virtuous society.
- We can be whole human beings at home, at work, in our communities, and in the world. As we experience "a quiet change of mind," we can trust that we are changing our lives and those of everyone around us and around the world. No one

else has responsibility for us. We are capable of choosing meaningful pain. We can have deep satisfaction knowing we will have made our unique contribution to the present and the future that no one can ever take away from us.

Jeanne Borei's Story: Building Community

"It seems as though systems are changing at fundamental levels, from the global arena to the individual person. This includes fundamental shifts in governments, organizations, schools, and our families. And I believe thousands of companies are going to die because of their unwillingness to change, despite all the obvious shifts that are taking place. We have personally experienced this. Our company, despite a reputation as one of the best and most respected training companies in the world, was beginning to have severe problems two years ago. We began to rebuild ourselves through a process called "community building."

We began to recognize serious problems, including financial ones, and we realized that if we were going to continue, some drastic changes had to be made. We weren't sure what those needed to be, but we felt very clearly that layoffs and the traditional cutback approach was not the way to go. I don't know how we knew that, but we did.

I went to a World Business Academy retreat in May 1991. There I experienced my first community building workshop based on M. Scott Peck's book *The Different Drum*. I discovered a new way of being—where two or more people, regardless of whether they knew each other or not, could be authentic and honest, and through that authenticity could reach true consensus and deal with task issues in a truly productive and effective manner.

I didn't realize that at the same time Bill Joiner, our president, was calling all the managers together to tell them our state of affairs. When he told me, upon my return, that he had had this meeting and asked for my input, I told him I had just experienced something that could give us hope. He latched on to every word, bit the bullet, and asked me to get in touch with the facilitators of the WBA session to see if they would be willing to take the managers through the process.

We gathered our team of 14 managers in September. Our president commented, "There's no going back now." We began what was literally a life-changing event for three-quarters of the managers. It made a definite difference in how we looked at each other as individuals and how we operated with each other as a group. It was the first time that, when we came back into the workplace, the employees in the company looked at us and noticed that there was something very different here.

Over a very short period of time, the employees began to notice that the managers were treating them differently, were seeing them differently, were honoring them for their diversity. The managers were willing to take risks by giving certain responsibilities to the employees and trusting them in new ways. We were treating each other differently, too. I had had a 10-year struggle with one of our managers and had no hope of healing that rift. The community-building process opened the door for the healing to start. The employees saw this immediately.

We knew we still had much work to do, but we weren't sure of the next steps. After a few months, we began to design tools and gauges to monitor ourselves so we didn't lose what we had gained at the workshop. Initially, we chose to meet in the formal community circle every other week. The point was to see whether we were hearing each other, respecting each other, and working with each other from a real place of truth and authenticity. The goal was to be able to do this on a daily basis: not just in our meetings, but in our interactions in the halls.

Four months later, we committed to take all the employees in the company through the experience. This was a crucial step. We realized that they would not have a complete understanding of what was really going on, nor would we be able to shift the company as we wanted, unless we had total employee involvement. So in early 1992, we took all the employees through the session. The initial employee response before going into the training was, "Oh, no." The response beyond that was one of curiosity and one of concern. They weren't sure whether, if they spoke honestly, there might not be some sort of retaliation.

One of the departments did come out of the experience in real confusion and pain. A great deal of baggage that had built up in that particular group over 19 years had never been dealt with. So it was like taking the surgeon's scalpel and very skillfully lancing open something that needed to be opened, so that the baggage could come out and the healing could take place. The workshop acted as a catalyst. It took weeks after to get that department to a place that I would call community. The group did get there.

What has occurred since the workshop is something that just continues to amaze me. In my vision, it's the way the world should be. In our company, we make mistakes every day, but where we are right now is light-years away from where we were two years ago. We have had traditional, quantifiable results and qualitative response about this. We had one customer come through not long ago who asked, "Do you pay these people to work here or do they pay you to work here?" I also have discovered that the creative juices have begun to flow more because there isn't the same fear of sharing ideas.

I cannot describe the difference in the management team, for instance. We have learned that if we do feel that someone else is not coming from a real place of authenticity, we can call, "Bullshit!" For example, I may feel that someone has a hidden agenda behind their remarks and can call him or her on it. I have yet to see any of the managers take any of that personally. That's a tremendous difference from where we were a couple of years ago. We were into defending turf. Today, we trust that we might be wrong and can examine that. If somebody is calling "Bullshit!" on me, I've learned not to blame that person. I stop and look very carefully. What have I just said or what have I just done? What is it in me that I can change? If there is a problem, the first place to look is at myself, before pointing fingers.

I had a wonderful conversation with Scott Peck not too long ago. He said that we were the first company in the world to do what we have done. I told him that is what makes it hard. It makes it scary for us because we're pioneers. Then he said, "That's why, right now, even your mistakes are important."

This idea of community is affecting everything we do. It causes us to ask whether we are being environmentally safe in the catalogs we produce. Are we using biodegradable products? Our sense of awareness has moved to a much higher level than it has ever been because we're beginning to gain a sense of clarity about who we are and what we do. We have decided to go into areas like Total Quality Management and Total Productive Management. I'm firmly convinced that none of that would stick if we didn't have the foundation that we do now. If TQM, TPM, and other similar programs are really going to make a difference in business, business is going to have to go another level deeper, and that level involves personal change.

Community building is critical to dealing with the changes and breakdowns in all levels of our society. A frequent comment from employees about our community building sessions is how much this process has helped them in their home life. I'm carrying it with me into a personal project in the Tennessee mountains. I am working to build a healthier community for troubled teenagers. Our children are extremely important and they need community, too. The idea is to help build a true community involving the police, the teenagers, and their parents. At the same time we'll be helping each teen discover his or her unique potential. This is one of those situations of "build it and they will come." The teenagers are turning up out of the woodwork, the parents are responding, and, in a remarkable way, the police have agreed to cooperate totally with what needs to be done. Magic is beginning to happen."

The Quest

When our work becomes real, our jobs will follow suit.

MATTHEW FOX

We are on a quest, you and I—a quest that has ever enlarging dimensions. The people and organizations in this book are good examples of the diverse ways the quest can play itself out. I believe that we are in this adventure together, whether we know it or not. This chapter helps us explore how to be more conscious of the quest in our personal, professional, and global life. It also suggests how to take the quest to a new level of discourse, systems understanding, and implementation.

A COMMON QUEST

I've asked many people who and what they most fundamentally want to be able to be and do at work. As we explore their initial responses and probe for what they mean by the words they chose, I find a common core that includes feeling meaningful, operating out of integrity, and being able to create a comfortable standard of living.

If I modify the question to ask them to think of work as their whole life's work, many people keep that same core and turn it into a larger cluster. They add two things—free time and making a contribution to something larger than themselves and the workplace.

The quest for this cluster reaches beyond the individual. More and more of us would like our organizations to want to do good in the world and be prosperous as well. That is true in government, education, nonprofits, and for-profits. So the personal desire parallels the organizational. On an even larger plane, we would like to believe that the world and all of life is meaningful and operating with integrity. What the total impetus of the quest is about is the birth of a higher order of work and life on this planet.

Some businesses, such as members of Businesses for Social Responsibility, the Greenleaf Center for Servant Leadership, and the World Business Academy, are trying to respond to this by redefining their purpose, making social and environmental causes part of their business agenda and allowing employees to participate that way. This helps employees feel their jobs are more meaningful. Ultimately, they hope to create a more sustainable economy because they know this one is running out.

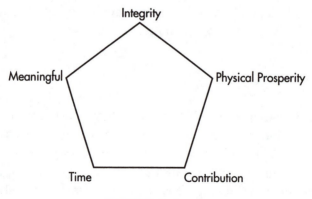

FIGURE 8-1

Meaning

The need for meaning is what drives our sense of purpose. There is greatness buried in each soul from the moment of birth. Purpose and meaning show up in our need to matter, to know we make a difference to someone or something beyond ourselves and even beyond our family. Purpose propels us forward to find that way of being that satisfies our need to do what we love and to do it in a way that serves some important need in the world. We are told to "follow our bliss" and sometimes we wonder why that doesn't always work. There is an implied assumption in this recommendation that needs to be explicit. There is no true purpose-filled bliss that isn't of service. There may be personal bliss, but that is different.

We must seek alignment and cooperation with others to be of service. Purposes are part of a system. It's Wynne Miller's earlier analogy to the puzzle in Chapter 3. If you're a piece of a puzzle and you try to find meaning and satisfaction without being in relationship to anyone or anything else, it won't happen.

Integrity

People talk about integrity using many different words. They talk about ethics, values, honesty, and excellence, as well as the negative impact of office politics and ego-driven decisions and individuals. As we explored these, it became clear the common issue was integrity.

Integrity means we are living out of our inner wholeness and expressing it with congruence in our outer world. It is much larger than just honesty. It's not that we are behaviorally perfect but that our intentions are usually in line with what we actually do. There is a consistency between professed beliefs and real behavior. Another way to say that is that our mind, heart, body, and soul are aligned around our sense of spiritual purpose as we do our daily living and working practices. And it requires a constant search to learn to understand more and to be open to changing our minds when confronted with new data.

Integrity issues surface for people related to their own behavior and that of organizations, governments, schools, and even churches. There is an increasing lack of trust in most traditional institutions that arises from perceived lack of integrity. It has to do with workplace politics, the behavior of public officials, the performance of schools, environmental degradation, and a vast range of other issues. People sense something is wrong when anyone or any group is working for his or her own self-interest to the exclusion of the well-being of the larger whole.

Time

I'll deal with the issue of time next because there is an interrelationship with integrity. Everyone is moving faster and juggling more than ever before, and many are working more than ever before. It's not surprising so many people wish for more time with the people and interests they love. Juliet Schor's book, *The Overworked American*, describes the situation behind this need in detail. The average American is working two months more per year than two decades ago. The practical challenges of this are staggering, especially for working parents and their children.

This is related to integrity from several perspectives. Most people say their family is their highest priority. Yet how they spend their time raises questions about consistency and therefore integrity. Schor's book goes on to describe findings of other economists. Economist Victor Fuchs has found that between 1960 and 1986 the time parents actually had available to be with children fell 10 hours a week for whites and 12 for blacks. Hewlett, another economist, links the parenting deficit to a variety of problems plaguing the country's youth: poor performance in school, mental problems, drug and alcohol use, and teen suicide. This causes enormous pain for everyone—parents, children, day care providers, teachers, and society. Most people feel stuck.

The whole family and work balance issue has yet to be confronted. The political agenda and some organizational agendas have begun to support family values, if we could decide what that means. Yet we dance around the edges of it by trying to give employees more tools to deal with a bad situation rather than confronting the bad situation. We teach people to be better organized, how to shop for quality day care and education, how to trade baby-sitting, and how to have quality time. Or we try to improve day care options. We need to consider a different path. I'll return to this in the section on system changes.

Contribution

The next highest desire of many people is to contribute to some larger community, whether that be their church, school, neighborhood, city, country, or the world. Many people have a passion around some cause, be it peace, the environment, education, children, the elderly, the homeless, or victims of war. This relates to the workplace need to be meaningful and expands it to a larger realm and customer. Many people feel there just isn't any time for these things any more. Others still participate but are exhausted.

Contribution has its roots in purpose, as described above, and the need to be of service. The need for volunteers continues to grow. I wouldn't be surprised if it weren't the fastest growing form of work. Given the increasing workweek, though, fewer and fewer people are able to respond to their own desire to help or to the growing need.

There is an additional root cause behind our desire to help. It is an increasing need to feel like we are part of a caring community. We need a sense of feeling connected to a meaningful group that is larger than family and friends. M. Scott Peck's books were mentioned in Jeanne Borei's story in Chapter 7. I strongly recommend them for an understanding of this phenomenon.

Physical Prosperity

On the most practical plane, we want physical prosperity. We have material needs that are totally appropriate, and these are expressed in my choice of the word *prosperity* (or *abundance*). The problem is that our culture has heightened perceived material needs to an unnecessary and dangerous degree. We are in danger of destroying all we have in the pursuit of more. We now live to serve the economy rather than for it to serve us.

It is easy to get trapped in vicious circles when it comes to money. It has come to mean so many things. It's a substitute for self-esteem, stability, safety, buying power, time, and even love. (I can't be home, so here's a present.) Our whole relationship to money must be scrutinized if we are to make some of the leaps to meaningful, healthier, and more profitable workplaces. I recommend the book, *Your Money or Your Life*, by Joe Dominguez and Vicki Robin. It also needs to be examined if we are to face the reality of the unsustainable imbalance in poverty, weapons, and money flows between the Northern and Southern hemispheres.

THE FEAR THAT BLOCKS THE QUEST

Fear and belief chains get in our way of following this quest. The overriding personal, organizational, and cultural fear is that we will have less than we have now if we engage in the quest. The "less" could be a job, power, material things, money, status, or security. It is the fear of the less that is at the core. We have trouble believing less could be more, that intangibles can more than compensate for tangibles, that virtue is its own reward, and that we could do good and be profitable.

The second fear is that it's hopeless anyway. The problems seem too big for us to impact. At some deep level, we wonder if the whole world isn't dying. Barbara Marx Hubbard's book, *The Revelation: Our Crisis Is a Birth*, speaks directly to my sense of this and offers hope. It provides a profound metaphor for thinking about where we really are. Hubbard suggests our whole world may be undergoing the pain of birthing a new world, rather than experiencing the pains of the dying process. So we might think of ourselves as the unborn child. At some point just prior to birth, she says we could imagine the following dialogue:

"Prepare for the end. . . . The future will be worse than the past,"
they said. The nervous system communicated a fear of The
End. . . . The voices of hope were drowned out by the cacophony
of despair. Depression, anger, alienation and pessimism
prevailed. . . . Suddenly all hell broke loose. The walls of our
secure world began to move. Terrible earthquakes rent the body
asunder. We were ripped from our source of nourishment.
Starvation, suffocation, deformation. We began to move out of
the womb. . . . We shall be destroyed. . . . [and then] . . . Each cell
awoke to a new potential, to growth of a new kind! The nervous
system reported breakthroughs instead of breakdowns. . . . And
with that the newborn child smiled.

It's ultimately an act of faith. The best things in life can't be proven.
The worst that could come from trying for the birth of a new way
of life would be a deepening of our own character and satisfaction. Not trying leaves us all right where we are. We have a choice
right now. We can operate out of fear and decide to let the system
run us, or operate out of the best we are and assist the system to
work for all of us—the organization, the individual, the family,
and the world. These are decisions that will have historic consequences.

The probability of some institution saving us is remote. My
message is that there is no one but us. You are it. We are all there
is. We *can* create a new workplace and through it influence the
world. The process described in Chapter 7 can be used by the individual for his or her own growth in this regard. It can also be
used for organizations and societal explorations and breakthroughs. It is the bridge that takes us to the type of system changes
that need to occur to give birth to a new world rather than be
drowned by this one.

As Rabbi Harold Kushner says in *When Everything You Ever
Wanted Isn't Enough*,

Only when we see ourselves in our true human context, as
members of a race which is intended to be one organism and
"one body," will we begin to understand the positive importance
not only of the successes but of the failures and accidents in our

lives. My successes are not my own. The way to them was prepared by others. The fruits of my labors is not my own: for I am preparing the way for the achievements of another. Nor are my failures my own. They may spring from the failure of another, but they are also compensated for by another's achievement. Therefore the meaning of my life is not to be looked for merely in the sum total of my own achievements. It is seen only in the complete integration of my achievements and failures with the achievements and failures of my own generation, and society, and time.

BREAKING FREE

To break free from our old work patterns as individuals, organizations or even as a society, will require a deeper understanding of human behavior as suggested by the Transformation Model presented in Chapter 7. It also requires a systems understanding of the interconnectivity of life. Some of this latter understanding comes from an appreciation of how nature works that modern physics is providing.

I am fascinated by the scientific research being done in quantum physics, in particular about self-organizing systems. I was introduced to these through Fritjof Capra's book, *The Tao of Physics* and Margaret Wheatley's book, *Leadership and the New Science*. When we look at things that appear as diverse as mountains, clouds, coastlines, vegetables, flowers, and even our own circulatory system we see the wonder, beauty, and complexity of nature. What scientists see are things called fractals, chaos, self-organizing systems, and attractors. What I'd like to direct the reader's attention to is that researchers point out that if we look closely we will see a pattern of repeating patterns at ever-smaller levels of scale. Think of a fern or a piece of broccoli or cauliflower and the repeating patterns we see there and you'll have a visual image of what they mean.

What I understand nature could be teaching us about life is that pattern formation in society operates much like these natural systems. There appears to be some kind of magnetic center that draws other elements towards it and forms a shape. This shape or pattern keeps repeating itself in social behavior just as in the cloud or broccoli formations. Wheatley wonders if there is a similar "magnetic force, a basin for activity, so attractive that it pulls all behavior toward it and creates coherence" in organizations. She recommends that a successful organization will have a strong vision and set of core values with much empowerment. The empowerment will create the chaos that is necessary for innovation and growth, while establishing an organizational set of parameters through vision and values that will keep the appropriate harmony, synergy, and direction. Vision and values create repetition in patterns but empowerment creates freedom to start new patterns. Thus one sees in nature a large degree of independence coupled with a harmonious system of interdependence and results.

I would say she is right and that we could take the same question to the level of local community and global behaviors. The same is true in the context in which I have been speaking. Where we have been control oriented and centralized, we need to allow more freedom and decentralization within the context of a higher-order attractor. By higher-order I mean a spiritual or community-good attractor or center. We have been organized around the principles of individual material acquisition, "more is better," and the centralization of responsibility and therefore power. The shapes these tend to create are larger and larger hierarchical pyramids where solutions are expected of some larger superior body—the boss. This pattern encourages a victim mentality and a narrow understanding of self-interest. It is repeated in the individual, family, community, school, country, and workplace, because social systems are fractal in nature, just like physical systems.

In that context, then, we need to begin discussions around what our new attractors and shapes could be. I offer the previous quest list—meaning, integrity, community prosperity, time, and contribution—as the list of new higher-order attractors. If we could get large-scale discussion of these, and individual as well as organizational movement to self-organize around them, we would be supplanting the former attractors that have created the current system.

What this suggests to me is that our current systems—organizational, personal, social, global—may have an inappropriate balance between chaos and control, may be self-organizing around the wrong attractors, or have an imbalance between them, or have fractal patterns of the wrong shape. I wouldn't doubt that we may very well have needed to have this happen for the sake of setting the next stage for human development. But clearly, we now need to shift direction given the state of the world and environment. It is a matter of survival.

System can be difficult to define. It is all the tangible and intangible relationships and activities that go into creating a way of life or specific goal. So all the inner workings of an organization can be thought of as a system in one context, while in another context these inner workings are a subsystem of the system that includes suppliers and customers. We can think of all life on this planet as a system; yet it, too, is a subsystem of the universe. For my purposes, I'll stick with the earth-level system.

A systemic change is an action that cascades through a system, affecting more than one discrete part. The most important change is actually the first one set in motion. This creates a multiplier effect. The initiating event can be an intentional act, and in that respect has a lot of thought and planning to it, but it also allows for a large dose of chaos. All the effects are not predictable. The intent needs to be of a higher order—a spiritual higher order, that is. So if we began self-organizing around the Five Quest Intents (meaning, integrity, community prosperity, time, and contribution), we would be on to something. Specific examples of these intentions turning into system transformers follow.

There are some strong chains that need cutting to create enough open space and freedom for that to begin. Possible ways to cut the chains and begin systemic transformation are suggested in the next section. This is not an exhaustive list but provides examples of the kinds of things we need to explore.

SYSTEMIC CHANGES: NEW HIGHER-ORDER ATTRACTORS AT WORK

- The stock market has tremendous influence on how companies behave. Much of the short-term thinking that is harmful to organizations, employees, the community, and frequently the environment is a result of the quarterly mentality forced on companies. Wall Street has not changed its thinking about the purpose of businesses. It still is stockholder oriented. This attractor inhibits the freedom of several of the new attractors to develop. It puts chains around the decisions and behaviors of companies who do want to operate out of a new sense of purpose and integrity. That, in turn, has a demoralizing effect on individuals. It also ties companies' hands in implementing some of the proposals that follow.

  So the systems question is, "Who influences Wall Street in such a way as to change our belief systems about the purpose of business, as well as business practices, which then, in turn, create more system change?" This may be one of those cases where we have met the enemy and it is ourselves. Private households, personal trusts, and nonprofit organizations account for 50 percent of corporate equities; employee pension funds account for about another 30 percent. Teacher retirement funds are the largest of the pension funds. Many of us in these categories are very concerned about the practices of business and how they affect our schools and communities, so it is time to examine our own goals and behavior and how that may drive us toward a world we are increasingly concerned about.

  What if someone could really educate these two primary groups, not their intermediaries, about the ramifications of their decisions and the power they have to affect society? What if we changed our investment goals and policies toward socially responsible companies that are trying to do good and be profitable? The existing data says we would do well.

- What about challenging the assumptions about work load demands, and being innovative on that end? Some organizations have had positive results with flex time, four-day workweeks, and job sharing, but these practices have not spread rapidly for all the "chains" we have already discussed.

  What if we really did switch heavily toward more freedom around the quantity of hours we work and how those hours are packaged? What if, like Germany, we went to a 30-hour workweek? What if, like in Australia, sabbaticals were frequent and common in all work environments? What if, like in Europe, vacations were longer and holidays more frequent?

  Possible system repercussions are enormous. The health and well-being of our children might improve dramatically. Learning might increase. Perhaps we would see a reduction in depression, suicide, anorexia, teen pregnancy, and drug use among the young. (Did you know that a large percentage of teen pregnancies occur between 3:00 PM and 5:30 PM Monday through Friday?)

  People might have more time to relax, read, volunteer, and even sleep. Sleep research points to a "sleep deficit" among Americans. A majority of us are currently getting between 60 and 90 minutes less sleep each night than we should for optimum health and performance. So productivity and quality might go up in the workplace as a result of working less.

  Stress and related illness could go down, which would affect health care costs, which, in turn, would reduce employer costs. People might smile more. They might have time for aging parents and for taking care of their own bodies. If enough people did this, companies might have to hire more people. We might reduce the number of people overworked and underworked at the same time. We'll need some new way of thinking about access to and cost of benefits for this change to be undertaken since business can't absorb all the costs.

- One of the obvious objections to the example of working fewer hours is "I can't afford to do that." There are two system changes that might help minimize that. One is to expand the experiments underway around the country with a new form of currency. We've forgotten that money is only a figment of our imagination that we have agreed to believe in. In fact, money is disappearing and being replaced by computer networks, anyway. So some people are creating a more liberating way to think about currency.

By combining elements of barter, volunteer time, debit card technology, and corporate discounts, people can contribute to their community and receive buying power in return. This is a new twist on doing what is meaningful and getting back something tangible. A person could work less, contribute to something they value, and receive at least some buying power. Someone unemployed can trade time for money and perhaps learn some skills at the same time. We could bring more people back into the economy. This is an example of Barbara Shipka's vision of contribution being larger than a job (see Chapter 5). Such systems are underway in a variety of U.S. cities and more are coming on-line.

- A second system shift that relates to buying power is to alter our perceptions of our needs. I'm not addressing this to people anywhere near the poverty line. I'm talking about those of us clearly above it. We've lost sight of the fact that we sell part of our lives every time we buy something. I coach too many people who are in bondage to a lifestyle that isn't bringing them happiness.

A large part of our problem in this regard is that we have conditioned ourselves around too narrow a definition of prosperity. Today we think lots of things will bring us prosperity: a bigger house, fancier car, more dinners out, more clothes. . . . In other words, prosperity is only in the physical world. So we never have it. We always need more. No wonder the indexes of happiness have not increased at all, even though physical prosperity has improved considerably.

I'd offer a different definition of prosperity: a feeling of inner peace derived from living with integrity. True prosperity means an enriched mind, body, heart, and spirit derived from a blend of the tangible and intangible joys of life. This comes as a result of having been of service.

This definition requires meaning, purpose, integrity, and prosperity to be part of one system: integrated and balanced, not separated. When this occurs, I see people who are happy and satisfied with life despite wide variations in physical prosperity. When integration and balance are not present, I see much depression, alienation, and destructive behavior despite great wealth.

Money is so paradoxical. Many of us are discovering that working less costs less per year, so the net effect on us is less than might be expected. Think about the costs you wouldn't have if you worked less, or in a different job, or in a different place. The net effect on your life may be minimal. Yet in other cases the nontangible return is so great that people are happy with the trade-off.

This is not to deny the reality of the extreme gaps between the rich and poor. It will be necessary for this gap to be narrowed both at the individual level and between have and have-not nations. This extreme is unsustainable. It will start with a reduction in the gap between executive pay and the lowest paid worker. The ridiculous contracts for sports figures and entertainers also must change. How to proceed after that is less clear to me at this time.

- Here's a business/environment/poverty system change. In terms of contribution, many people want to help restore the environment or aid those in poverty because these two issues are quite interrelated. The battle lines are drawn between economic development on the one side and the environment and wildlife protection on the other, and then we also start talking about integrity issues.

  This proposed system change is well documented in Paul Hawken's book, *The Ecology of Commerce*. What if companies and consumers thought of the manufacturing and use cycle as one continuous, no-waste cycle? In nature, he points out, there is virtually no waste. The waste of one system becomes the food for another related system.

What if companies owned their products forever? What if we thought of everything as rented at the consumer end, with an incentive for good treatment of products? For example, what if all cars eventually were returned to their manufacturers? Wouldn't that dramatically affect how materials were used, valued, reworked, reused? Wouldn't it have a profound impact on the environment, both in terms of depletion and pollution? It would enhance partnerships across industries, companies, and communities to seek to cooperate and feed each other's systems.

Also discussed in Hawken's book is the idea of making more products in each community, rather than shipping them all over the country and all over the world. There is so much waste in the distribution of raw materials and finished product, in packaging and advertising. These considerably raise consumer costs. It is environmentally unsound and takes jobs and money out of the local economy to buy something made elsewhere.

I have been thinking about this for some time in terms of jobs and businesses for those people who have been laid off, largely from factory jobs. They often do not have the education to change fields easily. Their skills are of a mechanical nature and there are few replacement jobs for them. If this were the 1600s or 1700s, many of them would have been merchants and craftspersons. We automated all those jobs, and then automated the automation, and thus turned the people out. I'd like to see some entrepreneurs come up with new tools for the small business craftsperson: things that allow them to meld customization with the personal care and quality of a craftsperson, with the speed and flexibility to make things economical for the customer and supplier. I wonder if it is possible to create a new type of crafts business for these people. I'd like to buy my custom-made shoes or table or awnings from someone in the neighborhood. It would help build communities and recirculate dollars within it, rather than exporting those dollars.

- A critique of the field of economics has been underway for this very reason for at least the last 20 years, since the brilliant British economist E. F. Schumacher published his book, *Small is Beautiful*. Hazel Henderson and other leading economists have furthered this reassessment. They share a number of questions and observations. We know the current system tends to bankrupt the future in terms of social conditions, the environment, and debt load. The hard-drawn lines between public and private sectors, the unrelenting narrow expectations of output from one system versus the other, and the resulting animosity and suspicion are preventing collaboration, creativity, and innovation in solving social problems. Many economists say we should question the morality of paying interest, which was considered usury for much of human history. And re-examining the whole issue of scale—size of healthy schools, homes, cities, workplaces, farms, and production practices—would be very useful.

  So what we need is a new attractor for economics that shifts the nature of the discussion from what is economical to what is useful in moving society forward. Currently, economics is interested in numbers, not human beings, and therefore we need a higher quality index than that of GNP to guide us.

- Groups within the health care industry tell us we could reduce our food costs, pollution, cruelty to farm animals, and world hunger, and minimize the motivation for the destruction of the rain forests, if we change one thing—our eating habits. And by the way, if those benefits aren't enough, we would be improving our own health. A shift to less meat and more vegetables, fruit, and grains would have tremendous system effects.

  John Robbins's book and video, *Diet for a New America*, discusses this in detail. I liked it most because it showed the kind of systems thinking I think is desperately needed. Robbins suggests that a diet change could lead to healthier lives. Few people contest this anymore, except those who have money to lose by a diet change. Those healthier lives help cut medical costs, which are skyrocketing. Many businesses are finding that health care providers are their largest suppliers. That is scary, whether you make cars or computers or do dry-cleaning. The government fiscal picture is also in trouble partially due to health care costs, and that means taxpayers are in trouble. And guess what it means for all the uninsured.

- Here is an intriguing spiritual shift. What if we could meditate our way into safe, nonviolent communities? I was reading Larry Dossey's book, *Recovering the Soul: A Scientific and Spiritual Search*. He described a meeting in Switzerland in 1974 involving the Maharishi Mahesh Yogi, the originator of transcendental meditation. The Maharishi suggested that if only 1 percent of a population began to meditate and experienced pure consciousness, the remaining 99 percent of the population would also be affected.

Dossey goes on to say: The idea was certainly unorthodox, but it could be tested, and sociologist Garland Landrift did just that. He found that in 1973, the most recent year for which all the needed data were available, among those U.S. cities with populations of 25,000 or more, eleven of them had 1 percent or more of their population practicing the TM technique. As a comparison he selected eleven other cities that had fewer than 1 percent TM participants, but that otherwise resembled the "1-percent cities" in terms of population, region of the country, college population, and previous crime rate trends. Landrift found that for the non-1-percent cities the crime rates between 1972 and 1973 followed the national trend, increasing an average of 8.3 percent. But in *each one* of the 1-percent cities there was a *decrease* in the crime rate of 8.2 percent. The likelihood that these findings could have occurred by chance was less than one in a thousand.

What if our cities, police departments, schools, or religious associations launched some kind of joint effort to create meditation groups of this kind? It appears to have low costs and would be very empowering to people. It's low risk in every way, except possibly the risk of public criticism from those who can't believe such things are possible.

- Within our organizations we could make a major shift in organizational planning and alignment. I've worked a great deal with many forms of strategic planning. At the heart of the intent behind many management-by-objectives programs, strategic plans, annual goal setting, and Hoshin planning in total quality is a common goal we have yet to achieve. They are all efforts to align people and to help them see their interconnectedness. Doing that reduces waste, lets the right and left brain work together, provides focus, and much more.

Most of these plans don't work out as well as we'd like. Interdepartmental or interdivisional conflicts and individual rewards get in the way, as well as honest misunderstanding or lack of information. One reason they don't work is that most are top-down driven and controlling. As Deming has pointed out, many of these approaches cause game playing and manipulation of data so that it appears we're reaching our goals. Often the new plans are overlays on top of the old paradigm, rather than new integrations. People seldom have ownership and commitment as a team. Instead, they have carrots to grab and sticks to avoid.

The most important element that is missing, though, is the individual personal passion of the employee. What we give people is the organization's vision and purpose and values. People need to look at their own visions, missions, and purposes, and to try to link those with the organizational ones. If we articulated a field of linked personal purposes, we could save a lot of time, energy, and waste in certain types of planning, incentives, and threats. When actions come out of our own motivation, they are much more powerful, insightful, and tenacious. We are working around our own attractor. When rewards and satisfaction come from the inside as well as the outside, we find much greater and longer lasting satisfaction. We would have very different organizations if we planned and set goals this way.

SPECIFIC ACTIONS FOR INDIVIDUALS

People often tell me their organization or community isn't ready for this and ask what they can do on their own. There are two primary strategic goals for individuals: Keep learning and growing by changing yourself to become more of your highest self. And remember that every moment you interact with anyone else is an opportunity of influence. At the level of implementation, these turn into actions like the following:

1. Engage in your own growth and learning by using the Transformation Web process of Practicing Purpose Navigation, Cutting Chains, Becoming a 360° Systems Opportunist, and Creating Higher-Order Unity. You will create more meaning in your life and enhance your ability to contribute.
2. Cultivate your spiritual and emotional self, as well as your intellect and physical skills. This enhances your ability to evaluate everything from the perspective of integrity.
3. Re-examine your material lifestyle in the context of increasing the quality of your life—create a different form of prosperity. Pretend you lost some percentage of your income and figure out how to adapt. Then put that percentage into your Freedom Savings account each paycheck. This creates the practical ability to seek all the other elements of the quest.
4. Spread the word. Share your own questions. Share this book. Pass it around. Find other things worthy to pass around to shake up everyone's thinking. Talk to your family, friends, peers, employees, managers. Create a community of like-minded people so you aren't alone. This is a significant form of contribution.

5. Relationships count for much more than we realize. There are many underground people out there, doing good by enlarging the lives of everyone they work with. A client who is a top performing sales manager recently told me, "I'm really an underground minister helping myself and my team grow, become more conscious, and transforming life. Everyone else, of course, thinks I'm leading a sales team to ever higher levels. I am, but in more ways than they mean." Live with integrity and influence anyone you can.

6. Come to peace with risk and change. Goethe, the German philosopher, reminds us, "that the moment one definitely commits oneself, then Providence moves, too. All sorts of things occur to help one that would never otherwise have occurred . . . all manner of unforeseen incidents and meetings and material assistance, which no man could have dreamed would have come his way. Whatever you can do, or dream you can, begin it. Boldness has genius, power and magic in it. Begin it now."

As for myself, I want to be like George Bernard Shaw, who said,

> I am of the opinion that my life belongs to the whole community
> and . . . it is my privilege to do for it whatever I can . . . .
> Life is no "brief candle" to me.
> It is a sort of splendid torch that I have got hold of for the moment,
> and I want to make it burn as brightly as possible
> before handing it on to other generations.

TEN GUIDING PRINCIPLES TO WHO WE COULD BE AT WORK

The laws of nature do not demand that we inherit the future. Rather, it is ours to create. We can create a dramatically different, healing workplace.

The great teachers have shown that if we seek change, we must first embody the change ourselves. By living it, we mirror it and influence others more deeply.

More and more people are asking, "Is this all there is?" We need to create more meaning in our lives and work. Ask, "What was I born to contribute throughout my whole life's work?"

The current system of business is unsustainable—personally, organizationally, and globally. Few are gaining while many are losing. Leadership is about recognizing this and posing questions that lead to new levels of insight.

Business is the most powerful institution on earth. Responsibility must be commensurate with power. Organizations must ask, "What higher purpose should our bottom line be serving?"

The data is in. Individuals and companies can do good and perform well financially. The question is, "Do we have the courage to try?"

How do you create courage and vision? Ask deep questions of yourself and allow a dialogue to emerge between mind, heart, spirit and body. Or, find a person who stretches your thinking and beliefs.

Great pain and cost result when internal and external realities are at odds. Integrity is the alignment of mind, body, heart, and soul. The whole needs congruence.

Pain is a natural part of life. Stop running from it. Use it for the gift it is—a signal and motivation to start the healing rather than to medicate the symptoms.

How to do more with less and avoid burnout? Stop separate "programs of the month." Learn systems thinking and how to create higher-order unity out of diversity. "Give me a lever long enough and I can move the world."
(Insight from Archimedes.)

Storytellers

Steven Wikstrom, Vice President of Manufacturing, Reell Precision Manufacturing Corporation

Terri Lynn, Chairman of the Board and Director of Creative Development, Universal Tradewinds, Inc.

George E. McCown, Managing Partner, McCown De Leeuw & Company

Robert Killeen, United Auto Worker Sub-Regional Director (Retired)

Patricia Raber Hedberg, Assistant Professor, University of St. Thomas

James Bowe, President, Career Management Systems

Susan M. Anderson, Executive Director, Bloomington Art Center

The Observer, Anonymous, Vice President Finance and Human Resources, Subsidiary of a *Fortune* 500 Company

Charles M. Denny, Chairman of the Board, ADC Telecommunications, Inc.

Susan James, Director of Marketing, Personnel Decisions, Inc.

Anthony L. Andersen, Chairman of the Board and CEO, H. B. Fuller Company

William C. Norris, Founder, Control Data Corporation; Chairman, William C. Norris Institute

Wynne Miller, Director of Human Development, ColorAge, Inc.

William W. George, President and CEO, Medtronic, Inc.

Wynn Binger, President, Construction Materials, Inc.

John Schaaf, President, **George Orr**, Vice President Human Resources, **Donald Sporer**, Vice President Sales, **Terry Busse**, Vice President Finance, American Paging, Inc.

Donald Price, Director Quality Assurance, **Jeffrey J. Zibley**, Director Human Resources, **Carol Lynn Courtney**, Organizational Development Specialist, Malt-O-Meal Corporation

Sandy Miller, Team Leader, **Robert Suelflow**, Quote Coordinator, Schott Corporation

David A. Koch, Chairman and CEO, Graco, Inc.

Herbert C. Johnson, Retired, President and CEO, Datamyte and MTS Systems

Paul Halvorson, Partner, Triad Group; Social Entrepreneur

Barbara Shipka, Corporate Consultant, Member, Board of Directors World Business Academy

Horst Rechelbacher, Founder and Chairman of the Board, Aveda Corporation

Robert Carlson, Former Sales and Marketing Executive

Anita Ryan, Owner, St. Paul Brass & Aluminum Foundry

Owen Schott, CEO, **James Meyer**, Vice President, Manufacturing, Schott Employees, Schott Corporation

Frederick M. Green, President and CEO, Ault, Inc.

Gail Straub and David Gershon, Cofounders, The Empowerment Workshop

Guy Schoenecker, Founder, President, and CEO, BI, Inc.

Magaly Rodriquez, Founder and President, Rapid Change Technologies, Inc.

Jeanne Borei, Director Human Resources, Tel-A-Train, Inc.

Bibliography

Arrien, Angeles. *The Four Fold Way*. San Francisco: Harper. 1993.

Autry, James. *Love and Profit*. New York: William Morrow and Co. 1992.

Barrentine, Pat, ed. *When the Canary Stops Singing*. San Francisco: Berrett-Koehler Publishers. 1993.

Block, Peter. *The Empowered Manager*. San Francisco: Jossey-Bass Publishers. 1990.

Block, Peter. *Stewardship*. San Francisco: Berrett-Koehler Publishers. 1994.

Bohm, David. *On Dialogue*. Sausalito: Noetic Sciences Review. 1992.

Bolman, Lee G., and Deal, Terrence E. *Leading with Soul*. San Francisco: Jossey-Bass Publishers. 1995.

Borei, Jeanne. "Chaos to Community." *World Business Academy Perspectives*, Vol. 6 No. 2. San Francisco: Berrett-Koehler Publications. 1992.

Borysenko, Joan. *Minding the Body, Mending the Mind*. New York: Bantam Books. 1987.

Bracey, Hyler, Jack Rosenblum, Aubrey Sanford, and Roy Trueblood. *Managing from the Heart*. Atlanta: Heart Enterprises. 1990.

Capra, Fritjof. *The Tao of Physics*. Boston: Shambhala. 1991.

Case, John. "A Company of Businesspeople," *Inc. Magazine*. Boston, April 1993, Vol. 15, No. 4, page 79.

Chappell, Tom. *The Soul of a Business*. New York: Bantam Books. 1993.

Covey, Steven. *Seven Habits of Highly Effective People*. New York: Simon and Schuster, Inc. 1990.

Cox, Craig, and Power, Sally. "Executives of the World Unite."*Business Ethics*, September/October 1992.

Coyhis, Don. *Teachings of the Medicine Wheel*. Boulder: Moh-he-con-nuck, Inc. 1993.

Dominguez, Joe, and Robin, Vicki. *Your Money or Your Life*. New York: Penguin Books. 1992.

Dossey, Larry. *Recovering the Soul*. New York: Bantam. 1989.

Dossey, Larry. *Healing Words*. San Francisco: Harper. 1993.

Elgin, Duane. *Voluntary Simplicity*. New York: William Morrow and Co. 1981.

Fox, Matthew. *The Reinvention of Work*. San Fransico: Harper. 1994.

Frankl, Viktor. *Man's Search for Meaning*. New York: Washington Square Press. 1985.

Gatto, John Taylor. "How Public Are Our Public Schools?" *Special Report: Real Choices in Education Conference, The Threefold Review*. 1992.

Gershon, David, and Straub, Gail. *Empowerment: The Art of Creating Your Life As You Want It*. New York: Dell Publishing, 1989.

Gibran, Kahlil. *The Prophet*. New York: Alfred A. Knopf. 1968.

Greenleaf, Robert. *The Servant As Leader*. Indianapolis: The Greenleaf Center for Servant-Leadership.

Handy, Charles. *The Age of Unreason*. Boston: Harvard Business School Press. 1990.

Hanson, Daniel S. *A Place to Shine*. Boston: Butterworth–Heinemann. 1996.

Harman, Willis, and Hormann, John. *Creative Work*. Indianapolis: Knowledge Systems, Inc. 1990.

Hawken, Paul. *The Ecology of Commerce*. New York: Harper Business. 1993.

Hubbard, Barbara Marx. *The Revelation: Our Crisis Is A Birth*. Novato, Calif.: Nataraj Publishing. 1993.

Kushner, Harold. *When Bad Things Happen to Good People*. New York: Avon Books. 1981.

Kushner, Harold. *When All You've Ever Wanted Isn't Enough*. New York: Pocket Books. 1986.

Leider, Richard J., and Shapiro, David A. *Repacking Your Bags*. San Francisco: Berrett-Koehler Publishers. 1995.

Levine, Stephen. *A Gradual Awakening*. New York: Doubleday. 1979.

Liebig, James E., in cooperation with the World Business Academy. *Merchants of Vision*. San Francisco: Berrett-Koehler Publishers. 1994.

Lindbergh, Anne Morrow. *Gift from the Sea*. New York: Vintage Books. 1978.

McLaughlin, Corinne, and Davidson, Gordon. *Spiritual Politics*. New York: Ballantine Books. 1994.

McVeigh, Patrick. "Mutual Fund Review." *Business Ethics*, January/February 1993.

Marks, Linda. *Living with Vision*. Indianapolis: Knowledge Systems, Inc. 1989.

Minnesota Center for Corporate Responsibility. *Toward a Moral Basis for Global Business*. Minneapolis: Minnesota Center for Corporate Responsibility. 1993.

Mollner, Terry. "Mondragon: Archetype of Future Business?" *World Business Academy Perspectives*, Vol. 6, No. 2. San Francisco: Berrett-Koehler Publications, 1992.

Morgan, Gareth. *Images of Organization*. California: Newbury Park: SAGE Publications, Inc. 1986.

Moyers, Bill. *Healing the Body and the Mind*. New York: Doubleday. 1993.

Palmer, Parker J. *Leading from Within*. 1990.

Pearson, Carol S., and Seivert, Sharon. *Magic at Work*. New York: Doubleday. 1995.

Peck, M. Scott. *The Different Drum*. New York: Simon & Schuster. 1987.

Peck, M. Scott. *A World Waiting to Be Born*. New York: Bantam Books. 1993.

Quinn, Daniel. *Ishmael*. New York: Bantam Turner. 1992.

Ray, Michael, and Rinzler, Alan (Editors for the *World Business Academy Perspectives*). "The New Paradigm in Business." New York: Jeremy P. Tarcher, Inc. 1993.

Rifkin, Jeremy. *The End of Work*. New York: Jeremy P. Tarcher. 1995.

Robbins, John. *Diet for a New America, How Your Food Choices Affect Your Health*. Walpole: Stillpoint Publishing. 1987.

Roddick, Anita. *Body and Soul*. New York: Crown Publishers, Inc. 1991.

Rogers, George L. *Benjamin Franklin's The Art of Virtue*. Eden Prairie, MN: Acorn Publishing. 1989.

Roskind, Robert. *In the Spirit of Business*. Berkeley: Celestial Arts. 1992.

Russell, Peter. *The Global Brain*. Los Angeles: J.P. Tarcher, Inc. 1983.

Russell, Peter. *The White Hole in Time*. San Francisco: Harper. 1992.

St. James, Elaine. *Simplify Your Life*. New York: Hyperion. 1994.

St. James, Elaine. *Inner Simplicity*. New York: Hyperion. 1995.

Savage, Charles M. *Fifth Generation Management*, rev. ed. Boston: Butterworth–Heinemann. 1996.

Schaef, Anne Wilson. *When Society Becomes an Addict*. San Francisco: Harper. 1987.

Schaef, Anne Wilson. *Women's Reality*. Minneapolis: Wilson Press. 1981.

Schaef, Anne Wilson, and Fassel, Diane. *The Addictive Organization*. San Francisco: Harper & Row. 1988.

Schor, Juliet. *The Overworked American*. New York: Basicbooks. 1992.

Schumacher, E. F. *Small Is Beautiful*. New York: Harper and Row. 1973.

Senge, Peter. *The Fifth Discipline*. New York: Doubleday. 1990.

Spears, Larry, ed. *Reflections on Leadership*. New York: John Wiley & Sons. 1995

Wheatley, Margaret. *Leadership and the New Science*. San Francisco: Berret-Koehler Publishers. 1992.

Whyte, David. *The Heart Aroused*. New York: Bantam Doubleday. 1995.

Index